Keep this book. You will
need it and use it throughout
your career.

MARKETING
in the
HOSPITALITY
INDUSTRY

Educational Institute Courses

Introductory

INTRODUCTION TO THE HOSPITALITY INDUSTRY
Fourth Edition
Gerald W. Lattin

AN INTRODUCTION TO HOSPITALITY TODAY
Third Edition
Rocco M. Angelo, Andrew N. Vladimir

TOURISM AND THE HOSPITALITY INDUSTRY
Joseph D. Fridgen

Rooms Division

FRONT OFFICE PROCEDURES
Fifth Edition
Michael L. Kasavana, Richard M. Brooks

HOUSEKEEPING MANAGEMENT
Second Edition
Margaret M. Kappa, Aleta Nitschke, Patricia B. Schappert

Human Resources

HOSPITALITY SUPERVISION
Second Edition
Raphael R. Kavanaugh, Jack D. Ninemeier

HOSPITALITY INDUSTRY TRAINING
Second Edition
Lewis C. Forrest, Jr.

HUMAN RESOURCES MANAGEMENT
Second Edition
Robert H. Woods

Marketing and Sales

MARKETING OF HOSPITALITY SERVICES
William Lazer, Roger Layton

HOSPITALITY SALES AND MARKETING
Third Edition
James R. Abbey

CONVENTION MANAGEMENT AND SERVICE
Fifth Edition
Milton T. Astroff, James R. Abbey

MARKETING IN THE HOSPITALITY INDUSTRY
Third Edition
Ronald A. Nykiel

Accounting

UNDERSTANDING HOSPITALITY ACCOUNTING I
Fourth Edition
Raymond Cote

UNDERSTANDING HOSPITALITY ACCOUNTING II
Third Edition
Raymond Cote

BASIC FINANCIAL ACCOUNTING FOR THE HOSPITALITY INDUSTRY
Second Edition
Raymond S. Schmidgall, James W. Damitio

MANAGERIAL ACCOUNTING FOR THE HOSPITALITY INDUSTRY
Fourth Edition
Raymond S. Schmidgall

Food and Beverage

FOOD AND BEVERAGE MANAGEMENT
Third Edition
Jack D. Ninemeier

QUALITY SANITATION MANAGEMENT
Ronald F. Cichy

FOOD PRODUCTION PRINCIPLES
Jerald W. Chesser

FOOD AND BEVERAGE SERVICE
Second Edition
Ronald F. Cichy, Paul E. Wise

HOSPITALITY PURCHASING MANAGEMENT
William P. Virts

BAR AND BEVERAGE MANAGEMENT
Lendal H. Kotschevar, Mary L. Tanke

FOOD AND BEVERAGE CONTROLS
Fourth Edition
Jack D. Ninemeier

General Hospitality Management

HOTEL/MOTEL SECURITY MANAGEMENT
Second Edition
Raymond C. Ellis, Jr., David M. Stipanuk

HOSPITALITY LAW
Third Edition
Jack P. Jefferies

RESORT MANAGEMENT
Second Edition
Chuck Y. Gee

INTERNATIONAL HOTEL MANAGEMENT
Chuck Y. Gee

HOSPITALITY INDUSTRY COMPUTER SYSTEMS
Third Edition
Michael L. Kasavana, John J. Cahill

MANAGING FOR QUALITY IN THE HOSPITALITY INDUSTRY
Robert H. Woods, Judy Z. King

CONTEMPORARY CLUB MANAGEMENT
Edited by Joe Perdue for the Club Managers Association of America

Engineering and Facilities Management

FACILITIES MANAGEMENT
David M. Stipanuk, Harold Roffman

HOSPITALITY INDUSTRY ENGINEERING SYSTEMS
Michael H. Redlin, David M. Stipanuk

HOSPITALITY ENERGY AND WATER MANAGEMENT
Second Edition
Robert E. Aulbach

MARKETING
in the
HOSPITALITY
INDUSTRY

Third Edition

Ronald A. Nykiel, Ph.D., CHA, CHE

EDUCATIONAL INSTITUTE
American Hotel & Motel Association

Disclaimer

This publication is designed to provide accurate and authoritative information in regard to the subject matter covered. It is sold with the understanding that the publisher is not engaged in rendering legal, accounting, or other professional service. If legal advice or other expert assistance is required, the services of a competent professional person should be sought.

> —*From the Declaration of Principles jointly adopted by the American Bar Association and a Committee of Publishers and Associations*

The author, Ronald A. Nykiel, is solely responsible for the contents of this publication. All views expressed herein are solely those of the author and do not necessarily reflect the views of the Educational Institute of the American Hotel & Motel Association (the Institute) or the American Hotel & Motel Association (AH&MA).

Nothing contained in this publication shall constitute a standard, an endorsement, or a recommendation of the Institute or AH&MA. The Institute and AH&MA disclaim any liability with respect to the use of any information, procedure, or product, or reliance thereon by any member of the hospitality industry.

©Copyright 1997
By the EDUCATIONAL INSTITUTE of the
AMERICAN HOTEL & MOTEL ASSOCIATION
1407 South Harrison Road
P.O. Box 1240
East Lansing, Michigan 48826

The Educational Institute of the American
Hotel & Motel Association is a nonprofit
educational foundation.

Printed in the United States of America
4 5 6 7 8 9 10 01 00

Library of Congress Cataloging-in-Publication Data

Nykiel, Ronald A.
   Marketing in the hospitality industry/Ronald A. Nykiel.—3rd
ed.
     p. cm.
   Includes index.
   ISBN 0-86612-143-9 (pbk.)
   1. Hospitality industry—Marketing. I. Title.
TX911.3.M3N94   1997
647.94'068'8—dc20
                                     96-30823
                                     CIP

Cover photograph courtesy of Foxwoods Resort, Mashantucket, Connecticut, and Tebo Photography, Westerly, Rhode Island

To my wife, Karen, our son Ron,
and my friends in the hospitality industry.
A special thanks to Trish and Sherri
for all their help in this endeavor.

Contents

Congratulations   xii

Preface   xiii

About the Author   xv

Study Tips   xvii

1 Understanding the Hospitality Industry   3

A Historical Perspective—The Growth of Industry Brands   3
A Marketing Perspective of the Industry   6
A Consumer Perspective of the Industry   7

2 Market Segmentation and the Hospitality Industry   11

Geographic Segmentation   11

*Regions, Zones, and Districts • Metropolitan Statistical Areas • Cities •
Zip Codes • Other Geographic Segmentation Tools*

Demographic Segmentation   15
Benefit and Need Segmentation   15
Psychographic Segmentation   16
Combining Segmentation Techniques   18
The Pendulum Swings Toward Value   18

3 Positioning in Line with Consumer Preferences   23

End Users   23

Business Travelers • Pleasure Travelers

Travel Intermediaries   25
Food Service Market Segmentation   27

*Desired Dining Experience • Price Sensitivity • Convenience and
Location*

4 The Channels of Distribution   33

Channels of Distribution   33

*Travel Intermediaries • Electronic Travel Distribution Systems •
Ground Operators • Air Carriers • Channels of Distribution in Europe
and Japan*

Government Regulation of Travel   38

United States • Foreign Governments

Vertical and Horizontal Integration 39

5 **Marketing in Perspective** **43**

Planning Resources for the Marketing Effort 43
Targeting Profitable Consumer Segments 44
Reaching the Market 45

6 **Applying Key Marketing Methodologies: Marketing Research** **51**

Marketing Research 51

*Types of Marketing Research • Marketing Research Techniques •
Marketing Research Presentation Tools*

7 **Applying Key Marketing Methodologies: Sales** **69**

Organizing the Sales Effort 69
Personal Sales 79
Telephone Sales 83
The Importance of Interdepartmental Communication 83

8 **Applying Key Marketing Methodologies: Advertising** **87**

Advertising 87

*Advertising Guidelines • The Six-Step Advertising Process • Do It
Yourself or Select an Agency? • Market Coverage • Media Selection •
Trade-Outs, Barter, and Co-Oping • Advertising Types and Themes •
Case Examples*

9 **Applying Key Marketing Methodologies: Public Relations** ... **113**

Public Relations 113

*What Public Relations Is • How Public Relations Can Be Applied •
Internal Public Relations • How Can Public Relations Be Measured? •
PR Examples to Think About*

Publications 123

10 **Applying Key Marketing Methodologies: Promotions** **129**

Promotions 129

*Keys to Successful Promotions • Types of Promotions • Methods for
Executing Promotions*

Internal Promotions 136
Case Examples 136

11 Applying Key Marketing Methodologies: Data Base Marketing **143**

Data Base Marketing 143

Data Base Systems • Keys to Successful Data Base Marketing

Sales Through Direct Mail 147

Keys to Direct Mail

12 Applying Key Marketing Methodologies: Packaging **153**

Packaging in the Hospitality Industry 153

Packaging Benefits • Packaging Participation • Types of Packages

13 Applying Key Marketing Methodologies: Collateral Materials and Promotional Support **165**

Collateral Materials 165

Types of Collateral Materials

Employee Motivation 174

Employee of the Month Programs • Employee-Interest Promotions • Employee Community Service Recognition

Clubs 176

VIP Clubs • Secretaries Clubs • Salesperson Appreciation Clubs • Meal-of-the-Month Clubs

14 Applying Key Marketing Methodologies: Understanding Rates and Fares **181**

Hotel Rates 181

Standard Rates • Other Rates • Ranges • Rate Strategies • Rate Comparisons

Airfares 187

Carrier Strategies

Rental Car Rates 188

Rental Car Strategies

Cruise Ship Rates 190

15 Applying Key Marketing Methodologies: Pricing Strategies . . **193**

Pricing Techniques 193

Technique 1: Offering a Price Range • Technique 2: Selling Up • Technique 3: Selling Down • Technique 4: Focusing on Revenue and

Profit per Unit • Technique 5: Using the Inflation Rate-Plus Factor • Technique 6: Using Intuitive Judgment and Flexible Breakeven Analysis • Technique 7: Rate Pyramiding • Technique 8: Analyzing Market Segments

16   Applying Key Marketing Methodologies: Revenue Maximization **205**

Market Mix 205

Example: The Church Convention

Pricing 207

Example: The Park, the Plaza, and the Palace

Yield Management 208
Revenue Maximization in Practice 210

17   The Total Hotel/Unit Marketing Plan **215**

The Marketing Plan 215

Marketing Plan Outline and Instructions • Competitive/Market Positioning Grid

Work Plan Example 223

18   The Total Corporate/Multi-Unit Marketing Plan **229**

Zero-Base Budgeting 229
Research and Required Information 230

Market Segmentation, Needs Identification, and Measurement of Customer Perceptions • Facts About the Competition • External Facts • Internal Facts • Other Hospitality Sector Applications

Marketing Plan 236

Analysis of Research and Information • Objectives • Marketing Program • Marketing Appropriations • Sales Goals • Action Programs • Communication of Assigned Responsibilities • Monitoring of Action Program

19   Practical Steps to Maximize Marketing **247**

Revenue and Profit Production Ideas 247
Methods to Distinguish Your Property 250
Ten Keys to Positive Consumer Reaction 253
Five Steps to More Competitive Marketing 255

20   Marketing, Operations, and Research **259**

Research 259
Operations 260

21   Travel Purchasing Systems: Automation and Beyond 267

Automation 267

*The Relationship to Marketers and Consumers • Reservations Systems •
Property Management Systems • Marketing Information Systems •
Travel Purchasing Systems and Beyond*

22   The New Paradigm 275

The Historic Foundations of Corporate Marketing Strategies 275

Internally Driven Forces • Externally Driven Forces

Corporate Strategies 277
Strategic Assessment 281
The New Paradigm 283

Bibliography 285

Glossary 289

Index 301

Review Quiz Answer Key 307

The Educational Institute Board of Trustees 309

Congratulations. . .

You have a running start on a fast-track career!

Developed through the input of industry and academic experts, this course gives you the know-how hospitality employers demand. Upon course completion, you will earn the respected American Hotel & Motel Association certificate that ensures instant recognition worldwide. It is your link with the global hospitality industry.

You can use your AH&MA certificate to show that your learning experiences have bridged the gap between industry and academia. You will have proof that you have met industry-driven learning objectives and that you know how to apply your knowledge to actual hospitality work situations.

By earning your course certificate, you also take a step toward completing the highly respected learning programs—Certificates of Specialization, the Hospitality Operations Certificate, and the Hospitality Management Diploma—that raise your professional development to a higher level. Certificates from these programs greatly enhance your credentials, and a permanent record of your course and program completion is maintained by the Educational Institute.

We commend you for taking this important step. Turn to the Educational Institute for additional resources that will help you stay ahead of your competition.

Preface

I<small>N ORDER TO UNDERSTAND MARKETING</small> in the hospitality industry today, one must have a thorough understanding of the marketplace. The consumers of lodging, food and beverage, and other travel-related products and services have changed. A look at the demographics, psychographics, user characteristics, or any other measure of the market will demonstrate that marketing hospitality products and services no longer consists of a simple sales call or a good advertising message. The key to marketing in the hospitality industry today is understanding that there is no *one* consumer; there are many, even within the same individual, as defined by a particular set of needs. Comprehending this concept, understanding the needs of consumers, knowing the segmentations of the market, and selecting the best marketing tool to reach your consumers are what this book is all about.

Let's think about the consumer for a moment. When this individual travels or makes use of the products and services offered by the hospitality industry, there is a response to a marketing message that can trigger a decision to purchase from you. This purchase translates into market share, sales, occupancy, average check, rate, profit, passenger miles, or whatever your measure of success is for your marketing program. The key to marketing today is to find the right marketing messages. When this individual travels for business purposes and dines out with clients, his or her needs may be very different than when he or she is traveling or dining out with family or friends.

The hospitality industry has responded to consumers and their changing wants and needs. In the food and beverage sector of the industry we have seen the all-purpose, all-occasion restaurant come and go—and come again. We have seen numerous fast-food concepts, theme restaurants, and even new dining environments emerge. In air travel, deregulation has led to everything from the specialized segmentation of carriers offering all one type or class of service to a plethora of discount and advance-purchase fares. In air travel the response has also included frequent-flyer programs, consolidations, the "hub" concept, and new automated technologies. In lodging, many segmented product specialties have emerged, ranging from budget to all-suite concepts. Major downtown mega-hotels arrived, departed, and returned. The motor inn replaced the motel and the motel returned. Concepts such as club/concierge floors, high-tech rooms, and contracted services emerged. While new chains popped up weekly in the mid-1980s, the results of the overbuilding of the 1980s and the recessions during that decade resulted in massive financial losses and property turnover. By the mid-1990s, demand for lodging was strong again, and occupancies, rates, and profits hit new highs.

This dynamic environment caused many changes in the hospitality products and services offered and in the marketing methodologies marketers used to address the needs of different market segments. Where is hospitality marketing now? More importantly, where should it be and what should it be doing? These questions will surface throughout this book. We will examine and dissect many marketing ideas and techniques—some that have succeeded and some that have failed.

Acknowledgments

Working in the hospitality industry is perhaps one of the greatest learning experiences an individual can have. Over the years I have learned from every travel experience and from each person I have met and worked with or for. The contents of this book were influenced by the exposure I have had to a number of people within the industry and in other professions.

I would like to thank the following individuals: Dr. Jim Myers, author of *Marketing Structure Analysis;* Peter F. Drucker, Professor of Marketing at The Claremont Graduate School, for sharing his knowledge on market positioning and brand preference; and Dr. Robert Buzzell, former Sabastian S. Kresge Professor of Marketing at the Harvard University Graduate School of Business, for helping me remain academically active in the field. To my good friend, Bob Aronin, thanks for the discussions on travel market intermediaries. To Eric Orkin, a sincere thanks for the healthy discussions on setting rates and managing revenue. My special appreciation goes to Bill Marriott, Chairman of the Marriott Corporation; Kemmons Wilson, founder of Holiday Inns and Chairman of the Wilson Companies; Mike Rose, Chairman of the Promus Companies; Juergen Bartels, Chairman of Westin Hotels and Resorts; Bill Hulett, former President of Stouffer Hotels and Resorts; and Jim Biggar, former Chairman and CEO of Nestlé Enterprises, Inc., for the opportunities they gave me to learn more about the industry and the knowledge I gained from exposure to their leadership.

Some of my greatest marketing successes were due to the receptivity of my friends in the media, so special thanks to *USA Today's* former president Cathy Black and current publisher Carolyn Vesper. Thanks to Steve Forbes, CEO of *Forbes* magazine, Danny Lehner and Marc Passarelli of In-Flight Services, and Martin Deutch, former publisher of *Frequent Flyer Magazine.*

A deep appreciation to Dr. Alan T. Stutts, Dean of the Conrad N. Hilton College of Hotel and Restaurant Management at the University of Houston; my colleagues in academia; and The Conrad N. Hilton Foundation. Thank you Ray Swan, former president of the Educational Institute of the American Hotel & Motel Association, for your persistence and help in making this book possible.

Finally, a special acknowledgment to my father for sharing with me his wisdom learned during 40 years in sales and marketing at Colgate Palmolive Company, and to my son, Ron, for helping me master the computer, teaching me some new marketing tricks of his own, and listening to both my good and bad promotional ideas during the course of my career.

Ronald A. Nykiel

About the Author

AUTHOR, business executive, lecturer, professor, and founder are all appropriate descriptions for Dr. Ronald A. Nykiel.

He began his business career with IBM in human resources. With Xerox and Marriott he held managerial positions in market research and strategic and operational planning. He has been a senior officer of Holiday Corporation, serving in a development and strategic planning capacity. As a senior officer of Ramada Incorporated, Nestlé's Stouffer Hotel Company, and Grand Met's Pearle Incorporated, he was responsible for all brand management and marketing functions on a worldwide basis.

Dr. Nykiel has served on the boards of associations, corporations, public television stations, and universities. He has consulted with two United States' Presidential Commissions, various other federal and state entities, and numerous corporations. He founded and is chairman of World Institute Associates, a global business strategy and marketing consulting firm.

He has addressed many corporate and association groups and has lectured at the Harvard Graduate School of Business and other prestigious universities on such subjects as corporate strategy, marketing, consumer behavior, brand management, service excellence, and executive development. He is recognized as an international authority in the field of hospitality, travel, and tourism marketing, and is the author of a leading hospitality industry marketing text. He has also authored a number of books on business strategy, non-hospitality marketing, consumer behavior, and service excellence. He has appeared on national television and radio broadcasts and has contributed to a variety of journals, magazines, and other publications.

Dr. Nykiel received his Bachelor of Arts degree in Liberal Arts from the State University of New York, his Master of Arts degree in Spanish from The Pennsylvania State University, and his Ph.D. in Management and Administration from Walden University. He also holds the Certified Hotel Administrator (CHA) and Certified Hospitality Educator (CHE) designations from the Educational Institute of the American Hotel & Motel Association. Dr. Nykiel is currently the Conrad N. Hilton Distinguished Chair and Professor of Hotel and Restaurant Management at the University of Houston's Conrad N. Hilton College. He is also the chairman of the Hospitality Industry Hall of Honor.

Study Tips for Users of
Educational Institute Courses

Learning is a skill, like many other activities. Although you may be familiar with many of the following study tips, we want to reinforce their usefulness.

Your Attitude Makes a Difference

If you want to learn, you will: it's as simple as that. Your attitude will go a long way in determining whether or not you do well in this course. We want to help you succeed.

Plan and Organize to Learn

- Set up a regular time and place for study. Make sure you won't be disturbed or distracted.

- Decide ahead of time how much you want to accomplish during each study session. Remember to keep your study sessions brief; don't try to do too much at one time.

Read the Course Text to Learn

- *Before* you read each chapter, read the chapter outline and the learning objectives. If there is a summary at the end of the chapter, you should read it to get a feel for what the chapter is about.

- Then, go back to the beginning of the chapter and *carefully* read, focusing on the material included in the learning objectives and asking yourself such questions as:

  —Do I understand the material?

  —How can I use this information now or in the future?

- Make notes in margins and highlight or underline important sections to help you as you study. Read a section first, then go back over it to mark important points.

- Keep a dictionary handy. If you come across an unfamiliar word that is not included in the textbook glossary, look it up in the dictionary.

- Read as much as you can. The more you read, the better you read.

Testing Your Knowledge

- Test questions developed by the Educational Institute for this course are designed to measure your knowledge of the material.

- End-of-the-chapter Review Quizzes help you find out how well you have studied the material. They indicate where additional study may be needed. Review Quizzes are also helpful in studying for other tests.

- Prepare for tests by reviewing:

    —learning objectives

    —notes

    —outlines

    —questions at the end of each assignment

- As you begin to take any test, read the test instructions *carefully* and look over the questions.

We hope your experiences in this course will prompt you to undertake other training and educational activities in a planned, career-long program of professional growth and development.

Chapter Outline

A Historical Perspective—The Growth of
  Industry Brands
A Marketing Perspective of the Industry
A Consumer Perspective of the Industry

Learning Objectives

1. Identify the major sectors of the
   hospitality industry. (pp. 3, 4)

2. Describe the rise of brands within the
   hospitality industry. (pp. 3–6)

3. Explain how marketing activities in
   the hospitality industry address the
   needs of many different types of
   buyers. (p. 6)

4. Explain why a consumer's perspective
   of the hospitality industry changes in
   relation to the purpose for venturing
   away from home. (p. 7)

Understanding the Hospitality Industry

A CONCISE DEFINITION for an industry that has experienced rapid development, like the hospitality industry, is virtually impossible. Moreover, definitions of the hospitality industry are often limited by the unique viewpoints of sectors within the industry. A hotelier might see the industry defined as rooms with food and beverage. A restaurateur might picture the industry as a quality dining experience with the focus on menu offerings and good service. An airline executive might believe that providing travel to people for business or pleasure defines the industry best. All of these viewpoints fit under a wider perspective that defines the hospitality industry in terms of products and services offered to consumers away from home. As shown in Exhibit 1, the industry, in its broadest perspective, encompasses travel, lodging, food and beverage, clubs, gaming, attractions, entertainment, and recreation.

This chapter provides a brief historical overview of the hospitality industry in terms of the emergence and growth of brands within some of the major sectors of the industry. The chapter also examines the multiple purposes of hospitality industry marketing and how marketing activities must address many different types of buyers—from consumers of products and services to owners and investors of the business. Finally, the chapter looks at how consumers' perspectives of the industry and of its product and service offerings change in relation to the reason or purpose for the consumers' ventures away from home.

A Historical Perspective—The Growth of Industry Brands

Restaurants with white tablecloths, hotels with grand ballrooms, business executives pampered by their favorite airlines with personalized matches and reserved seats—these are traditional and, to some extent, obsolete images of the hospitality industry. Today, more than just the personalized matches are gone. New images of the industry abound, created by the way in which airlines, hotels, and restaurants have developed and marketed products and services to meet the changing needs of consumers. Exhibit 2 briefly identifies some milestones of industry development prompted by the changing needs of consumers.

Historically, the consumer's perception of the industry centered on full-service independent hotels, business travelers, and the "glory" of travel. Conrad Hilton changed the image that consumers had of the lodging industry by creating one of the first powerful hotel **brands.** The chain of hotels and the name "Hilton"

Exhibit 1   Sectors of the Hospitality Industry

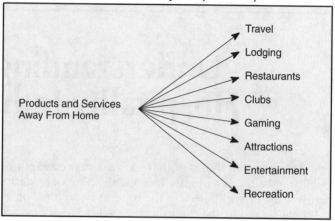

positioned the concept of a brand (Hilton) as synonymous with the word "hotel" in the minds of consumers across the country and eventually across the globe.

New concepts in lodging evolved as other great entrepreneurs conceived new products and services. Kemmons Wilson founded what would become the world's largest single lodging chain, Holiday Inns. In the 1950s, Holiday Inns developed a lodging product that met the needs of a rapidly growing consumer segment—the interstate auto traveler. The adventure of family vacations replaced the traditional image of the glory of travel. Across the market, the brand name "Holiday Inns" became synonymous with the word "motel." The continued success of Holiday Inn Worldwide can be attributed to its ability to change its product and associated levels of service to reach many market segments and fulfill many different consumer segment needs.

The hospitality industry grew rapidly due to the genius and hard work of other founders who built great hospitality companies. Willard and Alice Marriott developed food service concepts (such as the Hot Shoppe Cafeteria and in-flight catering) that met the needs of particular market segments. Their son, Bill Marriott, continued their work in the hotel and food business and made the "Marriott" brand known around the world.

New food concepts became globally recognized brands as companies targeted the ever-changing needs of consumers. McDonald's, Kentucky Fried Chicken (KFC), and other companies went beyond being just food concepts; they became delivery systems as well that specifically addressed the needs of consumers.

Today, Hilton, Holiday, and Marriott are multi-billion-dollar companies and are very different from what they were even just twenty years ago. For that matter, most of the growth firms in the hospitality industry today are very different from what they were ten years ago or even five years ago. Their products and services evolved from consumers' needs, their creativity resulted in new forms of businesses, and their profits from sales of products and services have grown substantially.

Exhibit 2   Some Milestones of Industry Development

1800s	Private rooms become the norm in hotels.
1859	First hotel elevator is installed in New York's Fifth Avenue Hotel.
1860–1900	The Manhattan cocktail is invented.
	The Tremont House in Boston becomes the first hotel to have indoor plumbing, free soap, and guestroom doors with locks.
	The Waiters and Bartenders National Union is formed.
1900	The American Hotel Association is formed.
1920	More new hotels are built (1920–1930) than during any other ten-year period before or since, resulting in a record low occupancy rate of 51% in 1933.
1929	The first airport hotel opens in Oakland, California.
1935	Howard Johnson initiates the first hospitality industry franchise.
1940	The first hotel management contract is signed by Inter-Continental Hotels.
1946	The hotel industry experiences its highest occupancy rate ever—95%.
1950s	Holiday Inns' roadside properties begin the era of the motel.
1960s	Market segmentation and product segmentation begin in earnest in the hotel industry.
	Motor hotels and roadside inns develop along the interstate highway system.
1970s	Spectacular design and architecture (exemplified by the Hyatt Hotel in Atlanta) establish a new era of the hotel.
1980s	Major developments in computers, telecommunications, and other technological areas result in sophisticated reservation systems.
	Industry deregulation arrives.
	Full product segmentation occurs in lodging with brands ranging from economy/budget lines to full-service hotels, all-suite properties, resorts, and mega-hotels.
1990s	Travel-related companies emerge as multi-billion dollar forces in lodging and air transportation.
	Travel purchasing systems emerge, as the marketing giants step in on the purchasing process.
2000s	Consumer-driven technology results in paperless airline tickets, keyless doors, at-home purchasing and delivery systems.
	Supersonic mass passenger aircraft coupled with computer-directed ground transport usher in a new age of travel.

Just as the lodging and restaurant sectors of the industry saw their "founders'" names become household words representing globally recognized brands, the same occurred in other sectors of the industry as well. The name "Walt Disney" became a brand in the entertainment and attractions sectors, and the name "Curt Carlson" became associated with the travel management and services sectors of hospitality. These individuals conceived products and services that turned into brands that not only fulfilled the needs of consumers but also stimulated others to develop more industry products and services and more brands.

Millions of consumers around the globe developed sets of expectations associated with the logos and signs of hospitality brands. The same development and growth of brands held true for airlines (American, Delta, United, etc.) and car rental firms (Avis, Hertz, etc.). Consumers responded to products and services that

Exhibit 3   The Audience for Marketing

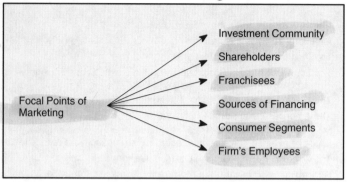

met their needs, and marketing quickly developed the "brand" names associated with those products and services.

A Marketing Perspective of the Industry

As products and services offered by the hospitality industry have evolved, so has the **marketing** of these products and services. Marketing focuses on the needs of the buyer. In today's hospitality industry, the audience of buyers has become complex. Not only do the firms' products or services have buyers, but so do the hospitality firms themselves. As shown in Exhibit 3, marketing must be aware of and relate to the total audience, including the firm's buyers (such as shareholders, the investment community, individual investors, and franchisees).

To explain the importance of these multiple purposes of marketing, it is necessary to briefly touch upon how the hospitality industry functions to achieve its growth and vitality. In order for a firm to function, sources of capital are required for investment. These sources come from internal profits generated by the firm and from a variety of outside investors. A hotel executive was asked who owned the most hotels in the United States today. His response was quick—the insurance companies who hold the mortgages. In the food sector, owners would be the banks, groups of local investors, and so on. The importance of the firm's buyers explains why hospitality industry firms spend marketing dollars on everything from image and awareness advertising to producing the firm's annual report to shareholders. The annual report represents a principal marketing vehicle to those who purchase pieces of the firm. Even more illustrative is the next tier of marketing to the franchise section of the audience of buyers. Annual franchise conferences often rival the best Broadway productions. The reason is simple. Hospitality firms are marketing to a very important audience—those who make the company grow.

To summarize, the hospitality industry marketing perspective is multi-purpose and must relate to many different audiences. The overall goal is not only the sale of the product or service, but the sale of the firm's image to its total audience.

A Consumer Perspective of the Industry

A marketing message that sells products and services is created by understanding the **consumer's perspective.** As a matter of fact, if the marketing process is thorough in its research and analysis of the consumer, then it can perform yet another service for the hospitality firm. This is to influence product development or to recommend changes to services offered so they are more in line with what consumers express as their needs. Marketing cannot succeed if the product or service offering is not in line with its consumers' needs.

The consumer's perspective centers on the needs fulfilled by a product or service. The marketing challenge is that not all consumers have the same needs. In fact, the same consumer can have a very different set of needs. Much depends on the consumer's purpose or the reason for using the product or service. For example, when an executive travels for business purposes, his or her needs may well relate to a nonstop air route, a full-service hotel with meeting facilities, and a gourmet restaurant. The executive, therefore, may have a set of needs that is best served by a specific airline and a specific upscale hotel. This same executive, when traveling with his or her family for purposes of pleasure, may have a set of needs that correspond to economy multiple-stop air travel and a budget lodging facility with a nearby fast-food restaurant. The point to remember is that a consumer's perspective of the industry and of its products and services changes in relation to the reason or purpose for his or her venture away from home.

When planning trips, the executive in our example may well identify specific airlines, lodging facilities, or restaurants by their brand names because the executive perceives that their product and service offerings will best meet his or her specific needs. The executive's expectation is that the brand will fulfill the needs.

The nature, care, and conveying of what the brand stands for and how it meets the needs of the consumer are what marketing is all about. The nature and care of the brand creates a perception by the consumer. This perception translates into a value. Investors pay a premium for this value, a sum of money beyond what they would be willing to invest in the same property or business unit if it were *not* associated with that brand. The perception created by packaging the brand helps to dictate the price consumers are willing to pay for the brand. Conveying how the brand meets the specific needs of buyers is the role of the various marketing methods and techniques.

Key Terms

brand
consumer's perspective
marketing

REVIEW QUIZ

When you feel you have covered all of the material in this chapter, answer these questions. Choose the *best* answer. Check your answers with the correct ones found on the Review Quiz Answer Key at the end of this book.

1. Which of the following would be considered a major sector of the hospitality industry?

    a. lodging
    b. clubs
    c. recreation
    d. all of the above

2. Which of the following would *not* be recognized as a brand name within the hospitality industry?

    a. fast-food operations
    b. Hilton
    c. Delta
    d. Hertz

3. Brands in the hospitality industry have been successful because:

    a. consumers associate value with the brand name.
    b. consumer needs evolve from branded products and services.
    c. branded companies pay little attention to the changing nature of consumer needs.
    d. all of the above.

4. Which of the following statements about marketing in the hospitality industry is *true?*

    a. Marketing efforts should focus on the needs of the buyer.
    b. Marketing efforts focus should on the needs of the hospitality company.
    c. Marketing efforts should focus on the needs of the marketing department.
    d. None of the above.

Chapter Outline

Geographic Segmentation
    Regions, Zones, and Districts
    Metropolitan Statistical Areas
    Cities
    Zip Codes
    Other Geographic Segmentation Tools
Demographic Segmentation
Benefit and Need Segmentation
Psychographic Segmentation
Combining Segmentation Techniques
The Pendulum Swings Toward Value

Learning Objectives

1. Describe the value of geographic segmentation for marketing in the hospitality industry. (pp. 11–15)

2. Explain how feeder cities and city pairs may help focus a company's marketing efforts. (pp. 11–13)

3. Distinguish destination cities from destination markets. (pp. 13–14)

4. Describe the value of demographic customer profiles for marketing in the hospitality industry. (p. 15)

5. Explain how the knowledge gained from benefit and need segmentation can bring hospitality marketers and operations managers into close working relationships. (pp. 15–16)

6. Describe the value of psychographic segmentation for marketing in the hospitality industry. (pp. 16–18)

7. Explain how combining different market segmentation techniques provides valuable research tools for marketing in today's hospitality industry. (pp. 18–19)

2

Market Segmentation and the Hospitality Industry

Mᴀʀᴋᴇᴛs ᴄᴀɴ ʙᴇ sᴇɢᴍᴇɴᴛᴇᴅ or subdivided in many different ways. This chapter briefly describes the traditional territorial concepts, as well as contemporary segmentation methods, and how each can be applied to the hospitality industry.

Geographic Segmentation

Geographic segmentation is the division of a market generally by region, zone, state, district, metropolitan statistical area, and postal zip code zones. There are many purposes and applications of this type of segmentation within the hospitality industry today. Establishing geographic market segments enables marketers to focus sales, advertising, public relations, and promotional activities in the most appropriate areas of a country.

Regions, Zones, and Districts

Regions are used primarily to establish geographic subdivisions of a country. Natural borders often define a region. For example, the area of the United States west of the Rocky Mountains is known as the western region. Regional subdivisions are useful to marketing in the hospitality industry because the bulk of travel by corporate sales forces is within a region. In fact, travel between cities within regions accounts for two-thirds of all travel in the United States. Regional advertising, sales efforts, public relations, and promotions can concentrate on where the business comes from and where it goes to in terms of geographic markets.

    Feeder cities are principal cities within a region that tend to "feed" travel to each other. For example, in the western region of the United States, travel from Los Angeles feeds such cities as Palm Springs, Las Vegas, Phoenix, and San Francisco, all of which in turn feed Los Angeles. Marketing efforts within a region may, therefore, concentrate on both the primary feeder market—say, Los Angeles—as well as the markets that feed Los Angeles.

    Some hospitality organizations with international operations may designate zones as sections of the world, such as the Southeast Asian Zone or the Northern European Zone. However, for most domestic marketing purposes, a **zone** is a geographic area smaller than a region. The area in the state of New York from Albany to Syracuse to Rochester might be classified as a zone.

    A district is a geographic area, generally smaller than a zone, with a concentration of customers. For example, a hotel-chain's midwest regional office may have, for marketing purposes, an Illinois-Wisconsin zone. This zone would have subdivisions called districts, such as Chicago, Milwaukee, La Crosse, etc.

Metropolitan Statistical Areas

The U.S. Census Bureau for many years gathered, compiled, and presented census data by what it defined as Standard Metropolitan Statistical Areas, or SMSAs. In 1990, the Census Bureau refined its definitions and terminology, eliminating the SMSA category by dividing it into Primary Metropolitan Statistical Areas (PMSAs) and Consolidated Metropolitan Statistical Areas (CMSAs). (The bureau also presents data according to two smaller classifications, Metropolitan Areas and Metropolitan Statistical Areas.) The precise definitions of these terms as used by the Census Bureau are beyond our scope here, but two points should be made. First, although the Census Bureau no longer uses the SMSA category, it had become so widely used and accepted that many people outside the government continue to use it; references to SMSAs remain common. Second, in the following discussion, we will refer generically to CMSAs and PMSAs (that is, those areas that used to be SMSAs) simply as **metropolitan statistical areas.**

Metropolitan statistical areas tend to be the population within a large county or within a number of small counties. However, the core of a metropolitan statistical area is usually a major city. For example, the New York City metropolitan statistical area, which is a huge market in terms of population, encompasses counties in three states and Long Island. Approximately 50% of the overnight travel in the United States is generated from 24 metropolitan statistical areas, some of which are listed below:

Los Angeles	Denver	Atlanta
Dallas	Chicago	Minneapolis-St. Paul
New York	Boston	Washington, D.C.
San Francisco	Houston	Seattle
Detroit	Pittsburgh	Miami/Dade County
Phoenix	Cleveland	

These areas become key strategic markets in which to sell travel products or services.

Metropolitan statistical areas play an important role in marketing for the travel sectors of the hospitality industry, such as airlines, bus companies, rail service, and lodging. Frequently, both print and broadcast media exposure are defined in terms of geographic areas related to metropolitan statistical areas. Also, there are direct correlations between the size of metropolitan statistical areas and the number and type of food service outlets such areas can absorb.

Counties are also important geographic areas because laws concerning business operations vary by county in relation to liquor license requirements, hours of restaurant operations, food service regulations, and so on.

City pairs such as Boston and New York City, or Washington, D.C., and New York City are cities between which a heavy travel pattern exists. Knowing major city pairs and understanding relationships between metropolitan statistical areas is essential for assessing the best use of marketing expenditures on a geographic

Exhibit 1   Map of Major Traffic Flows in the United States

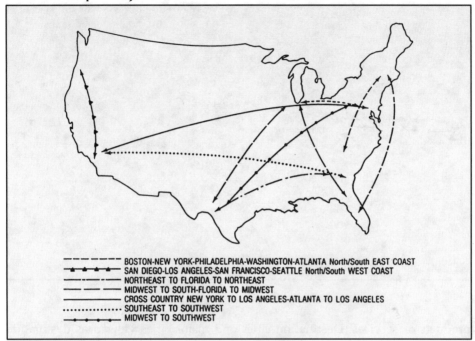

```
----------- BOSTON-NEW YORK-PHILADELPHIA-WASHINGTON-ATLANTA North/South EAST COAST
-▲-▲-▲-▲- SAN DIEGO-LOS ANGELES-SAN FRANCISCO-SEATTLE North/South WEST COAST
-------- NORTHEAST TO FLORIDA TO NORTHEAST
-------- MIDWEST TO SOUTH-FLORIDA TO MIDWEST
-------- CROSS COUNTRY NEW YORK TO LOS ANGELES-ATLANTA TO LOS ANGELES
·········· SOUTHEAST TO SOUTHWEST
-•-•-•- MIDWEST TO SOUTHWEST
```

basis. Marketing expenditures can concentrate on the city pairs that generate the largest number of consumers for travel products or services.

The travel between key strategic markets and city pairs is referred to as traffic flow. Exhibit 1 maps some of the major traffic flows in the United States. Exhibit 2 maps major world traffic flows. Examples of major world traffic flows are:

- East Coast of North America to Europe

- Europe to East Coast of North America

- Northern Europe to Southern Europe and the Mediterranean

- West Coast of United States to Japan and Asia

- Far East to West Coast of United States

- North and South United States to Mexico and Latin America

- Japan to Hawaii and West Coast of United States

- Japan to Asia and South Pacific

- United Kingdom to Germany, France, and Spain

Cities

Cities are often ranked in order of size of population, degree of affluence, type of industry base, or other criteria useful for the purposes of marketing specific

Exhibit 2   Map of Major World Traffic Flows

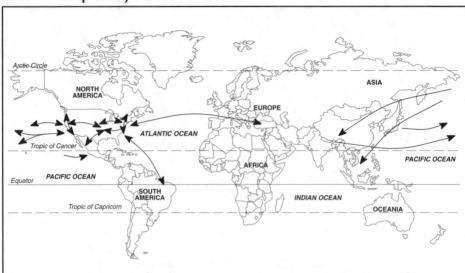

products or services. Destination cities and major cities viewed as destination markets are especially significant to marketing within the hospitality industry. Destination cities have unique attractions unto themselves that create demand for travel. For example, in the last 50 years, such major destination cities as Orlando, Las Vegas, Acapulco, West Palm Beach, Lake Tahoe, and Atlantic City have emerged (or re-emerged) as significant travel markets. While Las Vegas and Acapulco represent examples of pure destination cities, many major cities such as New York City and Los Angeles are viewed as destination markets. These cities create demand for travel not only from the unique attractions they offer, but also from their many centers of business and commerce.

Zip Codes

Zip codes—five-digit Unites States Postal Service designations with four-digit suffixes—correspond to some extent with cities and metropolitan statistical areas. However, zip codes further define an area into smaller sections, even to square blocks of a city. Zip codes and the first three digits of a zip code (known as the sectional center) have special significance for direct mail marketing. This significance has been greatly enhanced through the correlation of zip codes and demographic data from the U.S. Census Bureau reports.

Other Geographic Segmentation Tools

Other geographic segmentation tools that relate to metropolitan statistical area and zip code segmentation include Designated Market Areas (DMAs) and Areas of Dominant Influence (ADIs).

Designated Market Areas, conceived by the A. C. Nielsen Company, are composed of areas based on the dominance of clusters of television stations. DMAs are useful marketing tools in relation to media planning and for researching TV audiences.

Areas of Dominant Influence are geographic market designations developed by the Arbitron audience research firm. An ADI is a geographic area in which the majority of households are served by a given city's cluster of media. ADI boundaries are typically defined by the circulation patterns of magazines, newspapers, and other publications. ADIs can also be defined by zip code sectional centers and have excellent application for media planning in hospitality marketing.

Demographic Segmentation

Demographic segmentation is the categorization of consumers by like characteristics such as sex, age, income, home ownership, marital status, occupation, and education. Demographically different consumers reside within each region, state, district, zone, metropolitan statistical area, city, and even zip code. As a result of the comprehensive demographic data available through the U.S. Census Bureau reports and private research firms specializing in demographic market data, there are virtually hundreds of ways in which to demographically segment the market.

For years, direct mail operators, publishers, retailers of consumer goods, and others have developed **demographic profiles** of their consumers. These profiles vary in relation to the type of product or service marketed. To demonstrate how cost effective a good demographic profile and purchase pattern correlation can be, consider the example of the effective direct mail marketer. For some products, less than 35% of the zip codes generate more than 80% of the sales. A good mailing list correlates zip codes with demographic customer profiles and eliminates 65% of non-respondent market areas.

In the hospitality industry, there are direct correlations between income and the likelihood of using travel services. To a point, the higher the income, the greater the frequency of travel. In today's food service industry, fast-food restaurants, bars, and full-service restaurants develop demographic profiles of their customers.

Benefit and Need Segmentation

Benefit and need segmentation divides a market into groups of consumers on the basis of the benefits they seek, the needs they expect to satisfy, and, in some instances, the factors they hope to avoid. For years, the consumer-products industry has applied this market segmentation tool to determine what consumers look for in a product and what they avoid. This research is applied to everything from the color, smell, size, shape, and appearance of the product and package to the advertising message. Granted, a hotel, restaurant, or airline does not lend itself to this same level of refinement as far as the physical product is concerned, but each can be packaged and marketed using the same principles of benefit and need segmentation.

In the 1980s, a number of hospitality industry firms began to make use of benefits and needs research. For example, the airline shuttles between New York

City, Boston, and Washington, D.C., now serve a large group of consumers whose single greatest need is the convenience of no-reservation, multiple-departure-time transportation. Scheduling shuttles on the hour or on the half hour from early morning to late night fulfills the primary need of these consumers. Likewise, a fast-food restaurant may satisfy a number of needs or provide various benefits in terms of offering low prices, convenient location, and fast service.

Consider the situation of couples escaping for a weekend to a hotel. They seek a memorable experience in a relaxed atmosphere. Further, they try to avoid a child-oriented facility or one full of business meetings. If a lodging facility wants to successfully attract this market, it must recognize what these couples wish to avoid, as well as the benefits they seek. It is in this area of segmentation that marketing and product research must closely relate to operations and product development.

Marketing and operations work together to maximize the sale of products or services while satisfying the different needs of guests. Consider the hotel that promoted two types of "escape weekend" programs. One program was a "second honeymoon" escape, the other a family weekend escape. The second honeymooners were escaping from the children for peace, relaxation, and a memorable experience. The family escapees were out to have fun with their children and were looking for activities, excitement, and a very different kind of experience from that sought by the second honeymooners. The hotel's marketing and operations team came up with the solution. All families on an escape weekend were roomed in the wings of the property surrounding the pool, game room, and coffee shop. The hotel lodged all second honeymooners in rooms high up in the tower section of the hotel or near the indoor pool and bar. Also, the second honeymooners were served breakfast in bed and their dining reservations were made in the hotel's upscale restaurant, which was far removed from the coffee shop where the family escapees generally ate their meals.

Since each market segment frequently seeks different benefits or has different needs to satisfy, benefit and need segmentation presents a challenge to the hospitality industry. The business executive trying to impress a client and close a major contract needs an atmosphere conducive to a business discussion that will impress the client. An upscale hotel with a special table in the dining room might fulfill these needs. But the same environment that meets the executive's need while negotiating a business deal may be exactly what he or she wants to avoid when traveling for pleasure.

Psychographic Segmentation

Psychographic segmentation is a method of subdividing a market based on like needs and psychological motivations of consumer groups. Psychographic segmentation along with benefit and need segmentation provides insight into the psychological aspects of buyer behavior.

The firm of Yankelovich, Clancy, and Shulman (formerly Yankelovich, Skelly, and White) has been a leader in the development and use of psychographic segmentation through its research tool called MONITOR. MONITOR profiles the U.S. population by regularly measuring over 60 trends such as:

- Economizing on food purchases

- Dining out more or less often

- Planning more or fewer vacations

- Planning shorter or longer vacations

- Postponing major purchases

- Concern or lack of concern about credit usage

- Desire for more or fewer materialistic purchases

For participating clients, MONITOR psychographically segments the population based on groups holding common values. For example, the MONITOR program measures the percentage of the U.S. population holding traditional values of a Protestant work ethic. It also identifies other population groups holding common values and profiles them in categories of value segments with names like forerunners, new conformists, conservatives, and others. Each of these value segments is profiled demographically and geographically.

Many industries have applied the output from MONITOR to guide such marketing activities as product development, advertising, promotions, and the creation of brand images. The travel-related elements of MONITOR were sufficient to merit a separate study. In the early 1990s, the firm of Yesawich, Pepperdine, and Brown acquired the administration of the MONITOR studies that relate to travel.

Psychographic segmentation tends to focus trends into key areas such as activities, interests, and opinions. In programs like MONITOR, social attitudes help predict the propensity to travel, likely future rates of growth, willingness to pay, redefining the parameters of value, etc. Activity-related factors are also included, such as leisure-travel preferences and desired leisure activities. The degree and rank of interests are reviewed from year to year to determine attitudinal changes. Also, opinions on current issues and events influencing consumer behavior are identified.

While MONITOR looks at a comprehensive list of factors over a broad travel-related definition, other psychographic research programs focus on specific areas of the hospitality industry. *Values And LifeStyles* (VALS), developed by SRI International, focuses on the food service area. VALS categorizes the population (market) into different types (segments) with distinctive food preferences. VALS looks at attitudes and lifestyles as well as current and emerging trends to project potential buying habits and media preferences. VALS is used to assist food service companies in conceiving new restaurant concepts, food and beverage themes, menus, facilities, etc. VALS is also extensively used in media selection and planning and in the creative process connected with developing advertising and promotional campaigns.

Another attitudinal segmentation applied in food service marketing comes from CREST studies. CREST looks at QSC issues (quality, service, and cleanliness) as well as other issues like nutrition. CREST studies segment consumers into groups with distinctive attitudes. The studies then categorize groups with names such as nutritionally fit, conventional taste, restrictive dieters, busy urbanites, etc.,

Exhibit 3   Sample Frequent Traveler Profile

Age:	25 to 44 years old
Income:	$35,000 plus
Education:	College degree plus
Occupations:	Administration, Sales, Marketing, Engineers, Technicians, Business Executives, Buyers, Consultants
Industry Origins:	Electronics, Pharmaceuticals, Chemicals, Service, Manufacturing, Publishing, Banking, and Finance
Travel Habits:	Ten business trips plus, per year Heavy air travel Intra- and inter-regional travel Two pleasure trips plus, per year
Location:	Suburban and center city Corresponding sectional centers/Zips to above High income geodemographic census tracks

that are helpful to the marketing efforts of quick-service, casual, and upscale dining operations.

Combining Segmentation Techniques

Geographic, demographic, benefit/need, and psychographic segmentation techniques by themselves and in combination with each other are valuable marketing research tools in today's hospitality industry. For example, the **heavy user** is a recurrent consumer of a product or service who can be identified through demographics and other market segmentation techniques. To the fast-food industry, the heavy user is the regular at McDonald's, Burger King, KFC, and Wendy's. To airlines and lodging companies, the heavy user is the frequent traveler who could well become their repeat customer. Exhibit 3 presents a sample frequent traveler profile that incorporates demographic, geographic, and some psychographic data. Effective marketing tools for reaching the recurrent business traveler are mailing lists from major credit card companies and advertising media such as in-flight magazines.

Combining segmentation techniques helps to identify and monitor quantitative and qualitative trends. Also, hospitality organizations and market research firms work together to cut the market into increasingly finer segments, both in terms of its psychographic components (attitudes, opinions, interests, etc.) and its **geodemographic** nature (classifying how many people have characteristics of a like nature and where they reside). Since lifestyles change and new values and beliefs continue to evolve, understanding how consumers think and why consumers buy presents never-ending challenges for marketing in the hospitality industry.

The Pendulum Swings Toward Value

Price segmentation identifies groups of consumers within a market whose purchase of products or services is within the limits of certain dollar amounts. Such identification has always been important to the hospitality industry. In times of high inflation, business recessions, and economic turmoil, price segmentation becomes even more significant.

Groups of consumers are often segmented by price as a result of per diem allowances for travel, lodging, and meals. For example, government employees, salespeople, and military personnel are usually price-sensitive market segments because they have limited per diem allowances. Price sensitivity and related segmentation extends to virtually every area of the hospitality industry, ranging from the family who goes out for an inexpensive meal at the local fast-food restaurant, to the salesperson who wants a comfortable but inexpensive room within the per diem allowance of his or her firm, to the executive whose need to impress a client supersedes any interest in economizing.

While price sensitivity is always important, the overriding objective of marketing in the hospitality industry is to ensure customer satisfaction by providing *value*. Regardless of the market segment, hospitality organizations provide value by offering a quality product or service at a fair price.

One very interesting response to a research question demonstrates how the emphasis on value cuts across every segment of the market. The same question was asked of buyers of two automobiles, Volvo and Mercedes-Benz: "Why did you buy this car?" The response was the same: "Its quality and value." The same type of question was posed to a family eating at McDonald's: "Why did you buy your family dinner at McDonald's?" Although the family was from entirely different geographic, demographic, and psychographic segments than the Volvo/Mercedes consumers, the response was the same: "Because of its value—good quality at a fair price." Every demographic, psychographic, and economic indicator points to *value* as the key need that marketing must fulfill in the decade ahead.

Key Terms

benefit and need segmentation
city pairs
demographic profile
demographic segmentation
feeder cities
geodemographic segmentation
geographic segmentation

heavy user
metropolitan statistical areas
price segmentation
psychographic segmentation
region
zone

REVIEW QUIZ

When you feel you have covered all of the material in this chapter, answer these questions. Choose the *best* answer. Check your answers with the correct ones found on the Review Quiz Answer Key at the end of this book.

1. For the purposes of marketing, which of the following defines the smallest geographic area?

    a. a region
    b. a metropolitan statistical area
    c. a postal zip code
    d. a zone

2. The sectional center of a zip code is:

    a. the last three digits.
    b. the last two digits.
    c. the first three digits.
    d. the first two digits.

3. Which of the following is an example of a destination market?

    a. Las Vegas
    b. New York City
    c. Orlando
    d. all of the above

4. Which of the following statements is *true?*

    a. Natural borders define the boundaries of metropolitan statistical areas.
    b. Demographic segmentation reveals the benefits consumers seek and the needs they expect to satisfy.
    c. Frequent traveler profiles incorporate demographic, geographic, and psychographic data.
    d. Psychological aspects of buyer behavior are best discovered through geographic segmentation methods.

5. Which of the following statements is *false?*

    a. Print and broadcast media exposures are frequently defined in terms of geographic areas related to metropolitan statistical areas.
    b. City pairs are defined by patterns of heavy traffic flows.
    c. Designated Market Areas (DMAs) are useful marketing tools in relation to media planning and for researching TV audiences.
    d. Price segmentation studies separate price-sensitive consumers from those consumers seeking quality and value.

Chapter Outline

End Users
    Business Travelers
    Pleasure Travelers
Travel Intermediaries
Food Service Market Segmentation
    Desired Dining Experience
    Price Sensitivity
    Convenience and Location

Learning Objectives

1. Distinguish end users from intermediaries in the travel and hospitality market. (pp. 23–25)

2. Describe characteristics of business travel market segments. (pp. 23–25)

3. Describe characteristics of pleasure travel market segments. (p. 25)

4. Identify travel intermediaries for business and pleasure travel market segments. (pp. 25–27)

5. Describe user characteristics of consumer segments in the food service market. (pp. 27–29)

Positioning in Line with Consumer Preferences

T HERE ARE MANY KEYS to successful marketing in the hospitality industry. Most begin with an understanding of consumer preferences. Marketing's function is to target these preferences when communicating product and service offerings to specific consumer segments.

The first part of this chapter examines two broad consumer categories for the hospitality industry's products and services: end users and intermediaries. An **end user** is the ultimate consumer of the product or service offered. An **intermediary** is a person or company who influences the buying decisions of end users. Sections that follow focus on the needs of different types of end users and identify the major intermediaries specific to the hospitality industry.

The second part of the chapter looks more closely at segmentation in the food service industry. General consumer preferences are described in relation to desired dining experiences or purposes for eating away from home. Price segmentation of the food service market is also addressed, as well as the importance of convenience and location of food service operations to consumers who choose to eat away from home. Understanding consumer preferences is essential for properly positioning product and service offerings.

End Users

End users can be segmented in relation to their overall purpose for traveling—for business or for pleasure. Exhibit 1 identifies some major types of end users of lodging products and services. Each of these market segments is dynamic. Variations in the amount and type of travel are subject to internal factors such as a company's travel policy or an individual's tastes and habits. Variations are also caused by external factors such as the current economic situation as well as social and political events.

Business Travelers

In the business travel segment, there are three major subsegments of travelers:

- Meeting, conference, or convention attendees
- Travelers with relatively unrestricted expense accounts
- Price-conscious business travelers

Exhibit 1   End Users

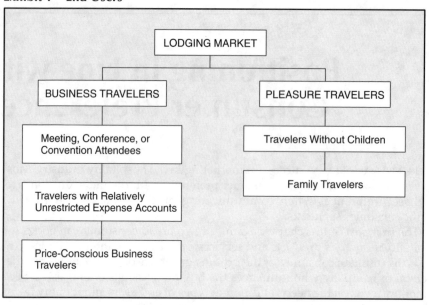

Meeting, Conference, or Convention Attendees. The individual business traveler attending a meeting, conference, or convention usually has little control over the selection of accommodations or the room rates he or she will pay. In some cases, the only choice the attendee may really have is whether to attend the function at all (although, in some instances, even attendance may be mandatory). Business travelers attending functions planned by associations tend to be more price conscious than those who attend corporate meetings or conferences. Almost always, the individuals in this subsegment make a reservation before arrival or are preregistered by their respective group, organization, or company.

The primary needs of this subsegment of the business travel market include not only comfortable meeting environments but also ample telephones and other communication devices to help them remain in touch with their businesses before sessions, during breaks, and after sessions. Attendees also need entertainment and other sorts of opportunities to relax after a day's intense round of meetings and functions.

Travelers with Relatively Unrestricted Expense Accounts. These individuals generally seek comfortable, dependable, full-service accommodations and are usually less price-sensitive than other types of business travelers. Individuals in this subsegment are likely to be business executives, international travelers, and high-income independent travelers. These end users are likely to prefer specific hotel locations or individual hotel brands. Their room reservations are likely to be guaranteed and placed through the services of a travel agent or secretary. Major needs and concerns of these travelers include security, convenient locations, and business-related services such as fax machines, message services, and guestrooms equipped to facilitate the operation of portable computers.

Price-Conscious Business Travelers. As corporations and government departments become more cost conscious, price-sensitive travelers are becoming a rapidly growing subsegment of the business market. These individuals may travel on a per diem basis. A **per diem** sets upper limits to the amount of money that individuals can recover from their organizations for expenses such as travel, lodging, and meals. While these travelers are sensitive to how much travel products and services cost, they still want as much comfort and service as their money can buy. Usually, a travel department, contracted travel agency, or department secretary makes their travel arrangements and room reservations, although these business travelers sometimes arrive at their destinations without room reservations.

Pleasure Travelers

In the pleasure travel segment, there are two broad subsegments of travelers: travelers without children and family travelers (travelers with children).

Travelers Without Children. Travelers without children include individuals, couples, and groups traveling for pleasure. They are not restricted by child-related responsibilities and may be interested in "living it up," enjoying various restaurant and entertainment facilities. These travelers are generally interested in comfort and service, but may also be price-conscious.

Family Travelers. Adults traveling with children are more restricted in their pleasure travel than are travelers without children. Family travelers are often more focused on the essential daily routines of feeding, caring for, and lodging their children than on "living it up." Important accommodation benefits include economical and casual restaurant facilities, in-room interactive television games, swimming pools, and other features that make the job of caring for the family away from home convenient and uncomplicated.

A subsegment of family travelers includes those vacationers who are extremely price-conscious and are not interested in paying for amenities or extras of any kind. They simply seek a place to eat and sleep that serves as a home base for their excursions. Another subsegment seeks simplicity, outdoor recreation, and freedom in their pleasure travel experience. These families are not interested in hotel services and seek unstructured, do-it-yourself vacations. They look to avoid the service, tipping, and costs of hotels and resorts, preferring instead to stay at campgrounds, beach cottages, mountain cabins, or condominiums.

Travel Intermediaries

Intermediaries are generally not end users of products or services, but they are important to marketing efforts because they assist and influence end users in their selections of travel and hospitality options. Exhibit 2 identifies some of the intermediaries for both the business and pleasure market segments.

Meeting planners are generally association executives, corporate executives, or training company executives whose major goal is to plan and execute successful

Exhibit 2   Lodging Market Intermediaries

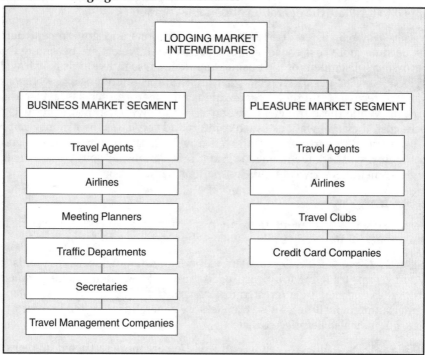

conventions, conferences, or meetings. Meeting room facilities, meeting-related services, and banquet operations are usually more important concerns than are the types of room accommodations or the variety of restaurant and food service outlets. Meeting planners are typically price-sensitive, but this may vary with the policies of their associations or corporations.

A number of major corporations have set up *traffic departments* to manage and schedule their high volume of company travel.

Secretaries are one of the largest groups of intermediaries in relation to business travel. However, the influence of secretaries on travel purchase decisions can vary tremendously, even within the same organization. In some cases, a secretary may be the decision-maker in booking travel arrangements, car rentals, and hotel accommodations. In other cases, a secretary may simply execute the travel decisions made by individual company managers and executives.

Travel management companies provide travel management services on a contractual or fee basis to corporations, government agencies, associations, and other organizations with business-related travel needs.

Travel agents arrange air, cruise, and rail travel and place reservations for car rentals and lodging accommodations for both business and pleasure travelers. They are interested in booking their clients with hospitality companies that are dependable in honoring reservations and that offer consistent levels of service. Travel agents prefer to work with hospitality companies that offer uncomplicated reservation processes and ensure prompt payment of commissions for booking business with them.

Capitalizing on the sophistication of their reservation systems, *airlines* may perform the role of a travel intermediary by handling requests for hotel and car rental reservations. Most airlines also sell to the pleasure travel market segment through other intermediaries such as travel and tour wholesalers, retail travel agents, travel clubs, and others. The airlines assist other intermediaries in selling to consumers and also offer flights and seat capacities that are sold as part of travel packages.

Travel clubs influence the travel purchase decisions of their members. As the pleasure travel market became more sophisticated, travel clubs emerged to meet both general and specific consumer needs. These travel clubs, such as Club Universe and Club Med, target the frequent pleasure traveler and offer club members special packages to desirable destinations. In addition, these packages are frequently tailored to specific interests, such as golf, tennis, visiting historic sites, or simply getting away from civilization.

Many *credit card companies* influence purchase decisions by promoting and selling consumer travel packages put together by other intermediaries, such as tour wholesalers. In addition, the larger credit card companies, banks, and even major department stores often have in-house divisions to promote travel and travel packages to their customers.

Food Service Market Segmentation

The food service or eating-away-from-home market can be segmented along many dimensions useful for the purposes of marketing. Exhibit 3 identifies some types of food service establishments that market to specific consumer segments. The sections that follow look briefly at user characteristics of consumers in the food service market in terms of desired dining experience, price sensitivity, and convenience and location.

Desired Dining Experience

Segmenting the food service market in relation to the overall desired dining experience subdivides the market into groups of consumers with specific purposes for eating away from home. For example, businesspeople may seek to impress clients, couples may seek romance, families may just want to get out of the house, and so on. Desired menu offerings and expected levels of service vary with the consumer's purpose for eating away from home. Marketing messages to food service segments are tailored to the consumer's desired dining experience and focus on the consumer's purpose for eating away from home.

The desired dining experience may also center on individual consumer tastes and types of food. Our culturally diverse society can be segmented by preferred cuisine (Mexican, Italian, Chinese, and so on) or even by taste preferences (from bland to spicy). A few of the numerous other ways to segment the market are: nutrition or health segments, diet-conscious segments, and segments based on preferred

Exhibit 3 Food Service Establishments with Specific Consumer Segments

```
                    ┌──────────────────────────────┐
                    │  Eating-Away-from-Home Market │
                    └──────────────────────────────┘

  ┌──────────────────────────┐        ┌──────────────────────────────────┐
  │ Traditional Market Segments │      │ Lodging-Related Market Segments  │
  └──────────────────────────┘        └──────────────────────────────────┘

   Fast Food Operations                     Hotel Restaurants
   Take-Out Delicatessens    ┌────────────────────────────┐   Local Restaurants
   Coffee Shops              │  Special Market Segments    │   Banquets
   Family Restaurants        └────────────────────────────┘   Room Service
   Dinner Houses              Airline Catering                 Bars
   Clubs                      Institutional Food Service       Catering
   Gourmet Restaurants        Sports and Entertainment         Buffets
                                 Complexes
                              Special Banquet Facilities
                              Catering
                              Contract Food Service
                              Concessions
```

type of food such as meat and potatoes, home cooking, pizza, pasta, beef, chicken, fish, and so on.

Price Sensitivity

Market segmentation by price and related demographic consumer characteristics has been the topic of many food service industry studies. Usually the higher the income (up to a certain point), the greater the propensity for consumers to dine out and spend. An exception to this tendency is the fast-food or convenience-food market segment, which includes customers of McDonald's, Burger King, Wendy's, as well as customers of pizza chains and locally owned and operated convenience-food operations. Within this segment, consumers not only seek convenience, they are also price conscious.

Exhibit 4 diagrams a three-tiered segmentation of the food service market based on price sensitivity. The first tier represents the fast-food or convenience-food consumer. The second tier identifies the medium-priced segment. These consumers seek a step up and a change of pace from fast-food and look for a dining "experience." Consumers within this tier are also value-oriented and expect quality at a fair price. The type of food service operations for the medium-priced segment might range from a prime rib house to a lobster barn to a specialty restaurant. Again, the consumer's purpose for eating away from home and preferences for different types of food are the key factors determining the buyer's behavior. The third tier is the least sensitive to price. This tier or subsegment includes two groups with different needs. The first is the special occasion group, exemplified by a couple celebrating a wedding anniversary by going to the "best" restaurant in town. Here, purpose overrides sensitivity to price. The second group is categorized by a

Exhibit 4 Food Service Market—Price Segmentation

	Price Sensitivity		
	Low	Medium	High
Tier 1 Convenience			Fast food chains Pizza shops Delicatessens
Tier 2 Value and Experience		Steak houses Seafood restaurants Specialty restaurants	
Tier 3 Special Occasion	Gourmet restaurants Upscale theme restaurants		

need to impress others. Conveying the impression of affluence often becomes the primary motive for selecting the "best" restaurant (which may equate to the most expensive restaurant, or the restaurant with the "best chef," etc.). This second group looks for gourmet menu items, upscale service, and unique ambience—all appealing to the dining experience they wish to have for themselves and helping to create the impression of affluence that they wish to give others.

Convenience and Location

When time is a critical factor determining where consumers choose to eat away from home, convenience and location become overriding consumer needs. This does not simply mean geographic location or proximity to a specific type of food service operation. In fact, convenience more often implies quickness of service. This is often the single most important factor for any food service subsegment when time plays into the decision to eat away from home.

Key Terms

end user
intermediary
meeting planners
per diem

traffic department
travel club
travel management company

REVIEW QUIZ

When you feel you have covered all of the material in this chapter, answer these questions. Choose the *best* answer. Check your answers with the correct ones found on the Review Quiz Answer Key at the end of this book.

1.   Which of the following would be considered an end user of hospitality products and services?

   a. travel agent
   b. convention attendee
   c. tour operator
   d. travel management company

2.   Which of the following consumer segments would most likely travel on a per diem basis?

   a. convention attendees
   b. government employees
   c. business travelers with relatively unrestricted expense accounts
   d. pleasure travel groups

3.   Which of the following intermediaries focus primarily on the needs of the business travel market?

   a. travel clubs
   b. airlines
   c. travel management companies
   d. all of the above

4.   Which of the following intermediaries focus most on influencing the buying decisions of consumers in the pleasure travel market?

   a. travel clubs
   b. meeting planners
   c. traffic departments
   d. travel management companies

5.   Which of the following statements is *true?*

   a. Desired menu items of consumer segments in the food service market vary with the consumer's purpose for eating away from home.
   b. Consumers in the fast-food market segment prefer convenience over value.
   c. Consumer expectations in relation to level of service do not change across market segments in the food service industry.
   d. none of the above

Chapter Outline

Channels of Distribution
    Travel Intermediaries
    Electronic Travel Distribution Systems
    Ground Operators
    Air Carriers
    Channels of Distribution in Europe
       and Japan
Government Regulation of Travel
    United States
    Foreign Governments
Vertical and Horizontal Integration

Learning Objectives

1. Describe channels of distribution within the hospitality industry. (pp. 33–38)

2. List and briefly describe U.S. and international governmental entities that regulate or influence travel. (pp. 38–39)

3. Describe vertical and horizontal integration in the hospitality industry. (p. 39)

4

The Channels of Distribution

Because the hospitality industry serves many consumer segments, it has established channels of distribution through which it markets its products and services. A **channel of distribution** is an entity through which all or parts of a travel product or service may be purchased directly or indirectly by the consumer. Advances in technology have created a dynamic environment within existing distribution channels, as well as adding new systems to the purchase process. The industry is also becoming increasingly more complex, in that often a variety of travel products and services are offered by the same firm or interrelated firms. The purpose of this chapter is to describe the hospitality industry's channels of distribution, touch on governmental regulation of travel, and discuss the evolution of integrated hospitality industry firms and their relationship to marketing.

Channels of Distribution

Channels of distribution within the hospitality industry include travel intermediaries (such as travel agents and tour operators), electronic travel distribution systems, ground operators, and air carriers. We will discuss each of these channels of distribution in the following sections.

Travel Intermediaries

In order to understand the complexity of how travel products can be purchased and marketed, let's return briefly to the consumer. Consumers may travel to visit friends and relatives, for business, for recreation, for sight-seeing and entertainment, for personal or family reasons, to gamble, or to visit a specific destination or attraction (see Exhibit 1). A travel product or service, be it for business or pleasure, can be purchased directly and usually in its entirety (from flight to lodging to meals) by individual consumers. However, today there is a much greater inclination among consumers to seek and use the services of either a captive or commercial **travel intermediary.**

A *captive intermediary* is an individual who does not receive a commission for handling travel arrangements for others. Examples of captive intermediaries include secretaries, office managers, and employees in company travel departments. A *commercial intermediary* is an individual (or entity) who works for a commission from a supplier of travel for handling the travel arrangements of individual or group consumers. Whether captive or commercial, the intermediary obtains the travel product and services through specific channels of distribution.

Examples of commercial intermediaries include the following:

Exhibit 1   The Purpose of Travel

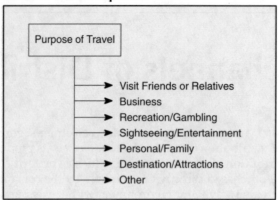

- *Retail travel agents (RTAs).* Retail travel agents sell tours, hotel rooms, airline tickets, steamship tickets, and so forth for wholesalers and tour operators. Retail travel agents earn all or most of their gross revenue from commissions. Travel agent commissions from travel suppliers vary by supplier and by country, but usually range from 10 to 40 percent.

- *Travel management companies.* Travel management companies provide a variety of travel management services, from financial management and credit card services to completely managing a firm's entire travel operation. Travel management companies have grown rapidly as travel becomes a focal point of cost management in corporations and government. Many large travel management companies also own or operate groups of retail travel agencies.

- *Tour operators-retailers.* **Tour operators-retailers** create "packages" for tourists that may include air, lodging, and ground services, and then offer them to consumers through a variety of such marketing tools as print and broadcast media, storefront operations, travel agents, and direct mail. In some countries (Germany and the United Kingdom, for example), these travel packages are sold through retail outlets directly to consumers on a large-scale basis.

- *Tour operators-wholesalers.* **Tour operators-wholesalers** create tour packages by buying the transportation, accommodations, and attraction components, then retail the packages through travel agents. Tour wholesalers service retail travel agents by preparing tour packages, ordering brochures and posters, and advertising. The difference between a tour operator-wholesaler and a tour operator-retailer is that the tour operator-wholesaler never sells directly to consumers, whereas a tour operator-retailer may.

- *Packagers/retailers.* Some packagers of tour products and services have now integrated vertically into retailing through their own outlets, after having moved into ownership of their own accommodations or transportation. One example of a packager/retailer is Club Med, which owns its resorts, charters transportation to them, and even markets/retails direct to individual consumers.

- *Incentive travel company.* Incentive travel companies specialize in putting together and selling travel awards, prizes, gifts, premiums, and so forth for individuals, groups, companies, and associations. The **incentive travel** trip or tour is usually sold to the user organization as part of a complete motivational package. Incentive travel is often used in a sales or marketing area to raise money for a group such as a church or other association, or to stimulate interest in a new product. In addition to the tour, incentive travel companies may also supply other administrative and creative capabilities to buyers.

- *Convention movers.* Convention movers specialize in moving people to and from conventions, usually using the major airlines and their regularly scheduled flights. Convention movers may also offer pre- or post-convention tours.

- *Travel clubs.* A relatively new merchandising method in group travel is the *travel club.* A travel club usually offers a group travel plan whereby membership in the club makes travel opportunities and vacation destination facilities available to members at discounted prices. The accommodations offered by travel clubs range from deluxe to very modest. Usually travel clubs offer a wide choice of locations, climate, terrain, and other vacation features. Unique atmospheres and sometimes specialized areas, events, and activities are often selling points of travel clubs.

- *Charter travel company.* A charter travel company specializes in putting together groups of people with common interests. The individuals are then eligible for charter flights, which are governed by specific regulations. A charter travel company also helps groups pay for and operate tours.

- *Electronic/on-line travel service providers.* Electronic/on-line travel service providers have emerged as informational sources as well as direct booking services on a subscriber basis. For example, American Express Travel Services and the SABRE reservation service are both available on-line direct to consumers through America On-Line. As the world continues to grow in computer literacy, so do these service providers.

Electronic Travel Distribution Systems

Electronic travel distribution systems were conceived in the 1960s when the airlines created their first computerized reservation systems. In the 1970s, airline reservation computer terminals were installed in travel agencies, and both car-rental and hotel reservations capabilities were added to the airlines' reservation systems. Thus, wherever an airline reservation terminal was installed, a new distribution location for booking travel emerged. As airline reservation systems expanded throughout the world, they created automated travel booking capabilities on a global basis.

In the 1980s, deregulation of U.S. airlines allowed for these now global electronic travel distribution systems to be developed as businesses unto themselves. Further dramatic expansion, combined with enhanced technologies, resulted in the majority of major travel agencies and corporate travel offices being automated and tied directly into the electronic travel distribution system of their choice. The U.S. systems are Apollo (also referred to as COVIA), SABRE, System One, and

WORLDSPAN. The Canadian system is Gemini; European systems are Amadeus and Galileo; and Asian systems include AXESS, Fantasia, and Abacus. Apollo, originally a United Airlines reservations product, and SABRE, originally an American Airlines product, each have approximately 30 percent of worldwide market share.

During the 1990s the global electronic travel distribution systems improved their hotel reservation capabilities, allowing for multiple room types, rate codes, negotiated rates, and other pertinent lodging information to be included in their programs. Today and in the future more "seamless" links and "mirroring" of hotel reservation, property management, central reservation, and yield management systems within the global electronic travel distribution systems are emerging as new networks are developed. Enhancements in product displays, pictures, voice, video, and other capabilities are being introduced into these global systems on a regular basis.

Ground Operators

Ground operators are those businesses that provide ground services related to a tour (rooms, meals, and so on) at destinations. A ground operator may be independent, part of a larger tour operator, or have some other direct or indirect relationship with a tour operator. In the case of large and some specialized (by destination) tour operators, a tour conductor—an individual who personally escorts a group of passengers for all or part of an itinerary—may have the expertise to provide most of these ground-operator services.

Air Carriers

The airline industry has helped to develop the entire hospitality industry. There are two types of air carriers that transport people: scheduled carriers and supplemental carriers.

Scheduled carriers provide air transportation at specified times over specified routes and have published schedules. Until the mid-1980s the fares and routes of U.S. scheduled carriers were regulated by the Civil Aeronautics Board (CAB). In an effort to streamline government, the president and Congress eliminated CAB. While some jurisdictional functions were transferred to the Department of Transportation and the Department of Justice, most were reduced to allow for what was referred to as *deregulation*. Under deregulation, mergers and acquisitions have prevailed as the combined pressures of fare wars, lack of capitalization, and extensive route competition have weeded out the weaker airline companies.

Under deregulation the Federal Aviation Administration (FAA), the Department of Transportation (DOT), and—in cases of mergers and acquisitions—the Department of Justice are the major government entities involved in regulating the carriers. The FAA and DOT still closely monitor routes, safety, air traffic control, airport development, and other aspects of the industry. Deregulation's impact was, and is, primarily felt in the rate area.

DOT must approve the participation of U.S.-flagged carriers serving international routes. ("U.S.-flagged carriers" are airlines based in the United States that are owned by U.S. corporations.) In addition, agreement must be reached with the

International Air Transport Association (IATA). IATA is the trade and service organization for most of the world's scheduled airlines serving international routes. The Air Transport Association of America is the trade and service organization representing U.S. scheduled carriers.

Supplemental carriers are a class of nonscheduled air carriers that hold certificates to supplement the regular service provided by scheduled carriers. Supplemental carriers are authorized to operate over broad areas. The National Air Carrier Association (NACA) is the trade and service organization that represents the U.S. supplemental carriers.

Channels of Distribution in Europe and Japan

While the channels of distribution or travel intermediaries just described represent methods of marketing travel products in the United States, they also exist in other parts of the world. The European and Japanese approaches to selling travel (including marketing and distribution services) are geared to a mature mass market. In Europe and Japan there is usually a more defined "holiday" period, which means that large portions of the population take their vacations at the same time of the year. The travel industry in Europe and Japan markets to these masses in every imaginable way—both through the media and directly through sales outlets. Tourism retains a high level of recognition in European countries. In addition to the operations of the national tourist offices, travel is marketed by the following techniques:

- Mass media (through catalogs, newspapers, magazines, direct mail promotion, radio, and TV)

- Merchandising (through travel and recreational clubs)

- Direct sales outlets (through storefront operations, tour operators, wholesalers selling directly to the public, banks, and—in Germany and Switzerland—sales in department stores)

Travel is marketed by airlines, travel companies (retail and wholesale), banks, tour organizers, tour operators, hotels, tourist ministries and departments, local tourist authorities, and other travel organizations. Low-cost holidays are made available to the public through the use of charter airlines and through tour operators or wholesalers who purchase seats, rooms, beds, food, and so on in bulk.

Travel marketers in the United States are starting to adopt some of the travel-marketing tactics that have proved successful in Europe and Japan. These tactics include innovations in promotion and advertising, pricing, packaging, and selling. In the area of promotion and advertising, U.S. airlines are making greater use of direct mail and special promotions aimed directly at consumers. The U.S. travel industry has become much more aggressive about luring consumers with attractive prices, using special promotional fares, excursion tours, and discount rates. Travel-industry advertising is putting more emphasis on travel packages, which include air fare, lodging, meals, car rental, and other services. There are also many new developments in merchandising, such as selling travel more directly to consumers through travel clubs, department stores, and bank credit card companies. In addition, there is a movement toward consolidation in the retail and wholesale areas that is resulting in changes in the traditional roles of wholesalers and retailers.

In addition to these outlets for travel products, there are many others through which a consumer may purchase travel. These include, but are not limited to, auto clubs, vacation clubs, time-sharing resort condominiums, and holiday club plans.

Government Regulation of Travel

There are numerous U.S. and international governmental entities that regulate or influence travel.

United States

A number of U.S. government organizations play a role in regulating the travel industry in the United States, including the following:

- Interstate Commerce Commission (ICC), which has jurisdiction over railroads and motorcoaches.

- Federal Maritime Commission (FMC), which has jurisdiction over U.S.-flagged ships.

- Department of Transportation (DOT), which has jurisdiction over the Federal Aviation Administration (FAA).

- Department of State, which negotiates bilateral agreements with other nations and handles matters of diplomatic concern.

- Department of Justice (DOJ), whose antitrust division sometimes participates in cases involving mergers, acquisitions, and expansion efforts. DOJ enforces antitrust laws.

- Department of Commerce, whose United States Travel Service (USTS) is designed to promote travel to and within the United States.

- Department of the Treasury, which concerns itself with the balance of payments.

- Congress, whose Senate Commerce Committee's Subcommittee on Aviation and Subcommittee on Foreign Commerce and Tourism have jurisdiction over legislation related to international travel.

Foreign Governments

Virtually all foreign governments play a major role in shaping policy on internal and external tourism. The degree of foreign-government involvement, which is substantially greater than in the United States, flows from several factors. One is that most foreign governments have a higher appreciation for the importance of tourism, particularly in an economic sense, than does the United States. Also, with very few exceptions, the flagged carriers of foreign countries are owned and controlled by their governments.

The ministries of tourism in foreign countries exert a great deal of influence on government policy. Most foreign governments, particularly in Europe, tend to be more involved than the U.S. government in guiding or dictating the direction of their tourism industries. European governments also tend to participate more in intergovernmental organizations, such as the International Civil Aviation Organization (ICAO), the European Civil Aviation Conference (ECAC), and the International Union of Official Travel Organizations (IUOTO).

In addition, many areas of the world support large influential associations that have travel at the forefront of their interests. For example, PATA—the Pacific Area Travel Association—is a large group promoting travel and tourism in the Pacific.

Most of the countries that are prominent in the tourism field encourage travel to their countries, particularly from the United States, but discourage travel by their own citizens to other countries. This attitude is prompted by economic and financial motives.

Vertical and Horizontal Integration

Vertical and horizontal integration is the interrelationship between two or more hospitality industry products or services performed or offered by the same firm or through a joint relationship with another firm within the industry. It may involve one or many of the channels of distribution. Vertical integration is exemplified by a company such as Holiday Inns, Inc., which offers a variety of lodging products, such as Holiday Inns Express, Holiday Inns, Crowne Plaza Hotels, etc. Horizontal integration is exemplified by a company such as Carlson Co., which operates lodging properties, cruise ships, restaurants, a travel company, and so on.

The hospitality industry is unique in that a large number of firms within the industry engage in more than one function from a product, service, and marketing perspective. For example, United Airlines offers airline passenger service, freight shipping, and reservation services. Airlines and hotels have marketing agreements with rent-a-car firms, resorts have agreements with airlines, rent-a-car firms with resorts, and so on.

The integration of more than one product, service, and/or marketing arrangement may be through ownership—there is a parent or holding company—or through an agreement among separate companies. For example, Marriott offers Hertz rent-a-cars at many of its locations through a joint marketing agreement with Hertz. It can be even more complex, in that one hotel chain might have marketing agreements with more than one rent-a-car firm, a variety of airlines, several tour operators, and so forth.

Key Terms

channels of distribution
incentive travel
travel intermediary
tour operator-retailer
tour operator-wholesaler

REVIEW QUIZ

When you feel you have covered all of the material in this chapter, answer these questions. Choose the *best* answer. Check your answers with the correct ones found on the Review Quiz Answer Key at the end of this book.

1. Someone who does *not* receive a commission for handling travel arrangements for others is called a _____ intermediary.

    a. carrier
    b. commercial
    c. casual
    d. captive

2. Companies that specialize in putting together and selling travel awards, prizes, gifts, premiums, and so on for individuals or groups are called:

    a. travel management companies.
    b. travel clubs.
    c. incentive travel companies.
    d. tour operators-retailers.

3. Electronic travel distribution systems are based on:

    a. the Internet.
    b. airline reservation systems.
    c. technology and hardware developed for the military.
    d. travel agency computer networks.

4. The U.S. Interstate Commerce Commission has jurisdiction over:

    a. railroads and motorcoaches.
    b. U.S.-flagged ships.
    c. airlines.
    d. a and b.

Chapter Outline

Planning Resources for the Marketing Effort
Targeting Profitable Consumer Segments
Reaching the Market

Learning Objectives

1. Explain why hospitality companies need flexible marketing strategies. (p. 43)

2. Describe how marketing efforts benefit from a zero-base budgeting process. (pp. 43–44)

3. Explain the function of internal and external analyses in determining company needs that marketing can fulfill. (pp. 44–45)

4. Describe how the concept of segment profitability applies to the marketing of hospitality products and services. (p. 45)

5. Identify some of the key motivational factors of travel retailers and wholesalers that could help shape a hospitality company's marketing efforts. (pp. 46–47)

Marketing in Perspective

TODAY MORE THAN EVER BEFORE, marketing strategies must be flexible. In a crowded and highly competitive marketplace, "change" is the key word in marketing. Marketers must have the flexibility to alter strategies and respond quickly to challenges arising either from changes in market conditions or from actions taken by aggressive competitors. This is why, over the last several years, we have seen a variety of hospitality marketing strategies such as frequent traveler programs and incentives for repeat customers, as well as price wars and discount advertising campaigns.

This chapter places marketing in perspective by examining the needs of hospitality companies for specific marketing efforts and how those efforts are funded through an effective budgeting process. While marketing activities focus on the needs of consumers, the budget funding those activities must focus on the specific marketing needs of the company. The chapter also explores marketing by showing how companies determine the best uses for marketing resources by targeting the most profitable market segments. The final section of the chapter briefly looks at how the most effective marketing techniques are selected for reaching appropriate market segments.

Planning Resources for the Marketing Effort

Hotels, restaurants, and other hospitality businesses face the same challenge: how to plan marketing activities that make the best use of the limited resources budgeted for the company's marketing effort.

This challenge is often complicated by poor budgeting practices. Time and time again, dollars for marketing are determined on the basis of amounts set by the previous year's budget—which, in turn, were based on the budget for the year before that. This kind of budgeting process fails to respond to the current and future marketing needs of a company. The hospitality marketplace is dynamic. The needs of consumers are constantly changing. A company's competitors are also constantly changing as they adapt their marketing messages and activities to address new consumer needs. A marketing budget formed on the basis of prior years' expenses often stagnates the marketing activities of a company in the ruts and routines of the past.

Resources for marketing efforts should be based on specific company goals that identify the kind of business that the company needs and when it needs that business. This approach to funding the marketing efforts of a company is part of a zero-base budgeting process. **Zero-base budgeting** requires the justification of all expenses. This approach assumes that each department, including marketing, starts with zero dollars and must justify all budgeted amounts. No expenditure is justified just because it was spent last year. Every expense is re-analyzed and justified each year on the basis that its expenditure this year will yield more favorable results than spending the same amount in another way.

Marketing planning begins with defining the products and services to be marketed and identifying the "core" dollars needed by marketing to maintain a desired level of business. For example, consider a casual-dining restaurant that serves lunch and dinner seven days a week. If the volume of business during weekday lunch periods is currently at or over capacity, then the restaurant may not need to allocate additional marketing dollars to increasing customer counts at lunch. The current level of marketing activity and expense may be sufficient to maintain the desired level of business. Similarly, consider a 1,000-room hotel that achieves near 100% occupancy during Monday and Tuesday nights, mainly from business off its reservations system. This hotel may not need to spend any marketing dollars for building business on these nights, other than the fee paid for accessing the reservations system. In both of these cases, an analysis of business activity shows where *not* to concentrate new marketing activities and identifies the "core" dollars needed to maintain a desired level of business. These amounts become justified under a zero-base approach to budgeting and are set as part of the overall marketing budget. The next step is to identify areas in which the company wishes to increase business and justify the marketing expenses that will be necessary to make the increases happen.

Targeting Profitable Consumer Segments

Planning resources for the marketing effort (beyond allocating core dollars needed to maintain current levels of business) begins with identifying specific company needs and targeting consumer segments that can most profitably meet those company needs.

Consider again the 1,000-room hotel that sells out nearly every Monday and Tuesday night. Let's assume that further analysis of the hotel's current pattern of business shows that, on average, only 330 rooms are sold on Friday nights and only 250 rooms are sold on Saturday nights. With 33 percent and 25 percent occupancy rates respectively, Friday and Saturday nights are clearly areas of company need for building more business. Marketing's task is to target specific consumer segments that could provide the most profitable business for the hotel on these nights.

Most of the business market segments can be eliminated; individuals from these segments do not travel much on weekends. In fact, this is probably why the hotel's occupancy rate is so low on Friday and Saturday nights in the first place. What's called for here is an internal and external analysis of pleasure market segments. The internal analysis identifies current customers—the pleasure travel segments that the hotel currently attracts with minimal marketing expense. Internal analysis also seeks to understand the needs of these customers and explain why they stay at the hotel on weekend nights. An external analysis studies the hotel's competitors. The objectives here are to determine which market segments the competition attracts and understand their customers' needs for weekend accommodations.

Based on the results of internal and external analysis, targeted pleasure market segments can be ranked in order of potential business volume. For example, a partial listing might include:

1. Second honeymooners
2. Families escaping for the weekend
3. Sight-seeing groups
4. Regional sports teams

Before allocating resources for marketing to any one of these segments, the profitability of each segment should be analyzed.

Segment profitability is determined by analyzing the revenue and profit generated through the sale of products and services to a particular type of consumer or market segment. As in all businesses, some customers are more profitable to serve than others. A hotel can determine the profitability of market segments by reviewing purchasing patterns of past customers. Historical information from guest folios shows the number and types of purchases made by customers grouped into the market segments under analysis. Although the profitability of market segments varies from property to property, the segment profitability ranking that follows could apply to many hotels:

1. International executives on unrestricted expense accounts with multiple night stays
2. Executives on relatively unrestricted expense accounts
3. Individuals attending a corporate group meeting, conference, or convention
4. Individuals attending an association group meeting, conference, or convention
5. Second honeymooners
6. Regional sports clubs and teams
7. Families with children
8. Individuals on restricted expense accounts

Given the need of the hotel in our example to build weekend business, the first reaction might be to focus resources on attracting business from second honeymooners. However, before spending precious marketing dollars, it's important to examine if it's possible to get a multiple sale for the same cost involved in securing a single sale. That is, can the marketing effort attract a group—such as family reunions—that will fill many rooms instead of filling rooms one at a time with marketing activities directed at individual second honeymooners? Perhaps the marketing effort should focus on attracting the local or state chapter of the Jaguar or Corvette Owners Club of America. Failing this, perhaps booking weekend business from sports clubs and teams would prove more profitable in terms of the return on investment of marketing dollars than promoting weekend stays to individual second honeymooners.

Reaching the Market

After identifying the business needs of the company and the most profitable market segments that could achieve the desired results, the next step is to determine

Exhibit 1   Marketing Within Distribution Channels

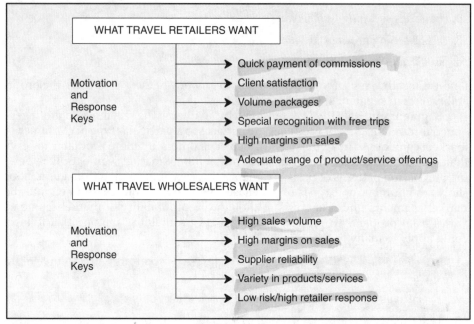

the marketing resources needed to effectively reach the targeted audiences. Different consumer segments respond to different marketing approaches. The wrong method or the wrong message can be counterproductive.

The most effective marketing methods or techniques are defined in terms of unique characteristics of the targeted market segments. Each market segment is motivated by a specific set of needs to purchase hospitality products and services. Lists of market segments, distribution channels, and marketing techniques are useless without understanding what is important to the consumer—what needs motivate market segments to seek hospitality products and services.

Let's assume that the marketing strategy of the hotel in our example is to build weekend business by attracting sight-seeing groups as well as sports clubs and teams. One of the marketing methods used to activate this strategy would be to reach travel retailers and wholesalers who book accommodations for these market segments. The intermediaries, however, are motivated by a very different set of needs than the clients they serve. Understanding their unique needs will help create the most effective marketing messages for them. Exhibit 1 lists motivational factors that are keys to eliciting effective responses to marketing efforts directed to travel retailers and wholesalers. This is only one example of how two different groups in the distribution chain are motivated by unique needs. Similar sets of motivation factors and response keys can be developed for other distribution channels as well as for each end user or market segment. The motivation factors and response keys direct the marketing effort toward the most effective methods for marketing.

Exhibit 2   Marketing in Perspective

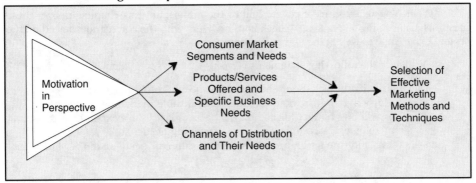

Exhibit 2 puts hospitality marketing in perspective by showing how the most effective marketing methods are selected only after developing a thorough understanding of three important areas:

1. The consumer market segments and their needs

2. The products and services offered by the hospitality company and its specific business needs

3. The motivation factors and response keys of the various distribution channels for hospitality products and services

Key Terms

segment profitability
zero-base budgeting

REVIEW QUIZ

When you feel you have covered all of the material in this chapter, answer these questions. Choose the *best* answer. Check your answers with the correct ones found on the Review Quiz Answer Key at the end of this book.

1.   Which of the following statements is *false?*

   a.   Marketing efforts should be based on specific company goals.
   b.   Today's dynamic marketplace demands flexible marketing strategies.
   c.   A marketing budget formed on the basis of last year's expenses is the surest way to meet the company's future marketing needs.
   d.   Travel intermediaries are motivated by different needs than the clients they serve.

2.   After a heated budget discussion during a senior staff committee meeting, the marketing executive of a hospitality firm outlined arguments in favor of adopting a zero-base budgeting process. Which of the following statements would *not* be included on that list?

   a.   Zero increases, zero decreases—we should continue to allocate resources to all departments based on amounts approved at the budget meetings we've held over the last two years.
   b.   Nothing is sacred—we all must justify every planned expenditure.
   c.   The budget formulas we used last year won't help us respond to changes in the marketplace.
   d.   None of the above statements would support a zero-base approach to budgeting.

3.   Which of the following would be identified through a hotel's internal analysis of market segments?

   a.   types of customers currently attracted to the hotel
   b.   profitability of new market segments that could be attracted to the hotel
   c.   the most effective marketing techniques to reach new customers
   d.   types of customers currently attracted by the hotel's competitors

4.   Which of the following statements is *true?*

   a.   Individuals in business market segments are good targets for hotel marketing activities that aim to increase occupancy during weekends.
   b.   An external analysis of a hotel's market segments identifies the most effective marketing techniques to reach new customers.
   c.   Travel wholesalers prefer packages that ensure high sales volume with high profit margins.
   d.   Zero-base budgeting determines the profitability of different market segments.

Chapter Outline

Marketing Research
    Types of Marketing Research
    Marketing Research Techniques
    Marketing Research Presentation Tools

Learning Objectives

1. Explain the purpose of marketing research, and describe types of marketing research. (pp. 51–53)

2. Describe three basic marketing research techniques. (pp. 53–55)

3. Describe marketing research presentation tools. (pp. 55–64)

6

Applying Key Marketing Methodologies: Marketing Research

Before you develop a marketing strategy and select a marketing tool to execute that strategy, you have to know your product/service, your target markets and their needs, and your competition. Your marketing strategies should be based on sound research, employ appropriate marketing tools, and be aimed directly at your target markets. The purpose of this chapter is to provide you with tools and techniques to research and analyze your product/service and the marketplace.

Marketing Research

One of the most difficult and important tasks in developing a marketing strategy is understanding objectively what your product or service really is in relation to your competition and the marketplace. The purpose of marketing research is to provide facts to help you make the proper judgments about your products, prices, and marketing strategies. Generally speaking, the more objective facts you have available to you, the sounder will be your selection of a marketing strategy.

There are many ways to classify, conduct, and categorize marketing research. In the following sections we will focus on the major types of marketing research, identify selected research techniques, and examine some tools for presenting marketing research data.

Types of Marketing Research

Broadly speaking, marketing research can be either quantitative or qualitative. Quantitative marketing research seeks to quantify data using numbers, projections, forecasts, etc. Qualitative marketing research seeks to identify, analyze, or profile consumers, working with consumer attitudes, behaviors, etc. Both quantitative and qualitative marketing research can be either primary or secondary. Primary research is research you conduct yourself; secondary research is research that someone else has conducted.

Marketing research can also be categorized with respect to:

- Markets
- Products or services
- Consumers

- The competition
- The environment
- Trends

Let's briefly examine each of these marketing research categories in the following sections.

Market Research. Also referred to as area demand analysis when dealing with lodging facilities, **market research** seeks to quantify and segment demand. The standard guest segments in the lodging industry are transient, group, business, and leisure. Demand also is usually classified with respect to weekdays, weekends, rate categories, and sources. Common sources of demand include local sources (areas near the hotel/motel), retail sources, service and manufacturing concerns, tourist attractions, convention facilities, cultural events, and sources related to traffic flow and transportation arteries.

Product or Service Research. Product or service research usually focuses on your product's/service's strengths and weaknesses in relation to the products/services of competitors. In the lodging industry this is often referred to as property research. Typically, a hotel's tangible features (physical assets) are profiled, such as number of guestrooms, square footage and layout of meeting space, recreational facilities, property amenities, etc. Likewise, intangibles (qualitative assets) are also profiled, such as guest perceptions, quality and customer service ratings, reputation, ratings by travel organizations (such as the American Automobile Association), and relative competitive positioning within the marketplace. Product or service research also takes into consideration factors such as substitutability—alternatives to the property of equal or similar rating; proximity—the advantages and disadvantages of the hotel's location; and rate data—rate surveys of similar properties. Some hotels only include rate surveys of those properties within a fixed percentage (for example, 15%) of their rates, while others profile the entire market.

Consumer Research. Consumer research takes many different forms in the hospitality industry. One of the most common with respect to hotels and resorts is referred to as **prospect research.** This research provides a profile of present and future guests. Sources of information include reservations data, registration input, check-out information, and origin- and destination-market data.

The origin market is where the traveler has come from. Origin-market data can be classified in a number of ways. The most widely used classifications are geographic, such as country, region, state, city, etc. Origin markets can also be classified by MSA (metropolitan statistical areas) and postal zip codes.

Since marketing frequently relies on the media as one method to reach prospective customers, present and future guests can be categorized by DMAs (Designated Market Areas—geographic areas reached by clusters of television stations, as defined by the A. C. Nielsen Co.) or ADIs (Areas of Dominant Influence—geographic areas defined by the circulation zones of major newspapers, as categorized by Arbitron, an audience research firm).

Consumer research seeks to identify the usage patterns of consumers, such as general travel habits and hotel or motel preferences. Consumer research also seeks to classify consumers by age, income, education, etc. (demographics), as well as discover their habits (psychographics) with respect to likes, dislikes, etc., always seeking to quantify where possible. Consumer research today explores everything from the purchasing habits to the attitudes and behaviors of consumers.

Competitive Research. One of the keys to successful marketing is understanding how your product or service compares to your top competitors' products or services. **Competitive research** compares your product or service to the products or services of competitors and tries to discover how consumers perceive and experience your product/service offering in relation to the competitors' products/services. Research questions are usually developed with respect to price/rates, quality of facility, service levels, convenience to purchase, etc. Competitive research reveals how your competitors are positioned—in relation to your product or service—to meet the needs of your key market segments, now and in the future.

Environmental Research. Marketing must take into account not only what consumers and competitors are doing, but also what is occurring within and to the total industry environment. **Environmental research** focuses on external forces (economic, social, political, technological, etc.) that are having or will have an impact on your product or service in some manner.

One key focus of environmental research is to look ahead at what form and shape opportunities and threats may take and how they will affect your activities. Frequently, competition research and environmental research are linked. The output of these research assessments is often referred to with the acronym **SWOT**, which stands for Strengths, Weaknesses, Opportunities, and Threats. These strengths, weaknesses, opportunities, and threats can then be analyzed to provide support rationale for developing marketing action plans.

Trend Research. Trend research focuses on both quantitative and qualitative trends. Quantitative trend research seeks to identify significant increases or declines in customer preferences, methods of purchase, usage/frequency, and other factors impacting future demand. Qualitative trend research seeks to identify changes in consumer attitudes, interests, tastes, benefits sought, and so on. Trend research findings help marketers make strategic marketing decisions.

Marketing Research Techniques

Many types of marketing research techniques can be used to help you make sound marketing decisions. Which technique works best depends on many factors, such as the product/service offering, nature of the problem or opportunity, amount of resources available, time or urgency, budget, etc. Basic marketing research techniques widely used in the hospitality industry today include surveys, questionnaires, and focus groups. Of course, there are many other quantitative and qualitative research techniques employed in the industry, but the purpose of this section is to familiarize you with these three basic techniques. Regardless of the research technique selected, the goal remains the same—to gain information and apply the findings to improve the marketing and/or marketability of a product or service.

Surveys. A **survey** seeks to elicit consumer opinion, uncover facts, and gain insights on potential trends. Surveys may be conducted in a variety of ways, at various locations, among customers or potential customers, or even among competitors' customers. Surveys may be conducted in person, by phone, electronically, or by mail.

A survey is a structured document, usually seeking to quantify its findings in terms of percentages of those who agree or disagree with particular statements. It also seeks to measure the depth of agreement or disagreement, often employing a point scale—for example, "Circle 1 if you strongly agree, 5 if you strongly disagree." Five-, seven-, and ten-point scales are commonly used. Surveys are also used to seek qualitative information, especially when open-ended questions are asked—i.e., "What else would you like to see or have," etc. Surveys may be conducted only once or periodically scheduled, such as an annual frequent-flier-program-preference survey. Multiple-period (semi-annual, monthly, etc.) surveys often seek to spot improvements or declines in such areas as property service levels or consumer preferences, thus providing a rationale for a marketing, operational, or development decision.

Questionnaires. Perhaps the most widely used research technique, **questionnaires** come in all types of forms and are used for multiple purposes. As data collection vehicles, questionnaires seek both factual information and opinion. Data that questionnaires are designed to collect include guest comments, customer profiles, product and service information, demographic and psychographic data, attitudinal information, consumer usage patterns and preferences, etc. The data collected may be used to measure property performance, improve products or services, qualify prospects, build leads, create mailing lists, determine consumer price sensitivity, analyze menus, and so on.

Like surveys, questionnaires can be conducted in person, by phone, by mail, or electronically. Questionnaires often are ongoing, such as guest-comment questionnaires, new customer/purchaser questionnaires, etc. Also like surveys, questionnaires can use scales or point systems to yield quantifiable data or rank items in order of importance.

Frequently, the terms "survey" and "questionnaire" are used interchangeably. However, questionnaires tend to be briefer than surveys and are usually less complex in content.

Focus Groups. A **focus group** is a marketing research technique that combines personal-opinion solicitation in the form of group discussion with a structured set of questions. During a focus-group session, a "moderator" conducts or facilitates the discussion using a script designed to elicit opinions from focus-group members on predetermined subjects. In some cases, time for more free-flowing discussion is built into a session. For additional analysis, focus groups may be recorded or observed via one-way mirrors. Focus group members may volunteer their time or be compensated.

There are a number of types of focus groups, ranging from single-area focus groups to regional/market-area focus groups to multiple focus groups. Single-area focus groups are focus groups drawn from one market; regional/market-area focus groups are single focus groups held in one or more regions of the country; multiple focus groups are more than one focus group held in multiple regions of the country. Also, there are product/service-user focus groups and non-user focus groups. Focus groups may be made up of your customers, your competitors' customers, prospective customers, or any combination thereof.

Focus groups by nature are more time-consuming for marketers to conduct and follow through on than surveys or questionnaires. Focus groups involve script writing, hiring a professional group leader, holding the focus group session itself, and then analyzing the focus group and its responses. In general, focus groups provide more in-depth qualitative findings related to attitudes and behavior than do questionnaires or surveys. Sometimes focus groups come up with useful questions that can be placed on subsequent questionnaires or surveys.

Marketing Research Presentation Tools

There are many presentation tools that marketers can use to help individuals understand and analyze research findings. Some of these presentation tools are simple graphics such as triangles or pyramids, circles or maps, linear diagrams, boxes or rectangles, and grids or matrices. Granted, some may view this as an oversimplification of the presentation process. However, the majority of research findings and models are visually presented using these simple forms. Let's look at a few research presentation tools that you will probably encounter during your career in the hospitality industry.

Pyramids. Pyramids are often used to depict size of markets, service levels, rates/prices, and product/brand positioning. Exhibit 1 presents a pyramid that profiles brands in the lodging industry by service levels and rates. This same presentation tool can be used to structure rates or profile market and price strategies.

Circles. Circles are frequently used for "mapping" purposes, wherein you are comparing your product/service to the expressed needs and wants of consumers and/or in relation to the products/services of competitors (see Exhibit 2). A "perceptual map" will help you focus on how well your product or service is doing in comparison to others in terms of quality and value, as perceived by your customers. In Exhibit 2, "quality" is plotted along the horizontal axis, "value" along the vertical axis. How your product/service is perceived by consumers is what locates you on the map. A perceptual map can help identify your problems and opportunities in relation to the market and your competition. A perceptual map can also be of great value in creating advertising or pricing strategies, or determining the necessity for product or service-level enhancements.

Linear Diagrams. Linear diagrams are frequently used to show "pathways" to targets, look at alternative strategies, develop networks and alliances, and aid in the decision-making process. One of the most popular linear diagrams is the "decision tree" (see Exhibit 3), most often used to view product/service extensions and expansions, market segment alternatives, product/service hybrids, etc. Decision trees show various possible "branches" that you might take to reach an objective or

Exhibit 1 Sample Pyramid

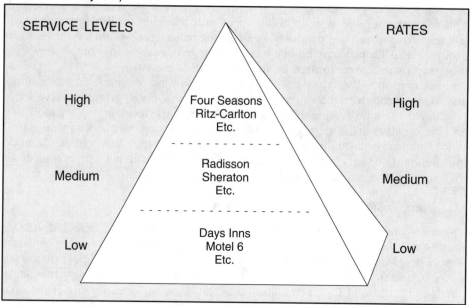

Exhibit 2 Sample Circle—Perceptual Map

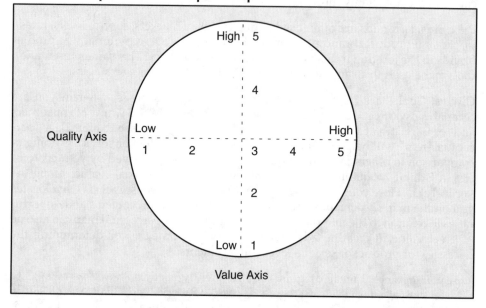

outcome. Decision trees have applicability in the product or service development process, operations, and marketing. Their benefit is to clearly show alternate or multiple routes to achieve goals and objectives.

Exhibit 3   Sample Linear Diagram—Decision Tree

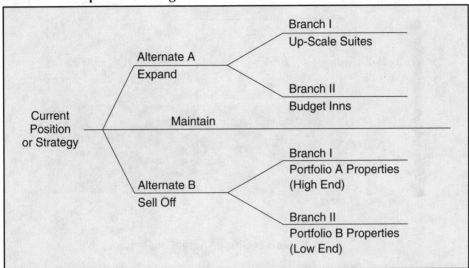

Boxes/Rectangles. For many years, boxes and rectangles have proved to be useful presentation tools for marketers. One of the most well-known "box" creations is attributed to the Boston Consulting Group and is referred to as the "portfolio approach to strategy formulation." This leading management consulting firm recommended that organizations appraise each of their products on the basis of market growth rate (annual growth rate of the market in which the product is sold) and the organization's share of the market relative to its largest competitor. Each product is then placed in the corresponding quadrant of the Boston Consulting Group Portfolio Box (see Exhibit 4). By dividing product-market growth into high growth and low growth, and **market share** into high share and low share, four categories of products can be identified: stars, cash cows, question marks, and dogs. These categories can be summarized as follows:

- *Stars.* Stars are those products in which an organization enjoys a high share of fast-growing (new) markets. Star products are growing rapidly and typically require heavy investment of resources. In such instances, the organization should mobilize its resources to develop stars in such a way that their market growth and market-share leadership is maintained. If the necessary investment is made and the growth proves enduring, a star product will turn into a cash cow and generate income in excess of expenses in the future.

- *Cash cows.* Cash cows are those products that enjoy a high share of slow-growth (mature) markets. They produce revenues that can be used to support high-growth products or underwrite those with problems.

- *Question marks.* Question marks are those products that only have a small share of a fast-growing market. Organizations face the question of whether to increase investment in question-mark products, hoping to make them stars, or

Exhibit 4   The Boston Consulting Group Portfolio Box

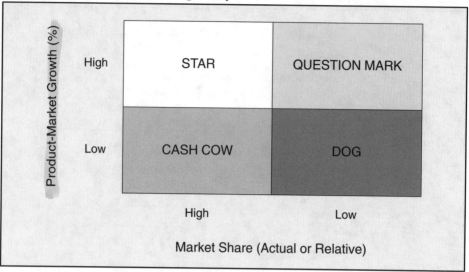

to reduce or terminate investment, on the grounds that funds could be better spent elsewhere.

- *Dogs.* Dogs are those products that have a small market share of slow-growth or declining markets. Since dogs usually make little money or even lose money, a decision may be made to drop them. Sometimes a business, for a variety of reasons, continues to sell dogs even though they are unprofitable. However, managers must remember that the resources that go into maintaining dogs are resources the business can't use for other opportunities.

The Boston Consulting Group Portfolio Box can also be used to analyze companies, brands, or markets.

Another box/rectangle tool is the G. E. Portfolio approach, which expands the Boston Consulting Group concept by adding the dimensions of market attractiveness and organizational strengths to the design. Both the Boston Consulting Group Portfolio Box and the G. E. Portfolio, as well as other boxes/rectangles, provide visual mechanisms that can help marketers understand data and formulate or select marketing strategies.

Grids. An extension of the box concept is the grid concept. Grids are excellent tools to help a business formulate marketing strategies and plans. The **Marketing Strategy Grid,** for example, is a dynamic tool that usually views both present and future market and competitive conditions (see Exhibit 5). It allows you to gain perspective on your own product or service through an honest and frank evaluation. In order to objectively select the appropriate marketing strategies, you must understand the conditions (present and future) of the market you are in, where the market is going, and how your product relates to both the current and future conditions as well as the competition's products.

Exhibit 5   Marketing Strategy Grid

Present Time
(Market Potential)

Strong   Moderate   Weak

1	2	3	Strong
4	5	6	Moderate (Competitive Position)
7	8	9	Weak

Future Time
(Market Potential)

Strong   Moderate   Weak

1	2	3	Strong
4	5	6	Moderate (Competitive Position)
7	8	9	Weak

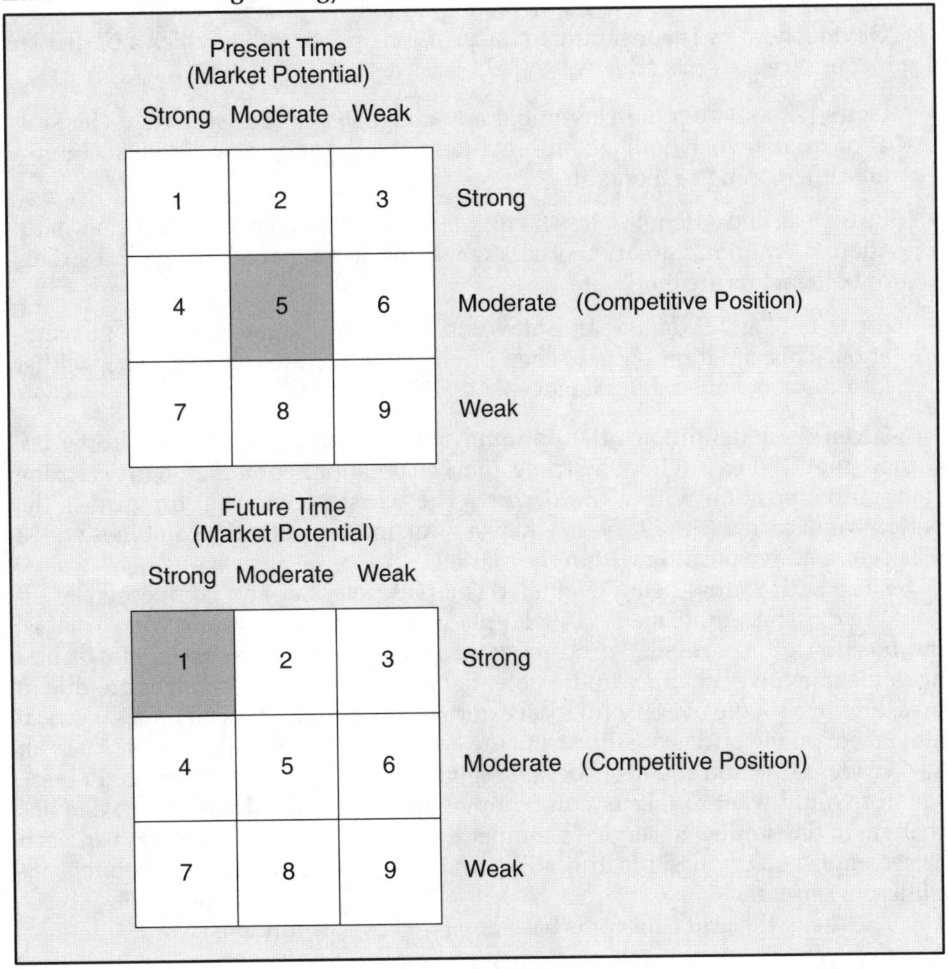

The Marketing Strategy Grid profiles the success of your product or service. A product's or service's position on the grid is a function of both the potential of the market and the competitive position within the market of the product or service. The horizontal axis of the grid denotes the potential of the market sector, while the vertical axis represents the competitive position of the product or service within that market sector. The possible rankings on both axes range from strong to weak. If you are ranking your property as a whole, your property's competitive position is a function of both quantitative and qualitative considerations, such as the amount and quality of competition; your property's competitive advantages as to location, access, image, facilities, size, rate, and so on; and your property's ability to meet the needs of available market segments. It is a good practice to develop two grids—one on your present competitive position, the second on your projected competitive position two to five years into the future. This will help you focus on the dynamics of your marketplace and competition.

Obviously, there is a meaning to the position on the grid in which a particular product or service is placed:

- Boxes 1, 2, and 4 denote a favorable, advantageous, or "go" situation. This situation occurs when both factors—market potential and competitive position—are either strong or moderate.

- Boxes 3, 5, and 7 denote a less favorable, less advantageous, or "caution" situation. A "caution" situation occurs when one factor is weak and one is strong, or both factors are moderate.

- Boxes 6, 8, and 9 denote an unfavorable, disadvantageous, or "no go" situation. This situation occurs when one or both factors are weak and neither factor is above the moderate level.

Given these definitions, the optimum position on the grid is the upper-left corner (the "1" box), where a strong market potential combines with a strong competitive position within the market. The worst position on the grid is the bottom-right corner (the "9" box), where a weak market potential combines with a weak competitive position within the market.

Since both factors being evaluated (market potential and competitive position) are dynamic, movement can take place within the grid framework—that is, the position of a particular product or service can vary over time. Horizontal movement involves changes in the potential of a market. Such changes are due to pressures in both the overall and local external economic and social forces. Vertical movement on the grid is possible from the lower six positions. These positions can be considered "action squares," because anyone with a product or service in these squares would want to take action to move up. Such vertical movement denotes changes in the product's/service's competitive position within the market and can be accomplished through the upgrading of management, marketing, products, facilities, or services.

The use of the grid concept is based on two key assumptions:

1. In order to best meet the needs of each market segment, as well as maintain a strong image and market share, we can assume that properties will always seek the 1, 2, and 4 positions (favorable positions) on the grid whenever possible.

2. The position on the grid in which you place your property assumes that no major capital improvement programs or other changes to the property will be undertaken soon, and few, if any, major changes will be made in the quality of management or the expenditures for marketing. As previously stated, you may wish to use two grids—one for the present and one for the future (usually within the next five years).

Let's review one example of how to apply this Marketing Strategy Grid to a hospitality industry property. The first step is to objectively evaluate your property and locate it within the grid. Let's assume you own a restaurant and its position on the grid is in box #1. This means your restaurant is in a strong market and is a strong restaurant, maybe even the best restaurant in that market. So, what are some marketing strategies you should employ?

One plan of action is to do everything possible to protect your position by maintaining not only the quality of your food and operation but also the core clientele who put you in that position. Special recognition programs for this core clientele could be developed. Another strategy that could be considered in view of a very solid #1 position would be to raise your prices to take advantage of your market position and maximize profits.

Not everyone is situated in the #1 position on the Marketing Strategy Grid. Let's look at a hotel that is in the #4 position on the grid. This hotel is an average hotel located in San Francisco—a strong market. The competition across the street is in the #1 position—a strong product in this strong market. What can this average San Francisco property do to maximize its profitability? Let's say that right now the market is running an 87 percent average occupancy, which is a very strong market. Demand is projected to continue strong, with a minimal amount of new guestrooms coming into the market. The hotel in position #1 on the grid is charging $70 to $95 per night and enjoys an average rate of $81.75. Our average hotel across the street in the #4 position is charging $40 to $48 per night and has an average rate of $44.85. Both properties are running at 87% occupancy.

The ingenious hotel marketing department in our average hotel came up with the following strategies: (1) change the hotel's image by adding a canopy and doorperson and refurbishing the hotel's public space, and (2) raise the rate structure to $60 to $75 per night. The result? No loss in occupancy (because of the strength of the market) and a bulge in profitability.

There are many different marketing strategies you can use. Which ones you choose depends on your property's position on the Marketing Strategy Grid. Upgrading (refurbishing) and raising prices represent two marketing strategies that worked in the preceding example; there are many other strategies to consider, based on your position on the grid. The following nine grids show the nine possible grid positions and accompanying marketing strategies appropriate to the positions:

Marketing Strategy Grids
(and Possible Marketing Steps)
Position #1: Strong Market—Strong/Best Product or Service

(Market Potential)

Strong	Moderate	Weak		
1	2	3	Strong	
4	5	6	Moderate	(Competitive Position)
7	8	9	Weak	

1. Maintain position.
2. Cultivate core customers.
3. Maximize profits through pricing.
4. Keep competitively ahead by adding services or upgrading product.
5. Expand your product or service (for example, more rooms, more restaurant seats, more flights, more gaming devices, etc.).

Position #2: Moderate Market—Strong Product or Service

(Market Potential)

Strong Moderate Weak

1	2	3
4	5	6
7	8	9

Strong
Moderate
Weak

(Competitive Position)

1. Go for market share via competitive pricing.

2. If the market movement tends to be strong in future years, improve to a #1 position.

3. If the market movement tends to be weak, go after additional marketing segments (for example, build core market, consider alternate pricing strategy, etc.).

4. Become the "only" place in town to stay or eat, become the "only" airline to take.

Position #3: Strong Product—Weak Market

(Market Potential)

Strong Moderate Weak

1	2	3
4	5	6
7	8	9

Strong
Moderate
Weak

(Competitive Position)

1. If the market is moving toward becoming moderate or strong, build market core now and retain loyalty of consumers.

2. Go after all market segments with multiple pricing strategies and/or product and service offerings.

3. Strongly emphasize cost control and targeted promotions.

Position #4: Strong Market—Moderate/Average Product or Service

(Market Potential)

Strong Moderate Weak

1	2	3
4	5	6
7	8	9

Strong
Moderate
Weak

(Competitive Position)

1. Maximize profits through pricing slightly below the #1 competitor.

2. Consider upgrading your product or service to move closer to or into the #1 position if the future markets look strong.

3. Go after the "value-oriented" market segments.

4. Distinguish your product or service as an acceptable replacement for the #1 competitor.

Position #5: Moderate Market—Moderate/Average Product or Service

(Market Potential)

Strong Moderate Weak

1	2	3	Strong
4	5	6	Moderate
7	8	9	Weak

(Competitive Position)

1. If the direction is toward a stronger market, put the product or service in a stronger position with upgrading.

2. Expand the number of market segments you are attracting with specialized promotions.

3. Go after market share through competitive pricing.

Position #6: Weak Market—Moderate/Average Product or Service

(Market Potential)

Strong Moderate Weak

1	2	3	Strong
4	5	6	Moderate
7	8	9	Weak

(Competitive Position)

1. If the market is moving toward becoming moderate or strong in the future, maintain your core market through recognition programs and go after your weakest competitors with special pricing to gain share.

2. If the market is stagnant, and it appears that it will remain weak in the foreseeable future, gear your marketing programs to capture as many segments as possible.

3. Create your own markets via specialized promotions and programs.

Position #7: Strong Market—Weak Product or Service

(Market Potential)

Strong Moderate Weak

1	2	3	Strong
4	5	6	Moderate
7	8	9	Weak

(Competitive Position)

1. Upgrade the most visible aspects of your product or service.

2. Once the upgrading is completed, increase your rates or prices to take advantage of overflow or strong sell-out times or periods.

3. Become the best at servicing the market segments your stronger competitors are not paying attention to.

4. Theme your promotions toward special functions and go for volume.

Position #8: Moderate Market—Weak Product or Service

(Market Potential)
Strong   Moderate   Weak

1	2	3
4	5	6
7	8	9

Strong

Moderate

Weak

(Competitive Position)

1. If the market is not moving toward being strong, look at special rate or price schemes to build share.

2. If the market is moving toward strong, make every effort to upgrade the product or service offering to move along with the market.

3. If the above is true, work promotions, sales, and advertising to convey your product's or service's availability and value orientation.

4. Consider marketing your product or service around a theme such that you serve segments but obtain greater volume from competition by this specialization.

Position #9: Weak Market—Weak Product or Service

(Market Potential)
Strong   Moderate   Weak

1	2	3
4	5	6
7	8	9

Strong

Moderate

Weak

(Competitive Position)

1. It is time to dispose of your product or service.

2. Consider alternate uses for your product or service that make sense in this poor environment.

The marketing strategies accompanying these nine sample grids are only suggestions. There are many variables to consider, and each product or service may have a uniqueness unto itself that needs to be taken into consideration prior to selecting a strategy. The Marketing Strategy Grid is a tool designed to help you think about how to maximize your marketing strategies for the most productive results. In the final analysis, it is management's judgment that will dictate the strategy selected; the Marketing Strategy Grid only helps sharpen that judgment.

Key Terms

competition research
environmental research
focus group

market research
market share
marketing strategy grid

product or service research

prospect research

questionnaire

survey

SWOT

trend research

REVIEW QUIZ

When you feel you have covered all of the material in this chapter, answer these questions. Choose the *best* answer. Check your answers with the correct ones found on the Review Quiz Answer Key at the end of this book.

1. Research that you conduct yourself is called _____ research.

   a. primary
   b. quantitative
   c. secondary
   d. qualitative

2. Marketing research that compares your product or service to the products or services of competitors is called _____ research.

   a. market
   b. product or service
   c. competitive
   d. consumer

3. Which of the following statements about surveys is *false?*

   a. Surveys can be conducted in person, by phone, electronically, or by mail.
   b. Surveys are only conducted among your own customers.
   c. Surveys may be conducted only once or conducted periodically.
   d. a and b.

4. A product classified as a star by the Boston Consulting Group Portfolio Box is a product that:

   a. only has a small share of a fast-growing market.
   b. enjoys a high share of a fast-growing market.
   c. only has a small share of a slow-growing or declining market.
   d. enjoys a high share of a slow-growing market.

5. The worst position on the Marketing Strategy Grid—the position where a weak market potential combines with a weak competitive position—is the number _____ box.

   a. 1
   b. 4
   c. 7
   d. 9

Chapter Outline

Organizing the Sales Effort
Personal Sales
Telephone Sales
The Importance of Interdepartmental
　　Communication

Learning Objectives

1. Describe common sales tools and procedures used in hotel sales departments. (pp. 69–79)

2. Summarize three keys to personal selling. (pp. 79–83)

3. Summarize keys to telephone sales. (p. 83)

4. Describe the importance of interdepartmental communication to the sales process. (pp. 83–84)

7

Applying Key Marketing Methodologies: Sales

THE PURPOSE OF THIS CHAPTER is to examine the sales function. We will discuss organizing the sales effort, personal sales, telephone sales, and the importance of communication to the sales process. We will concentrate on the hotel sector of the hospitality industry because it encompasses more sales functions than most other sectors.

At the outset it should be noted that the sales forms shown in the chapter are examples only. Similar forms are available from many vendors. Computerized forms are also available that can be tailored to meet the unique needs of individual hotels or hotel chains. This chapter discusses the basic sales methods and forms with which a hotel sales department should work, but keep in mind that hotels and hotel chains modify these methods and forms to suit their own needs.

Organizing the Sales Effort

This section discusses the basic tools and procedures that a hotel sales department works with to sell meetings, conventions, and other group events. The following is a sales-tool checklist for hotels:

_____ **Sales Brochures.** Do you have a brochure that includes the following: a description of the hotel's meeting rooms, including seating charts showing different arrangements (theater style, U-shaped, schoolroom, etc.) and room capacities; a list of the property's amenities; property services available; directions to the hotel and a map; transportation services; the hotel's phone number and address; and sales personnel to contact?

Comment: There are many examples today of beautiful four-color hotel brochures. Look them over and you may find nice pictures, but if any of the above elements are missing, they are not good _sales_ brochures.

_____ **Activities and Amenities Guidebook or Brochure.** Do you have a guidebook or brochure for guests that describes what activities are available at or near the property? Does it address entertainment options for the spouse and children? The guidebook/brochure should contain a list of shops, recreational offerings, nearby attractions, and so on.

Exhibit 1   Sample VIP Reservation Request Form

Name:_____	Arrival Date:_____
Title:_____	Time:_____
Organization:_____	Departure Date:_____
Address:_____	Time:_____
Phone:_____	No. in Party:_____

Purpose of Visit:　　　　　Personal
　　　　　　　　　　　　　Inspection
　　　　　　　　　　　　　Other (State):_____

Accommodations Requested:	Single	Queen
	Double	King
	Double/Double	Jr. Suite
	View	Suite

Rate Instructions:　　　　　Comp.
　　　　　　　　　　　　　Special (State):_____
　　　　　　　　　　　　　Billing Instructions:_____

Instructions:	Wine & Cheese	Std. Fruit
	Std. Liquor Tray	Wine Only
	Champagne	Other (State) _____
		_____

Requested by:_____　　　Date:_____
Approved by:_____　　　Date:_____

Comment: No one wants to meet in or bring his or her family to a hotel surrounded by an entertainment and cultural wasteland. Telling what is offered—not only at your facility, but also nearby—can help you *maximize* your market.

_____ **VIP Reservation Request Form.** This important sales tool is designed to record a VIP's name, title, organization, address, and phone number; arrival and departure dates and times; the number of people in the VIP's party; the reason for the visit; accommodation instructions; rate instructions; special requests, such as wine, flowers, etc.; the name of the person who will make sure all of the above occurs; and the appropriate approval. (See Exhibit 1 for a sample VIP reservation request form.)

Comment: Take your time to ensure that this form is filled out entirely and correctly. If at all possible, personally review all VIP requirements with the manager on duty at the projected time of arrival of your VIP guests.

_____ **Tentative Confirmation Letter.** Do you have a model tentative confirmation letter, and does it include the following: date(s) of proposed meeting; arrival and departure dates; clearly stated rates; number of rooms and type being held; and an outline of the meeting requirements, including set-up of the room, meal functions, equipment reserved, and coffee-break information? (See Exhibit 2 for a sample tentative confirmation letter.) This letter is important because it is the basis for your eventual "contract" with the customer. A brochure about the property and its amenities can be sent along with the letter.

Comment: Cover all the facts, and don't forget to say "thank you."

Sales Checklist. A sales checklist is a working document that should be stapled to the client's file folder. It provides room for recording (and changing, if necessary) all arrangements, so that anyone in the sales department can see exactly what the customer wants, with whom the customer has spoken, and what has been said to date. The sales checklist should have space for recording a salesperson's name; the dates the tentative confirmation letter and reminder/final confirmation letter were mailed; dates for the meeting, and whether those dates are confirmed; room data, including rates agreed to, front office instructions (copies of the tentative confirmation letter and reminder/final confirmation letter should be attached), special housing procedures, and complimentary room information; billing instructions; catering department instructions, including dates, rates, and liquor/beverage special arrangements; exhibit requirements; research data on arrival/departure times, flights, and van/limo transportation requirements; and miscellaneous comments such as special rooms, amenities, anticipated problems, etc. (See Exhibit 3 for a sample sales checklist.)

Comment: Leave no stone unturned. Make sure personal contact is made by a salesperson with every other area in the hotel so that all the details are covered.

Contact Report. This is a simple chronological listing of the contacts made with an organization. It should contain the following: organization name; key contact's name, title, address, and phone number; secretary's name; and a chronological list of contacts in the form of brief sentence recaps. (See Exhibit 4 for a sample contact report.)

Comment: This report not only helps salespeople avoid overkill (contacting a prospect too often), it can also serve as a "tickler file" because you can use it not only to record the last contact made, but also to record the date by which you want to make the next one.

Reminder/Final Confirmation Letter. This letter should contain all the final details and include all items listed in the original tentative confirmation letter. It serves both as a reminder to the customer and as another opportunity for the salesperson to ensure that all details and customer requests/requirements are in order. It also helps to prevent the surprise of a late cancellation or no-show. The reminder/final confirmation letter should be signed by both parties; it serves as a "contract" or binding letter of agreement.

Exhibit 2   Sample Tentative Confirmation Letter

October 11, 19___

Mr. Phil Jackson
Vice President of Marketing
Michigan Insurance Co.
811 Anchor Way
Lansing, Michigan

Dear Phil:

It certainly was a pleasure speaking with you yesterday concerning the possibility of the Grand Plaza Park Hotel hosting the Michigan Insurance Company in February of 19___.

I'm now holding 120 rooms on a tentative basis for arrival on Wednesday, February 4th, and departure on Saturday, February 7th, 19___.

The following rates will be in effect for your meeting:

Singles:	$95.00
Doubles or Twins:	$105.00
Junior Suites:	$125.00
Parkside Suites:	$150.00
Skyline Suites:	$175.00

The following is my understanding of your meeting requirements. On February 4th you will need a reception/dinner for 120 guests. On February 5th, 6th, and 7th you will need a meeting room set for 120 guests, from 8:00 A.M. until 3:00 P.M.

Bill Robinson, our Director of Banquets and Convention Services, will be in touch with you to further finalize all details such as coffee breaks, audiovisual equipment, etc.

It is my understanding that all room, tax, and incidental charges will be charged directly to the Master Account.

Phil, it is my further understanding that you will be forwarding a rooming list; we need to be in receipt of this rooming list no later than January 6, 19___ to ensure proper confirmation. After that time, rooms will be on a space-available basis.

I've enclosed detailed brochures on both the meeting facilities and property amenities that we have available, and we will make every effort to make your meeting a success.

Phil, enclosed is an additional copy of this letter that can be signed and returned as definite confirmation.

Again, thank you for calling and we look forward to working with you and the Michigan Insurance Company in 19___.

Sincerely,

Paul J. Winslow
Director of Marketing

PJW:ms
#432

APPROVED BY:

_____
Phil Jackson, V.P. Marketing

_____
Date

Exhibit 3   Sample Sales Checklist

Salesperson Responsible _____   Date _____

Confirmation Letter Sent _____   Date _____

Key Dates: CONFIRMED _____   YES _____   NO   If Yes, when _____   To _____

  If No, Tentative _____   To _____

        Logged in Master Book _____ Yes _____ No

Room Data: _____   To Front Office with Confirmation Letter

_____   To Front Office with type, number, and special requirements

_____   Specified rates for all room types to Front Office and Bookkeeping

_____   Special Housing Procedures—list, VIPs, etc.

_____   Complimentary rooms—numbers, location, list match

_____   Final confirmation _____ date _____ initials

_____   Final log in Master Book

_____   Reservation cards _____ reply required

Billing Instructions: _____   Individual

_____   Master Account number _____

_____   Other (Specify) _____

Catering: _____   Program listing confirmed with client

        Date confirmed _____   Copy sent _____

_____   Rates per person or meal confirmed

_____   Liquor/Beverage special arrangements

Exhibit Requirements:

_____   Yes _____   No   (If Yes, dates and schedule recorded)

_____   Rates _____   Move in _____   Move out

_____   Special needs list _____

_____

Key Data: _____   Arrival time/flights recorded

_____   Departure time/flights recorded

_____   Van/limo pick-up/drop required

Comments: _____   Special people requirements, i.e., disabled, children, etc.

        Specify _____

_____

_____   Anticipated problems (if any, identify problem) and who is responsible to pre-resolve) _____

_____

_____ **Telephone Assurance Procedures.** These procedures help sales-people make follow-up telephone calls to clients to make sure that the reminder/final confirmation letter the clients received is accurate and

Exhibit 4   Sample Contact Report

Date: _____	Organization _____
	Key Contact _____
	Title _____
	Address _____
	Phone No. _____
	Sect'y Name _____

Interview and Comments: _____

Date: _____

Date: _____

Date: _____

Date: _____

Date: _____

Do's _____   Don'ts _____

mutually agreed upon. This is one final chance for the salesperson to change items or even sell up.

_____ **Meeting/Convention Definite Booking Form.** This form is designed to provide a permanent record of a definite booking of a meeting or convention. It should be cross-referenced with the organization's file number. The following items should be on the meeting/convention definite booking form: the salesperson's name; group name and address; key contact person's name, title, address, and phone number; attendance anticipated; rooms promised; main arrival date; main departure date; room blocks identified and cut-off date for holding; final decision date; single and double rates; suite rates; billing instructions; complimentary rooms; and special instructions, if any. (See Exhibit 5 for a sample meeting/convention definite booking form.)

_____ **Key-Contact Assignment.** For the duration of the meeting or convention, one person—preferably the salesperson who made the sale and handled the arrangements—should be available to the customer at all times to take care of any and all problems. This is perhaps the single greatest key to a successful customer experience.

Exhibit 5   Sample Meeting/Convention Definite Booking Form

File # _____   Salesperson's name _____

Definite _____   Date _____   Approval _____

Booking group name and address _____

_____

_____

_____

Key contact name, title, address,   _____
and phone

_____

_____

_____

Key Data: Attendance   _____

Rooms Committed   _____

Main Arrival Date   _____   Time _____

Main Departure Date _____   Time _____

Hold Rooms Until   _____   Contact _____

Rates Promised: $_____ Singles $_____ Doubles

$_____ Jr. Suites $_____ Suites

Billing: _____ Individual _____ Master Account

_____ Special Instructions—Detail_____

Reservation Process: _____ List by sales office

_____ Other

Comps: _____ #_____   Names

_____ Approved

Sun.	Mon.	Tues.	Weds.	Thurs.	Fri.	Sat.	Auth. Sign. _____	
							Room Req.	Date:
Check In _____. Check Out _____.								

Comment: When something goes wrong, make sure you are there to personally handle it. Don't tell the customer to "call maintenance" or "call catering." *Do it yourself.* Remember, you work for the customers, they don't work for the property!

_____ **Events Timetable/Workplan Form.** This document should be posted and reviewed by everyone involved in serving the group. It should contain the group's name; key contact persons and telephone numbers; signing officers for billing and approval purposes; billing instructions; event name; room block information; audiovisual and other equipment requirements; special instructions; billing policy on

Exhibit 6   Sample Events Timetable/Workplan Form

Group/Party Name: _____
Key Person(s): _____   _____
Telephone Number(s): _____

    ☐ Do above have signature authorization for account?
    ☐ Master Account/Billing Ref. # _____
    ☐ Individual Account/Instructions _____
                                  _____

Event: _____
Rooms Assigned: _____
A-V Requirements: _____   ☐   _____   ☐   _____   ☐   _____   ☐   _____
Special Instructions: _____
Comp. on Meeting Room: ☐
Charge on Meeting Room: ☐ If Yes, state agreement _____

Day	Time	Event	Description (All details specified)	Person Resp.

the meeting room (comp or charge); and a listing of key events, in chronological order, with specific descriptions on set-up, cocktails, bar service, menu, and other details, along with the person responsible for each event. (See Exhibit 6 for a sample events timetable/workplan form.)

Comment: Having a completely filled-out events timetable/workplan form to which the entire hotel will march can help make for successful meetings and satisfied customers.

Exhibit 7   Sample Post-Meeting/Convention Report

File # _____

Organization _____

Arrival _____   Departure _____

Contact _____   Title _____

Address _____   Phone _____

History _____

_____

_____

Action Steps   1. _____   Person Resp. _____
                2. _____   Person Resp. _____
                3. _____   Person Resp. _____

Follow-Up: Dates: _____   Steps: _____   Call _____
                  _____   _____   Letter _____
                  _____   _____   Visit _____

Rooms Booked _____   Rooms Used _____   _____ Comps.

Early Arrivals _____   Late Check-Outs _____

Rate History _____ S _____ D _____ JS _____ S _____ Other

Meeting Room _____   Charge _____   Set-Up

Catering Functions _____   No.
                   _____   Menu Ref. # for File

Special Remarks _____

_____

Booked By _____

_____ **Billing Procedures.** Does the sales department have clear billing procedures for everyone to follow? Billing should be concise, accurate, and to the letter of the agreement—with no variations or surprises. Clear and accurate billing ensures not only a satisfied customer but quick payment.

_____ **Post-Meeting/Convention Report.** This report is filled out after the event to make sure the billing was accurate and the customer was satisfied. This report contains a reference file number; the name of the organization; arrival and departure dates; the contact's name, title, address, and phone number; a brief history of the account/event; action steps for follow-up regarding future business, including dates and the people responsible for the follow up; guestrooms booked and actually used, including complimentary rooms; early arrivals and late check-outs; rate history; meeting room charges; history of catering functions; and special remarks, such as customer comments, complaints, and important non-routine requests that occurred. (See Exhibit 7 for a sample post-meeting/convention report.)

_____ **Thank-You Process.** The thank-you process should consist of two specific actions. One, it should include a personal letter from the salesperson who actually booked and handled the business. And two, the salesperson should call the client to express thanks. This also gives the salesperson an opportunity to clear up any complaints on a one-on-one basis.

_____ **"Please-Come-Back" Letter.** This is the letter that closes the sales loop and just may bring you valuable repeat business. This is an opportunity to thank the client again and ask for the chance to satisfy the client's meeting needs in the future.

If you have all of these checklist items in place and believe you are organized to sell, you're wrong! What happens when you are not at your desk and Mr. VIP calls? Are your department secretaries trained? You should make sure that they are. Just as the department's salespeople need a manual or workplan, so do its secretaries.

A desk manual should be part of every sales secretary's office equipment. Included in this manual should be telephone answering instructions, greeting procedures for walk-in customers, and instructions on how to fill out various sales-department forms:

• *Telephone answering instructions.* Answering the telephone properly is perhaps the most important, yet often mishandled, activity in any sales department. Secretaries should be provided with a form on which they can record a caller's name, address, title, company, and phone number, along with the caller's meeting dates and general requirements. Also on this form should be a clear statement on rates—either giving secretaries a very broad range of rates to quote, or simply advising them to tell callers that rates are negotiable. This form should also contain the general property brochure's descriptive data about the hotel, and a salesperson's name that the secretary can give to the caller, along with a time at which this salesperson will get back to the caller.

   Hotels lose untold amounts of business because telephone answering instructions do not exist or are not used. It should be made clear to all sales department secretaries that such instructions are part of the job and should be followed.

• *Greeting procedures for walk-in customers.* A warm, friendly, but businesslike greeting procedure should be outlined for all personnel who greet walk-in guests. If no salesperson is immediately available, a sales secretary should provide the walk-in with coffee and a brochure or other collateral material about the hotel. The goal is to keep the walk-in "warm"!

• *Form instructions.* All secretarial personnel (as well as the sales staff) should be trained and provided with an instructions guide on how to fill out sales-department forms such as requisition and purchase order forms, brochure request forms, tentative convention booking forms, cancellation forms, and VIP reservation request forms. They should also know how to make, trace, and kill a file.

Organizing for the sales effort is an important and essential step. The checklist presented in this section lists basic tools and procedures salespeople can use to do the sales job properly and book business. The results of using these tools and procedures religiously will be an organized, efficient sales department—and satisfied repeat customers.

Personal Sales

There is a great deal of literature on **personal sales**—face-to-face sales calls. Some authors expound on the value of good grooming and a professional appearance, others go into sales psychology, and still others talk about such subjects as how to use biorhythms to make a sale. Many of these sales theories have merit and can help you sell.

However, the basics of successful personal selling can be stated quite simply. You must have thorough knowledge of your product or service, thorough knowledge of your client's needs, and thorough knowledge of your sales image—that is, how you come across to clients. If you know your product or service and know how to identify your client's needs, oftentimes you can match your product/service to the needs of the client and make the sale:

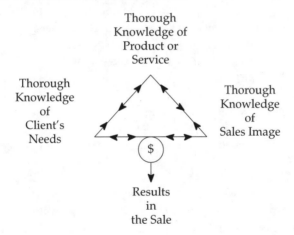

Can it really be that simple? The theory is simple, but it takes careful study and a lot of hard work to put it into practice. Let's look a little closer at the three keys of personal sales.

Key 1: Thorough Knowledge of Your Product or Service. You don't possess thorough knowledge of your product or service until you know your product/service so well that you seldom, if ever, have to look up a fact or get back to a client. For example, let's say you are selling group business for a major hotel and calling on Ms. Haskell, the national sales manager for EBM Corporation. Can you readily state your hotel's room prices; amenities; meeting room sizes, set-ups, capacities, and ceiling heights; audiovisual equipment capabilities; and so on? If so, you thoroughly know your product/service.

Checklist to Increase Sales

_____ 1. Shop your competition. Compare rates and make adjustments to yours when necessary.

_____ 2. Focus on maximizing revenue, rather than just rate or occupancy.

_____ 3. Communicate with reservations personnel. These employees are the hotel's front line to the customer.

_____ 4. Give every group something. To close a sale, have some items to "give"—coffee breaks, suites, etc.

_____ 5. Sell up—to a higher-rated room or better menu item.

_____ 6. Sell down. If rate resistance is encountered, try to move the function to a "valley" period and sell it.

_____ 7. Regularly review your sales files. Look to convert tentatives to definites, or check why a piece of business was lost.

_____ 8. Review all key accounts. Are they being called on regularly and by the correct person?

_____ 9. Track multi-room-night transient guests. For all transient guests producing 50-plus room nights a year, establish an account and track it; treat these guests as you would your best group customers.

_____ 10. Review the function book on a regular basis. Sell into valley periods and push weak or questionable tentatives out of prime periods.

_____ 11. Review all lost-business reports. Ask how you can get this business back next time—and do it.

_____ 12. Keep in touch with and entertain key contacts. These contacts include local car rental, airline, and motorcoach managers.

_____ 13. Develop a support letter. Ask your general manager or owner to give you a support letter. It may make the difference to a group you're going after.

_____ 14. Free yourself and all others in sales from all non-selling activities. The more time spent selling, the more sales that are realized.

_____ 15. Regularly meet with key meeting planners. Show your personal interest.

_____ 16. Send a post-meeting follow-up thank-you letter and "How-may-we-help-you-again?" questionnaire to clients.

_____ 17. Check your competitors' reader boards every day. (A "reader board" is the board on which meetings are listed in a hotel.) Make notes and prepare a game plan to land these organizations for next year or next quarter.

_____ 18. Get to know those who are in the know—your local community's newspaper, city magazine, radio, and television personalities. They are often the first to know who is coming to town or what big event is about to occur.

_____ 19. Know your transient guests. They can lead you to your next group booking. Get to know them and their local contacts.

_____ 20. Monitor and befriend the top-producing travel agents for your hotel.

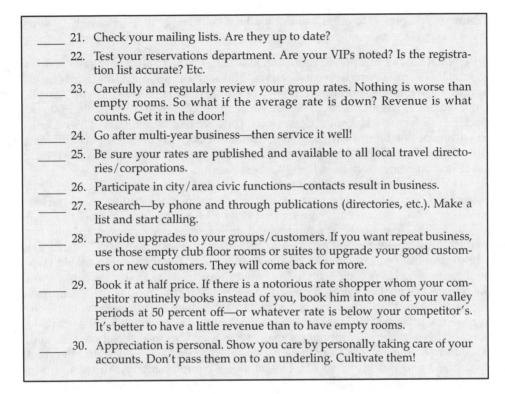

_____ 21. Check your mailing lists. Are they up to date?

_____ 22. Test your reservations department. Are your VIPs noted? Is the registration list accurate? Etc.

_____ 23. Carefully and regularly review your group rates. Nothing is worse than empty rooms. So what if the average rate is down? Revenue is what counts. Get it in the door!

_____ 24. Go after multi-year business—then service it well!

_____ 25. Be sure your rates are published and available to all local travel directories/corporations.

_____ 26. Participate in city/area civic functions—contacts result in business.

_____ 27. Research—by phone and through publications (directories, etc.). Make a list and start calling.

_____ 28. Provide upgrades to your groups/customers. If you want repeat business, use those empty club floor rooms or suites to upgrade your good customers or new customers. They will come back for more.

_____ 29. Book it at half price. If there is a notorious rate shopper whom your competitor routinely books instead of you, book him into one of your valley periods at 50 percent off—or whatever rate is below your competitor's. It's better to have a little revenue than to have empty rooms.

_____ 30. Appreciation is personal. Show you care by personally taking care of your accounts. Don't pass them on to an underling. Cultivate them!

Key 2: Thorough Knowledge of Your Client's Needs. If you have thorough knowledge of your client's needs, then you've done your homework—you know what EBM Corporation does, who Ms. Haskell is, what types of meetings she usually holds, and how much she usually spends. Even if you do not know all of this, you will find it out within the first few minutes of conversation with Ms. Haskell's secretary or Ms. Haskell herself. You should identify the client's requirements before you try to sell him or her your products/services. Even more important than this is to understand that Ms. Haskell has more at stake than you might think. A successful meeting within the stated budget makes Ms. Haskell look good to Mr. Big—remember that when you sell. The old expression, "We know you want a successful meeting; our success and yours are one and the same" should be remembered and perhaps even stated at some point whenever you are trying to sell meeting space.

Key 3: Thorough Knowledge of Your Sales Image. This is a tough thing to learn, especially if you are not looking closely at yourself. What image do you convey to clients through your dress, speech, mannerisms, and so forth? To what image do you think Ms. Haskell will respond during a sales call? If your image and Ms. Haskell's image are not the same, you need to adjust yourself to fit Ms. Haskell's image. Yes, it may even mean getting a haircut and shoe shine. You can know your product and your client very well and still lose the sale because you aren't aware of the image you project to others, or don't adjust your image to more closely fit your client's expectations.

A Personal Sales Example. Recently a text was published with many sales articles written by hospitality industry executives. The articles contained lots of advice on how to make a successful sales call. There were such statements as, "If you're well-groomed and wear an immaculate suit or dress, you're more than likely going to land the sale"; or, my favorite, "Convey yourself as a real swinger; most men like to be with people who are with it!" Well, you and I both know that many different attitudes and beliefs exist among prospective clients, and the sale does not totally hinge on you being a "swinger" or "the best-dressed kid."

This kind of advice reminded me of something I once saw on a flight between Boston and New York. A few rows up on the other side of the curtain was Mr. Hospitality, a hotel sales executive going first class all the way. It really hurt to watch him in action. He not only was wining and dining some decision-makers for a big medical group meeting, but he even had a better property than Ms. Tryharder, a salesperson from another hotel who was flying coach. There sat swinging Mr. Hospitality, sipping his second scotch, the entertainment of the first-class cabin. And the prospects were just eating it up—or so he thought. His grand finale in impressing his new "buddies" (he certainly wasn't treating them as prospects) was the old third-drink trick. As the flight attendant went past him, he extended his arm and bumped his just-about-empty glass against her back, dropped the glass, and said, "Good grief, woman, you've spilled my drink!" The embarrassed flight attendant apologized and quickly gave Mr. Hospitality a complimentary third drink. Mr. Hospitality figured this really impressed his buddies—by this point booking the business was a mere formality, he thought. When the plane landed, Mr. Hospitality sprayed his mouth with a breath spray, popped in a piece of gum, and headed for his hotel with the prospects in tow, to further impress them. Poor Ms. Tryharder had to wait until later that day to meet with these same prospects and try to convince them that her slightly inferior property with a slightly higher rate was where they should book their meeting.

In the afternoon the prospects arrived at Ms. Tryharder's property across town. Ms. Tryharder answered every question, displaying thorough knowledge of her product and thorough knowledge of the prospects' needs. Ms. Tryharder really did her homework, and it was about to pay off.

As Ms. Tryharder seated the prospects in her office and poured them a cup of coffee (which they really needed after their liquid lunch with good ol' Mr. Hospitality), she said casually, "Your attendees will be bringing their spouses, won't they?" The prospects said, "Definitely." Ms. Tryharder reached into her desk and laid out a map of the city with entertainment and shopping areas clearly marked. The clients thanked Ms. Tryharder and asked, "What are all the red zones on this map?"

"Those are high-crime areas," Ms. Tryharder replied.

"That spot where all the red zones come together—isn't that where we were this morning, at Mr. Hospitality's hotel?" the prospects asked.

"Well, yes," Ms. Tryharder said, "but don't worry, Mr. Hospitality's hotel has excellent guards and even patrol dogs—they've thought of everything."

The next morning Ms. Tryharder's phone rang at 9:00 A.M. sharp. It was the prospects, wanting to book the meeting at her hotel. The prospects thought Ms. Tryharder's hotel might suit their needs a little better, in view of the fact that spouses were accompanying the meeting attendees.

Think about this story as you go out to sell, and remember the three keys to personal selling:

1. Thorough knowledge of your product/service
2. Thorough knowledge of your client's needs
3. Thorough knowledge of your sales image

Telephone Sales

Many times a hospitality industry product or service is sold without the opportunity for a direct face-to-face sales call. Booking business by telephone is an art in itself. There are a few golden rules to **telephone sales** that will help you achieve success. The first three are identical to the three keys we discussed in the previous section—thorough knowledge of your product or service, thorough knowledge of your client's needs, and thorough knowledge of your sales image. Let's look at these keys as they apply to telephone sales.

First, just as in personal sales, you should know your product or service thoroughly. You don't want to hesitate or be forced to say, "I'll have to get back to you with those dimensions." *Second,* know about your prospect by doing research before you call, not while you're talking to him or her. *Third,* make sure your sales image is professional and positive—your sales image can be transmitted and detected over the telephone by your vocal expressions and telephone mannerisms.

The *fourth* key to telephone sales is perhaps the most important of all: Listen! Think of our earlier personal sales example and imagine what it might be like if Mr. Hospitality and Ms. Tryharder had to close the sale over the telephone. There's Mr. Hospitality on the speaker phone, telling his prospects a few jokes, reminding them of his famous third-drink trick, and talking so much that he misses it when the prospects mention that their spouses will be traveling with them to the meeting. Then there is Ms. Tryharder, listening intently to the prospects, ready with information about entertainment options for their spouses, and giving the prospects a clear, accurate, and prompt response to every question. Ms. Tryharder's phone call is going to end like this: "Let me recap your needs, item by item," and then, "Now that we have all the details, should we book you on a tentative basis for the 3rd through the 5th of next month?" Ms. Tryharder has just completed the *fifth* key to telephone sales—asking for the sale. The *sixth* key is to say "Thank you." Ms. Tryharder will then proceed to make sure the booking becomes definite, the prospects' needs are met, and the meeting is a success.

The Importance of Interdepartmental Communication

It is critical that all departments within a hotel communicate with each other. Communication is especially important to the sales department. After all, sales impacts every department and area in the hotel. For example, if catering is not part of the sales department (i.e., it's the responsibility of the food and beverage department or is a stand-alone function), sales department communication with catering is especially critical, as both sales and catering could sell the ballroom on the same date to two different groups. While this may be an obvious example, there are many other crucial hotel interrelationships that the sales department should be constantly aware of during its daily activities.

For example, the reservations department is an often-ignored part of the overall sales process. Never forget that reservations is not just a mechanical or computerized system—it is a key point of customer contact. If you are in direct sales, be sure you spend a portion of each week talking with the reservations department. Tell the reservations department which groups are coming, what to do when the reservations start pouring in, and—if necessary—how to do it. Room availability, payment procedures, rate/revenue management, and group check-in/check-out times are some of the key areas to cover. Make sure you know the reservations personnel well enough to ask for a favor every so often. Just like other employees, reservationists like to feel appreciated, so giving them a little extra attention once in a while can really pay dividends. Horror stories about reservations are more abundant than those told about hotels or rooms. You, the sales professional, have an obligation to see that your customers' reservations are handled flawlessly.

Here are just a few more examples illustrating the importance of interdepartmental communication:

- Sales and the rooms department must be in sync on VIP needs, meeting times, etc.

- Sales and the food and beverage department must be clear about group meal functions, break times, menus, etc.

- Sales and the engineering department should review any special technical needs (lighting, HVAC, etc.) of incoming groups

- Sales and the security department must communicate with respect to VIPs, valuable equipment, etc.

Key Terms

personal sales
telephone sales

REVIEW QUIZ

When you feel you have covered all of the material in this chapter, answer these questions. Choose the *best* answer. Check your answers with the correct ones found on the Review Quiz Answer Key at the end of this book.

1. Which of the following rate information would be appropriate to include in a sales secretary's telephone answering instructions?

   a. Secretaries should be given a very broad range of rates to quote.
   b. Secretaries should be given two or three rates to quote.
   c. Secretaries should be advised to simply say that rates are negotiable.
   d. a or c.

2. Which of the following statements about your sales image is *true?*

   a. Your sales image is made up of such things as your dress, speech, and mannerisms.
   b. You shouldn't adjust your sales image to meet the expectations of your clients.
   c. It's easy for most salespeople to learn about their sales image.
   d. Your sales image is not an important factor in making a sale.

3. Which of the following is a key to telephone sales?

   a. asking for objections
   b. listening
   c. thoroughly knowing your product or service
   d. b and c

4. Which of the following statements about communication and the sales department is *true?*

   a. Communicating with other departments is not important to the sales department.
   b. There is no need for salespeople to communicate with personnel in the rooms department.
   c. If the sales department doesn't communicate with catering, a meeting room might be sold on the same day at the same time to two different groups.
   d. The sales department should communicate with the food and beverage department about special technical needs a group might have, such as unusual lighting or HVAC requirements.

Chapter Outline

Advertising
    Advertising Guidelines
    The Six-Step Advertising Process
    Do It Yourself or Select an Agency?
    Market Coverage
    Media Selection
    Trade-Outs, Barter, and Co-Oping
    Advertising Types and Themes
    Case Examples

Learning Objectives

1. Summarize advertising guidelines, and describe a six-step advertising process that can help you develop a successful advertising campaign. (pp. 87–90)

2. Describe criteria for selecting an ad agency, list different ways to cover your markets through advertising, list media selection criteria, and describe how you can exchange your product or service for advertising space or broadcast exposure. (pp. 90–96)

3. Summarize advertising types and themes, and describe examples of hospitality industry advertising campaigns. (pp. 96–109)

8

Applying Key Marketing Methodologies: Advertising

This CHAPTER CONCENTRATES on helping you understand the basic elements of a successful advertising campaign. The chapter will examine when, how, and where to advertise, and look at the various media available. It will also examine how to create an advertising proposition and support it with an advertising platform. The chapter concludes with a discussion of ad themes or types and a section that takes a look at examples of hospitality advertising.

Advertising

There are many lists of "do's and don'ts" for advertising, yet few of them acknowledge the product or service itself, and the role that advertising plays in the overall marketing of that product or service. However, there are some advertising guidelines that can help you acknowledge both your product or service and your total marketing plan.

Advertising Guidelines

The following list of advertising guidelines can help you put together successful advertising campaigns:

1. Know your product or service
2. Advertise as part of the total marketing strategy
3. Develop a proposition
4. Create a platform
5. Be realistic about the level of expectation
6. Review for customer needs

We will briefly discuss each of these guidelines in the following sections.

Know Your Product or Service. What do you know about the product or service you want to advertise? What consumer needs does it fulfill? Do you understand how consumers currently perceive your product or service in terms of price, quality, relationship to competition, consistency, and inconsistency? Knowing the role your product plays in the market and how the product is perceived by consumers is essential to creating effective advertising. Without these basic facts, you cannot

87

get a clear, realistic picture of where your product stands in the market and where you want it to be.

Advertise as Part of the Total Marketing Strategy. What role do you anticipate advertising will play in your total marketing strategy? Do you even need to use advertising as a marketing tool? If so, should you use advertising with a narrow range but direct aim, or do you want to target a large region with more general advertising tools? Later in the chapter a number of case studies will be presented demonstrating how certain advertising tools work better for certain situations.

Develop a Proposition. Have you developed a general **proposition** to be conveyed in your advertising message? A proposition is the strongest truthful statement you can make to the consumer on behalf of your product or service. Your proposition should agree with and support your overall marketing strategy, and meet the purpose of your advertising. For example, if you are trying to persuade people to use your product or service, does your advertising include a toll-free telephone number that consumers can call to order your product or service or get further information?

Create a Platform. Once you understand your product or service, the consumer's perspective of it, the role your advertising will play as part of your total marketing strategy, and you have developed your proposition, focus on the advertising **platform.** The platform is an item-by-item list of facts that support your proposition. Platform statements illustrate the strength of your proposition. For example, when Hyatt Hotels says, "We offer you a touch of class," the company supports that claim with some spectacular photos that demonstrate some "touches of class."

Be Realistic About the Level of Expectation. Regardless of your advertising purpose and its strategic role in your overall marketing plan, there is one key principle that you should remember when advertising hospitality industry products and services. *Never promise more than your product or service can deliver.* The **"level of expectation"** principle can be graphically presented as follows:

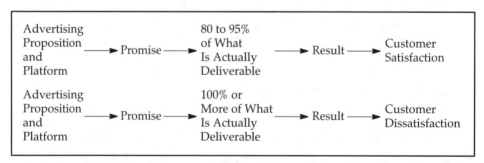

Keep this idea in mind whenever you plan advertising. Think about how you would feel in this situation: You see an ad stating "all of our Florida Rent-A-Car customers have a new Lincoln* assigned to them upon arrival." When you arrive at the rental agency, you get a two-year-old Pinto with an explanation that the fine print on the contract says "*subject to availability, etc., etc." Many hospitality companies have made the mistake of promising more than they could deliver. The result was customer dissatisfaction.

Review for Customer Needs. Does your advertising strategy relate to your customers' needs? Your customers' needs should be the focus of your advertising strategy.

Once you understand the six guidelines just described, you can begin developing an actual advertising campaign.

The Six-Step Advertising Process

The following is a six-step advertising process that can help you develop a successful advertising campaign.

Step 1: Identify Your Purpose. Clearly identify *one* purpose you expect your advertising to serve. What do you want your advertising to do for you? Advertising is usually used to:

- Inform consumers that your product or service is available and tell them how to get it
- Persuade consumers that your product or service is better than your competitors'
- Remind consumers to use your product or service

Identify the purpose for advertising your product or service and then make sure that the ads you create fulfill that purpose. For example, if you want to *inform* consumers that you are offering a new service, your ads should not focus on reminding consumers you're still in business.

Step 2: Target Your Audience. Assuming you know what you want to say and why you want to say it (your purpose), the next step is to precisely *identify to whom you want to say it.* You want to advertise to people who will buy your product or use your service. "Who are these people?" and "How do I reach them?" become the next critical questions to answer. Market research can tell you who and where your target consumers are, and proper selection of advertising **media** can help you reach them.

Step 3: Select a Medium. You want to reach as many potential customers as possible without spending a fortune. What is the most effective, efficient, and affordable medium you can select for advertising your product or service? Depending on your product or service, and your target consumers, it may be television, radio, or magazine advertising; in other situations, it may be direct mail, directories, outdoor advertising, or the yellow pages. Your choice of media also depends on how much money you have to spend and the role advertising is to play in your total marketing plan.

Step 4: Create the Ad. The advertising you develop largely depends on all other steps and guidelines previously cited. Despite wide interest in great creative advertising, your product or service, purpose, and budget are the practical parameters of what you can and cannot do with your creative strategy. Make sure your ad is appropriate for your audience, product, service, and budget. It is very difficult to show your customers your expansive beach when all you can afford is a 30-second radio spot or a three-line ad in a directory.

Step 5: Place and Time the Ad. Thanks to your (or your agency's) creativity, you have a great ad ready for the market. Don't blow it now! The proper selection of *where* your advertising goes and *when* it is aired is critical to the success of your advertising campaign. When you select *where* to place your ad, consider:

- Markets

- Media selection, be it an outdoor billboard near the airport, an all-news radio program, a cooking show on cable television, or *Sports Illustrated*

- The page and page **placement**

To determine *when* to run the ad, think about:

- Time of year

- Month

- Week

- Day of the week

- Hour of the day

- The minutes during the hour of the day, such as after the sports on FM radio at 4:20 P.M.

Step 6: Fulfill Expectations. You ran a great ad at the right time and place, and now the phone is ringing off the hook. Is there *anyone* there to answer it? Make sure you can fulfill your ad promises after you have motivated the consumer to purchase. Meeting the expectations generated by your advertising should always be considered within the total context of your advertising strategy.

Do It Yourself or Select an Agency?

Depending on your skills and the size of your budget, you may want to do an advertising campaign yourself or contract with an advertising agency to handle the campaign for you. The scope and breadth of hospitality industry advertising is immense, ranging from local newspaper ads to national television campaigns. If you cannot afford the luxury of hiring an agency, here are a few suggestions to help you handle your own campaign.

First, start your own *master notebook*. This notebook should contain examples of clean ads that you have developed and used. The notebook will help you review the effectiveness of your ads and should include such information as how and where your ad came together. Include a section in the notebook labeled "Monitor" to record the history of your advertising and a statement of results. For example, it could read as follows:

Tues., February 20. Print Ad "A-1"—*Telegraph,* Entertainment Page
Wed., February 21. Print Ad "A-l"—*News,* Sports Page
Thurs., February 22. Print Ad "A-l"—*Telegraph,* Lifestyle Page

Results: Meals sold for February 20–22 up by 25% over same period
last year and/or week.

or

Beverage revenue up 16% February 22 and 28% February 23 compared
with same period last year and/or last week.

This simple procedure will give you and your property a history of which ads were run, where they were run, and the results.

Also, consider including in your master notebook examples of your competition's best advertising. Analyze the file to determine what advertising strategies your chief competitors are using, trends they're following, and what you can do to combat your competitors' moves. For example, let's say your competitor has advertised "2-for-1" sales. Analyze their ads to determine if you can offer a similar or better sale. Look for patterns as to when these sales are run. For example, you might discover that your competitor runs a "2-for-1" ad the fourth week of every month. You might counteract this strategy by advertising your own "2-for-1" sale during the third week of the month.

Selecting an Agency. If you can afford to hire an ad agency, you should probably do so, even if you believe you have the capability of running your own advertising campaigns. Why? Because advertising professionals are best equipped to navigate through today's complex and sophisticated marketing arena.

Selecting an agency is more like selecting a business partner than selecting just another supplier of services, so ask a lot of questions before forming this vital partnership. Agencies will provide you with their credentials in terms of work they have performed, awards they have won, current and past clients, and so on. Look closely at these credentials and talk to the agency's former and current clients to get a balanced perspective of the agency's strengths and weaknesses. Evaluate an agency's strengths and weaknesses in relation to your own. Where do you or your company need more help—for example, in creativity? in media planning? etc. The following is a list of some of the functional areas within ad agencies; keep in mind that not every agency can be outstanding in every area:

- Account management/account executive area—the staff members in this area have the overall management responsibility for a brand, product, or client company; they are the primary contact persons with clients ("accounts") and manage the "account teams" (the persons who do the work for the clients)

- Research—provides quantitative and qualitative data on the market, needs, benefits, competition, customers, etc., using an array of services and techniques

- Creative (the imagination function)—generates ideas to link the brand or product to consumers' needs

- Casting—identifies people, voices, actors: the ingredients that make an ad or commercial work

An Advertising Checklist

An advertising checklist can help you determine if your advertising is organized and effective. The following checklist can be adapted to your own advertising efforts and may prove to be a useful tool for your organization. A checklist can do more than save you money; it can provide a cross-check to ensure that advertising, sales, and public relations personnel are all working together to execute your marketing plan.

Advertising Audit/Checklist

_____   Do your advertising plans support the objectives and strategies of the current marketing plan?

_____   Does your chief marketing officer understand the responsibilities of everyone involved in executing the advertising strategy for your product or service?

_____   Is the sales manager or director involved in the planning and execution of the advertising strategy and program? To what extent?

_____   Do your key marketing and advertising people have good rapport with the media? Are they capable of executing trade-outs or barter agreements?

_____   Do you have a "master notebook" containing up-to-date examples of your advertising?

_____   Do you have a monitoring and results-measurement system in place to determine the outcome or effectiveness of your advertising expenditures?

_____   Do you have a "clippings" file? Is someone specifically assigned to analyze what the competition is doing?

_____   Are request forms, exceptions reports, insertion orders, sample copy, and sample ads readily accessible?

_____   Is there a master file for all media and trade-out contracts?

_____   Have you prepared advance advertising schedules?

_____   Are advertising work request forms used? Are they sent in with sufficient lead time? Are copies on file?

_____   How is the advertising production budget managed? Have all ads and expenditures received proper approvals?

_____   Are insertion orders submitted to the media on time? Are copies of completed orders properly distributed?

_____   Do all key marketing personnel understand the conditions of all media contracts—print, broadcast, outdoor, airport display, and trade-outs?

_____   What is the condition of outdoor signs? When were they last checked? When are they scheduled for reprint?

_____   Is an advertising verification process in place? Are all ad invoices from the media supported by tearsheets or affidavits? Are copies of invoices and tearsheets on file? Are they checked for accuracy against insertion orders?

_____   Are rates and discounts verified? By whom? Are rate changes supported by new rate cards?

_____   Have there been any major changes in the approved advertising schedules? Is everyone aware of these changes?

_____   Have all deficiencies from the previous audit been corrected?

- Media—looks for the best reach and frequency to reach your target audience, given your budget

- Production—pulls together creative, media, and other agency areas and delivers the final product

Perhaps the most important question to ask is: Who will actually work on your account—an experienced creative team or new hires?

Make sure that the agency you select knows something about your market and your customers. Good research, either conducted within the agency itself or contracted out to another research supplier, can increase your agency's and your own knowledge of target markets. If an agency immediately wants to talk creative strategy, media, or contract, take another look. A good agency will listen and learn as much as possible about your product or service, markets or consumers, and about you and your overall marketing philosophies before moving on to actual strategies.

One way to choose an agency is to place your business "out to bid" or "out for proposal." An amazing amount of good work done absolutely free of charge can come from "bid presentations." Consider more than one agency in the proposal stage so that you will have a basis for comparison.

Only you can judge how long to stay with an agency or how often to switch. Make changes only when your objective measurements indicate that it is time for a change. Objective measurements include declining sales, lower levels of brand awareness among customers and potential customers, negative customer feedback about your advertising, excessive errors in the advertising copy, missed deadlines, and so on.

Market Coverage

Next, think about where to expose your product or service to the consumer. Look at each case individually. There are no real golden rules for determining how and where to cover your market. You don't always have to stick to the same media or technique. In the following sections we will discuss some definitions to help you understand different techniques for reaching your markets through advertising.

Nationwide Campaigns. Simply stated, nationwide campaigns give you coast-to-coast coverage or **exposure** of your product or service. If your market is nationwide or if you are trying to develop a national market presence, it might make sense to look at this type of total market exposure. Nationwide campaigns are particularly useful for large chains seeking to increase their brand awareness levels or provide an "image" for their brand. Also, nationwide campaigns can be used to introduce a national product simultaneously in all markets.

Major Markets. Based on research or because of budget constraints, you might want to advertise only in those major markets you want to penetrate with your campaign. This is a cost-effective advertising technique and there are many examples of how this technique works. For example, major market selection would make sense for a restaurant chain with facilities in 20 major markets, all located east of the Rockies.

Regional Markets. Advertising can be purchased or selected on a regional basis also. There are many ways to identify marketing regions for your product or service. For example, one large chain of cafeterias selects only the southwest region for advertising exposure, since this is the primary market for its locations and customers.

Population Markets. Population markets are major concentrations of population that can be categorized according to size, such as standard metropolitan areas with populations of over 1,000,000, over 750,000, over 500,000, and so on. Populations may be measured in terms of viewers, readers, listeners, exposures, etc., depending on the type of media you are considering.

Viewer/Reader/Listener/Subscriber Market Areas. Television stations, radio stations, magazines, and newspapers can provide detailed descriptions of the number of people within their range or on their circulation lists. In addition, they can provide you with various *buyer characteristics* that will help you choose the best match of media to your product or service consumer. Using this advertising method allows you to better define a market area for your advertising message.

Feeder Markets. Feeder markets—markets (geographical areas) from which your guests travel—are usually likely targets for your advertising.

Cities. Advertising can be placed in individual cities or even in areas within an individual city. Using local market research can be a valuable aid to selecting the proper media for each city.

Today's sophisticated market analysis and customer research should help you select the best method or combination of methods to maximize the effectiveness of your advertising dollar.

Media Selection

Carefully evaluate media selection before creating your advertising. *Broadcast media,* which include television and radio, provide one type of exposure for your product or service. *Print media,* which include magazines, newspapers, supplements, catalogs, directories, yellow pages, brochures, flyers, and so on, provide other types of exposure for your product or service.

Before you select media for delivering your advertising message, carefully analyze the various media to determine the number of potential customers they can reach, your expected return on investment, and the best, most cost-effective method to convey your advertising strategy. Again, consider your needs, purpose, and budget as part of your media analysis.

Trade-Outs, Barter, and Co-Oping

One way to reduce your advertising costs is to exchange your product or service for advertising space or broadcast exposure. There is an infinite variety of **trade-outs** or **barter** agreements you can negotiate with advertising suppliers, ranging from a "one-for-one" trade to a "five-for-one" or even greater trade. A one-for-one trade means that you will provide a set dollar amount of your products or services for an equal dollar value of space or air time, for example, $1,000 worth of your

Exhibit 1 Sample of a Cooperative Advertisement Campaign

Courtesy of Sheraton

product or service for $1,000 worth of space or ad time. A two-for-one trade means you provide $1,000 worth of your product or service for $2,000 worth of air time or space, and so on. If negotiated properly, trade-outs can be an effective way to stretch your advertising dollars and increase your business.

Another way to stretch advertising dollars is to **co-op**, or join with other companies to advertise, thereby sharing the costs (see Exhibit 1). Resort areas frequently run cooperative advertising campaigns that promote the region or area and also list or mention specific products or services. A more popular use of co-oping is seen when two or more firms advertise each other's services or products, either individually or collectively, in the same advertising campaign. For example, Marriott Hotels and Hertz Rent-A-Cars, or American Airlines and Avis, feature the other's products and services in cooperative ad campaigns.

Advertising Types and Themes

An ad is not just the product of an idea. Effective advertising begins long before the "great idea" stage. As previously discussed, you need to answer some key questions regarding the purpose of the advertising, the platform, and the proposition. Even a "great idea" must have a purpose, or the ad campaign will be ineffective. Later in the chapter we will look at some examples of great advertising ideas. As you will see, "great ideas" can backfire if the consumer's reaction to an ad differs from the reaction the advertisers were trying to evoke.

In the following sections we will discuss some examples of ad campaign types or themes.

Reputation Builders. These ads feature *testimonials,* self-claims, or other-party claims, or cite leadership or professionalism as a way to enhance the reputation of the product or service advertised. One common reputation-building technique is to have a recognized celebrity speak on behalf of the product or service, or lend his or her photo or signature as an implied endorsement of the product or service. A slightly different version of the celebrity testimonial is the self-testimonial ad, in which the CEO, president, or chairperson of the company speaks on behalf of the company's product or service. (This is also sometimes referred to as the "ego trip.")

Another form of the reputation builder is the *professional trust ad* in which the platform itself is self-implied professionalism. The ad features the entire property or company staff in uniform standing at attention, just waiting to professionally serve guests.

Finally, we have the "image" form of a reputation builder, in which one or more images are used to represent your product or service: for example, rich-looking flower arrangements, monogrammed towels, a Rolls-Royce at the portico to convey luxury or class, and so on (see Exhibit 2).

Product/Service Touters. A product or service touter ad can take on a number of looks (see Exhibit 3). The *direct* look features the product or service and boldly states the reasons for its greatness. Touting the actual elements of the platform produces results similar to those of the reputation-builder ads—they both enhance the product or service. Another form of touter ad is the *comparative approach.* Here, the ad compares the product or service with a competitor's product or service to demonstrate that its benefits outstrip the competition's.

A touter ad may feature an unusual product element or characteristic. For example, an amenity of unusually high quality may be the ad's focal point. Sometimes a touter ad will feature a scene, such as an elegant-looking couple or a luxury setting, as the positioning statement for the product or service. Product/service touter ads can have multiple elements, such as "we were rated highest by an independent survey, our service is extraordinary, and our facilities are world class."

Exhibit 2   Sample of a "Reputation Builder" Advertisement

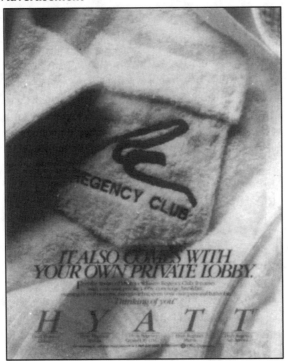

Courtesy of Hyatt Hotels Corporation

Brand Identifiers. In today's crowded marketplace, getting your brand known—also known as achieving *brand awareness*—is not an easy job. What may be even more difficult is to effectively convey what your brand stands for, or your *brand identity*. To achieve brand awareness and brand identity:

- Include statements that boldly feature the brand

- Develop a *brand identifier*—a character, voice, image, phrase, etc., that becomes synonymous with the brand (see Exhibits 4 and 5)

- Make an introduction or announcement about the brand: "USAir now serves Cleveland"

- Develop a niche by providing a unique service

Offers. In an offer ad, the platform becomes part of the proposition. One common type of offer is the straight *price offer:* "Newark $49 Round Trip." In a price offer, the actual price, not necessarily the product or service itself, is featured and highlighted as the key motivation for consumers to buy. Another variation of the straight price offer is the *price offer plus*—something additional is included with the product at no additional cost. For example, you might include with your product a

Exhibit 3   Sample of a Product or Service Touter Advertisement

A NEW GENERATION
DISCOVERS THE BREAKERS.

For decades The Breakers has offered visitors to Palm Beach an extraordinary dining experience—superb cuisine served in a classic setting. The tradition continues with dining and dancing in the legendary Florentine Room. Sunday brunch in the oceanfront Beach Club is a Palm Beach favorite. Guests may also enjoy casual dining options. The Fairways Cafe and the Beach Club are ideal for luscious lunches, while evenings are celebrated with live entertainment in the Alcazar Lounge.

For reservations, please call (407) 659-8480 and discover the timeless qualities of great dining and entertainment at The Breakers.

THE BREAKERS®   One South County Road, Palm Beach, Florida 33480

Courtesy of The Breakers, Palm Beach, Florida

complimentary meal such as breakfast, a room or seat upgrade, or an economy rate for a luxury car rental.

Today, one of the strongest-hitting offer ads focuses on *repeat* or *"build"* promotions such as frequent traveler or frequent guest promotions. These ads feature offers or benefits for customers who repeatedly use one product or service.

Human Scenarios. A long-standing type of advertising is the *human scenario*. A person or group is the focal point of the ad, either directly or by identifiable event or circumstance. For example, an employee or group of employees is featured, accompanied by a gratuitous statement or slogan, or an exceptional employee is portrayed as representing the norm.

On a more sophisticated level (and more risky if it doesn't work well) is a "situation identification" (see Exhibit 6). Here, a "wrong-way" scene is shown and a statement is made that this situation won't occur with your product or service. These often humorous ads should be carefully considered, because they can backfire.

**Exhibit 4   Sample of a Brand
Identifier—Advertisement I**

Courtesy of Embassy Suites, Inc.

And last, but certainly not least, is the age-old "suggestive" approach featuring or implying the promise of romance or sex to the consumer (see Exhibit 7). This type of ad features an attractive person or implies how people who use the product or service become more attractive, successful, etc. The "hook" is a consumer's imagination.

Benefit. The *benefit* ad reflects the advertising platform in that it states, item-for-item, why consumers should purchase your product or service. Sometimes the ad will focus only on a primary benefit, such as a straight location pitch: "Located at Dallas-Ft. Worth Airport." At other times the benefit becomes engulfed in an overall umbrella, such as with most destination ads. More complex benefit ads present multiple benefits: "Free Gifts for You. Free Avis Upgrades for Your Clients" (the "you" refers to travel agents—see Exhibit 8.) Often, meeting-related ads are benefit-oriented; they seek to convey the benefits sought by the meeting planner.

Series. Perhaps one of the most famous series ads run in print was for Porsche. Actually numbered 1, 2, and so on, these bold ads stated the "numerous" reasons that Porsche was a superior automobile. The series ad campaign, while used in the automotive industry and outside the U.S. market, has been rarely used in the domestic hospitality industry (see Exhibit 9).

Exhibit 5   Sample of a Brand Identifier—Advertisement II

In Over 140 Countries Around The World, There's Nothing Lost In The Translation.

Wherever you find Avis, you'll find the same philosophy: a commitment to trying harder than ever to provide you with the quality and service you expect.

You'll find 4,800 locations in over 140 countries. Connecting them together throughout the world is our Avis Wizard® system, which provides on-line, real-time reservations just about anywhere you could think of, and links all rental data so your commission information is secure. It also makes getting into and out of a rental car as fast and easy as possible.

With our Preferred service at over 700 locations worldwide, it means a car that's ready to go. And our Roving Rapid Return® makes dropping off the car just as easy. At our Worldwide Reservation Center, our Language Service Desk can help answer any question you may have in many different languages.

So you can see that no matter where your clients are headed, when we say "We try harder," the translation will always be the same.

To book Avis reservations worldwide, check your **ZI** location files. Or call an Avis employee-owner at **1-800-331-2212** for U.S. rentals, or for International rentals, **1-800-331-1084**.

Avis features GM cars.
© 1994 Wizard Co., Inc.

AVIS®

We try harder:®

Courtesy of Avis

Line Art and Silhouettes. More of a technique or production treatment than ad type or theme, line art and silhouettes have become more and more popular in advertising (see Exhibit 10). Their popularity stems largely from their effectiveness in a newspaper or other black-and-white setting.

Trade. With more travelers turning to travel intermediaries to help them with purchasing decisions, trade ads take on new importance. Today, hospitality companies understand the growing importance of travel intermediaries and are seeking to gain their attention. Naturally, many elements of the previously described ad types are incorporated into a trade ad. The theme of the trade ad depends to some extent on the travel intermediary. For example, a trade ad aimed at travel agents might

**Exhibit 6   Sample of a Situation
Identification Advertisement**

Courtesy of The Westin Galleria and Westin Oaks

focus on the commission check (see Exhibit 11); an ad aimed at meeting planners may take a different approach: "Meet with us—we know your job is on the line."

Let's examine some of these ad types and approaches in more depth as we look at a few select case examples in the following sections.

Case Examples

Case Example A: The B-52 That Bombed. In the late 1970s, major hotel chains frequently used national television for their major advertising campaigns. Holiday Inn, whose aggressive new marketing team was out to gain market share, spent the most money on national campaigns. Holiday Inn launched a new advertising campaign called "The Best Surprise Is No Surprise," which was carried by nationwide television, in print media, and even on napkins and matches. The theme of the campaign was simply to tell consumers that their lodging experiences at Holiday Inn would contain no negative surprises. Sub-themes, such as no lost reservations, no dirty rooms, and so on, were included in the ads. Moreover, this was a hard-hitting campaign, in that it took an "us" versus "them" approach. "Us"—Holiday Inns—were always the good examples, and "them"—other hotels—were always the bad examples. Holiday Inns saturated the airways with "The Best Surprise Is No Surprise at Holiday Inns."

What was the response to this massive campaign? What worked and what didn't? There were many positive factors in the campaign, including:

Exhibit 7   Sample of a Suggestive Identifier Advertisement

Courtesy of Couples

- Quality creative work
- Excellent selection of broadcast and print advertising
- Consideration of the overall marketing strategy
- Excellent execution, placement, and timing
- Complete coordination throughout the marketing areas and within the in-house promotional materials

Exhibit 8 Sample of a Benefit Advertisement

Courtesy of Avis

Exhibit 9 Sample of a Series Advertisement

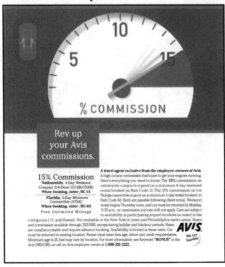

Courtesy of Avis

Exhibit 10   Sample of a Line Art or Silhouette Advertisement

Courtesy of Le Parker Meridien New York

- Pre- and post-measurement mechanisms in place to determine the very positive results expected

Technically, the campaign had many plus marks. This was no surprise. After all, Holiday Inns was the biggest advertiser in the industry and had money to spend on quality advertising. However, although the campaign had its strong points, a few very important items kept the campaign from being a success. *First,* the campaign violated the key principle of advertising: never promise what you can't deliver. The level of expectation generated by the ads wasn't met at the property level. The result was guest dissatisfaction, as well as an increase in the volume of complaint mail. *Second,* the platform (the item-by-item list that supports

Exhibit 11   Sample of a Trade Advertisement

Courtesy of Hertz

the proposition) was not 100% fulfilled at the operational level. There were still surprises, especially in a chain with 1,700 properties where quality control and consistency are major challenges. *Third,* the campaign implied that the rest of the industry, both other chains and independents, would give the consumer all kinds of bad surprises. In essence, the advertising "knocked" or degraded the competition. It is unwise to offend everyone else in your industry!

This ad campaign was widely recognized and talked about. Was it successful? Yes, in terms of volume, placement, and air time. However, the campaign failed in terms of its results—negative reactions from consumers and the industry.

Case Example B: Testimonials and the "Ego Trip." Advertising agencies often have success with their clients when they use the chief executive officer of their client-company as the main star in the firm's ad campaign. Naturally, the CEO believes in his or her product or service and doesn't mind gaining personal exposure.

Perhaps the most famous example of a testimonial ad campaign came from Chrysler in the 1980s, with CEO Lee Iacocca as the chief spokesperson. This wasn't just a CEO's ego trip—it was a credible, well-executed ad campaign. The man, the product, and the ads all gelled into a believable story that successfully targeted consumers' patriotism and their desire for the underdog to win. That campaign will probably be remembered as one of the all-time winners.

Before the Chrysler campaign, Marriott launched a self-testimonial campaign with similar success and credibility. The campaign focused on Bill Marriott, Jr., and his personal involvement in ensuring that things were right in Marriott hotels. As he said, "That's my name on the door." The campaign's theme was really product consistency and the tie-in was the boss making sure the product was right. As self-testimonial ads go, this campaign was pretty good. The Wendy's ads featuring CEO Dave Thomas are examples of a current hospitality industry testimonial ad campaign that is enjoying success.

In the hospitality industry, the CEO testimonial ranges from the straightforward to the absurd. One risk inherent in self-starring testimonial campaigns is that not everyone loves the star. Those who knew Bill Marriott knew he worked hard and really did inspect his properties to make sure things were done right. On the other hand, other self-testimonials have backfired. For example, Leona Helmsley's many appearances as the "queen" did much to publicize the Helmsley Hotel chain. However, much of the publicity was viewed negatively by consumers, who were turned off by Helmsley's self-proclaimed status as "queen." And, naturally, if your CEO ends up serving a prison sentence, as Ms. Helmsley did, your self-starring testimonial campaign will end immediately.

There are other examples of testimonials that fail. The fundamental problem with such ads is human nature and credibility. Is the proposition there? If so, is it believable? Where is the platform? And where are the real people—the consumers? What measurable results are derived from such ads?

There is a big difference between CEO product testimonials that really work and ads that are just "ego trips" for the CEO. Yes, it is important that consumers know that managers and employees care about the product or service they offer, but the question to ask is, Does this testimonial ad express the benefits the consumer seeks from the product or service?

Case Example C: Level of Expectation. Occasionally, an advertising campaign can be so well done that the product or service cannot live up to the level of expectation created by the campaign. For a number of years, Sheraton ran a television campaign featuring an attractive female vocalist singing Sheraton's praises. The ads always featured quality photography of superior rooms, food, and beverages, and gave viewers the clear impression that Sheraton Hotels and Inns offered a "classy," quality experience. Unfortunately, the ads also built an unrealistically high level of expectation, one that would be difficult for any hotel or inn to fulfill.

For years Sheraton advertised its 800 number, creating perhaps the single greatest number of exposures for any toll-free number. The number has been in print advertising, on matchbooks, in TV commercials, and even sung as part of a commercial jingle. Think about it: Do you remember the 800 number? How many other consumers do you think remember the number? Probably not very many. There are approximately five million frequent travelers in the United States. For the same cost, how many times could a gold-embossed reminder card with the 800 number have been mailed to each traveler?

Case Example D: Humanizing the All-Beef Patty. On the food and beverage side of the hospitality industry, one firm has won practically every possible advertising award. McDonald's advertising campaigns have humanized the all-beef patty and fast-food experience. Be it a birthday party or a promise to a small child, McDonald's has gone right to the heart of the consumer. The products, service, and level of expectation are all positively recognized by consumers. The creative character of the advertising, the tie-in to promotions, the responsiveness to overall marketing strategies, and technical elements are works of precision. In addition, McDonald's has successfully improved its customers' eating experience by upgrading facilities and logically expanding the menu offerings, without sacrificing quality or confusing their image. The proposition is there, as is the platform to support it. Most important of all is the fulfillment of expectations in terms of value. McDonald's value is an inexpensive, quality product that is easy to obtain and enjoy. McDonald's is also a master of market segmentation—ranging from small children to grandparents, teens to adults. With its advertising, McDonald's manages to connect with market segments in a way that makes the most effective use of advertising resources.

Case Example E: Building an Image Out of Brick, Glass, and Mortar. The design of a product or service can be an advertisement in itself, if it is so unique as to trigger a response in the consumer's mind. Pizza Hut, McDonald's, Taco Bell, and even L'eggs Panty Hose receive advertising benefits from their physical packaging. How many consumers recognize a McDonald's or a Holiday Inn by its sign alone?

For years, Hyatt Hotels spent very little money on advertising, yet their image as a classy hotel operation continued to build in the consumer's mind. Hyatt's advertising centered on unique designs for its properties (see Exhibit 12), which were so out of the ordinary that they advertised themselves. Hyatt fully capitalized on these spectacular properties and succeeded in its effort to place the company in a class by itself. Simply because of its product design, Hyatt stands out to consumers who seek a first-class lodging experience.

Case Example F: "Friendly," "Nice," "People Pleasin' People." Consumers in the hospitality industry often look for a home away from home when they travel. They want to feel comfortable and secure in the places they stay. Several travel industry advertising campaigns recognized a person's need for warmth and support when

Exhibit 12   Sample of a "Building an Image" Type Advertisement

Courtesy of Hyatt Hotels Corporation

away from the security and comfort of his or her own home and environment. These campaigns have become classics of hospitality advertising.

United Airlines' "Friendly Skies" advertising campaign was one of the first in the industry to recognize the psychological needs of traveling consumers. The United Airlines' ads were a direct response to consumers' fears of cold or impartial treatment or the uncertainties associated with traveling. American Airline's "Doing What We Do Best" and Holiday Inns' "People Pleasin' People" ads picked up on the same theme.

Similarly, Ramada's "Nice People Doing Nice Things for People" campaign really drove home the message that Ramada was one hospitality business that was really hospitable. The advertising was sincere and, again, directly related to consumer needs for a warm, friendly environment away from home. Unlike advertising that preached about "standards," "policies," and other items of little interest to consumers, this "nice people" advertising directly addressed a consumer need.

Case Example G: The Cat that Made the Brand Roar. Earlier in this chapter we displayed an ad showing Garfield the Cat as the spokesperson for Embassy Suites (Exhibit 4). This ad campaign presented a dilemma similar to the one discussed in the Helmsley campaign. Like Helmsley "the Queen," the Garfield campaign excelled at building brand awareness. In fact, there may never have been another ad campaign that created such high brand awareness so quickly. From that perspective, the campaign was a stroke of genius. It used an endearing character: Garfield was easy to love, easy to look at, and—most important of all—easy to remember.

So what was the problem? Simply this: Does Garfield the Cat do justice to the Embassy Suites' brand or product identity from a positioning perspective? Garfield became synonymous with Embassy Suites' all-suite hotel concept; however, he did not portray the upscale image that would support the $100-plus-per-night rates that Embassy Suites might have capitalized on. As a brand name, "Embassy Suites" conveys the top of the line. However, the Garfield "fat cat" campaign portrayed Embassy Suites as appealing to the middle-tier consumer who wanted to step up—but pay less. If you have a great name and a superior product concept (all-suites), why not design a campaign that merits or conveys a higher rate and image awareness? In the case of Embassy Suites, its predetermined product positioning was mid- to upper-mid-market. Thus, despite Embassy Suites' fine product and great positioning name, the "fat cat" campaign was perceived as on target with the chain's product positioning. Moreover, as mentioned previously, the Garfield ads broke through the clutter and was a tremendous success at building brand awareness.

Case Example H: Breaking Through the Clutter By Building a Niche. Beginning in the 1960s, the "Camel Scoreboard," which provided baseball scores in local newspapers under the "Camel" banner, gave Camel cigarettes strong brand awareness among consumers. Camel broke through the clutter of competitors by carving a niche with a service. By appearing regularly to consumers, Camel retained a high level of brand awareness in a fragmented and oversaturated market, and the Camel brand survived.

One hotel company was able to carve a niche in its overcrowded marketplace in a slightly different way. In the late 1980s, Stouffer Hotels became the sponsor of the "Business Travelers' Weather" page. This page appeared in two major papers, the *Wall Street Journal* and *USA Today*. Stouffer Hotels also sponsored the "Business Travelers" Forecast on CNN, The Weather Channel, and on local TV news programs. Because the name "Stouffer" was associated with one of the daily concerns of travelers, the hotel achieved dramatic increases in brand awareness, despite a tough name with which to work. Stouffer's weather forecasts accomplished exactly what "Camel's Scoreboard" and Garfield the Cat had done so well—they created brand awareness by breaking through the clutter, carving a niche, and being unique.

Key Terms

co-op	placement
exposures	platform
level of expectation	proposition
media	trade-outs/barter

REVIEW QUIZ

When you feel you have covered all of the material in this chapter, answer these questions. Choose the *best* answer. Check your answers with the correct ones found on the Review Quiz Answer Key at the end of this book.

Multiple Choice

1. When you advertise your product or service, you should:

    a. never promise more than your product or service can deliver.
    b. always include the price of your product or service.
    c. never compare yourself to competitors.
    d. always include at least one testimonial from a satisfied customer.

2. If you negotiate a one-for-one trade with an advertising supplier, that means:

    a. you are exchanging one of your employees for one of your supplier's employees for a stated period of time.
    b. you will provide a set dollar amount of your products or services to the supplier in exchange for the same dollar amount of advertising—for example, $1,000 worth of your products/services for $1,000 worth of advertising.
    c. you are giving the supplier whatever it is you are advertising as payment— for example, if you are advertising a cruise for $799, one person on the advertising supplier's staff gets to take a cruise for that price.
    d. you will provide a set dollar amount of your products or services to the supplier in exchange for twice that dollar amount of advertising—for example, $1,000 worth of your products/services for $2,000 worth of advertising.

3. An advertisement that features a company's CEO talking about the company's products or services is a _____ ad.

    a. brand-identifier
    b. human-scenario
    c. reputation-builder
    d. trade

4. In the late 1970s Holiday Inn produced a national ad campaign that featured the following slogan: "The Best Surprise Is No Surprise." The campaign told consumers that there would never be a negative surprise—a dirty guestroom, a lost reservation, etc.—at a Holiday Inn. What was the problem with this campaign?

    a. Holiday Inn promised more than it could deliver.
    b. The campaign slogan was so long that consumers had a hard time remembering it.
    c. Holiday Inn should not run national campaigns.
    d. There was no problem with this campaign.

Chapter Outline

Public Relations
    What Public Relations Is
    How Public Relations Can Be Applied
    Internal Public Relations
    How Can Public Relations Be
        Measured?
    PR Examples to Think About
Publications

Learning Objectives

1. Describe public relations. (pp. 113–114)

2. Explain how public relations can be applied, summarize tips for direct-contact PR, and describe strategies for successfully dealing with the press. (pp. 114–121)

3. Describe internal public relations, explain how public relations can be measured, and list examples of hospitality industry publications. (pp. 122–125)

9

Applying Key Marketing Methodologies: Public Relations

THE PURPOSE OF THIS CHAPTER is to help you understand how public relations can help improve sales and boost employee morale. We will focus on internal or "within-the-house" public relations applications as well as the full range of external public relations techniques and methods. We will also take a look at examples of public relations programs that have proven their worth in the hospitality industry. Finally, we will discuss how to tie your public relations effort to your needs and how to measure the results.

Public Relations

Public relations is a marketing tool. It is a communications vehicle connecting the hospitality industry and a variety of audiences. The public relation's perspective must include the *total audience*, which includes the investment community, shareholders, and franchisees, among others, as well as travel intermediaries and individual consumers of hospitality products and services. Public relations can effectively reach and affect everyone in this broad external audience. Furthermore, public relations can prove to be a very effective internal marketing device with which to communicate with and motivate employees.

You may frequently hear the expression that "so and so really got publicity from that event." **Publicity** is only one facet of public relations. Publicity can be free, but it can also be negative as well as positive—think of all the publicity surrounding hotel or casino fires. We'll discuss publicity in more detail later in the chapter.

There are many fallacies about public relations: "PR is B.S."; "Public relations is undefinable—it doesn't do anything and can't be measured"; "It's a waste of time and money"; "Anyone can do PR work." People who make these comments either do not understand public relations or have only been exposed to disorganized public relations efforts. It's true, public relations does not directly make sales; however, it can be very influential in seeing that sales are made. Let's look at some ground rules for various aspects of public relations, and explore what public relations is, how it can be applied, and how it can be measured.

What Public Relations Is

Public relations is a powerful marketing tool that is capable of reaching all marketing audiences. In positive applications, public relations is on the offensive; in negative situations, public relations can provide a strong defensive strategy.

Public relations involves dealing with all publics, including individual consumers and potential consumers, the financial community, the local community, the media, and even your own employees. Effective public relations can provide a competitive advantage within your own business area—be it hotels, airlines, restaurants, or travel services. This competitive advantage is frequently overlooked, even by public relations personnel. In essence, a well-executed public relations program can provide a good image within your industry segment. That image pays dividends in consumer preference for your product or service, and it may also result in attracting and retaining good employees.

Public relations can create a favorable environment for your company, product, or service. It creates this favorable environment most effectively if it is part of the firm's overall marketing plan. Objectives, strategies, target markets, expected results, timetables, and measurement can and should be established for all public relations programs. Of equal importance in a formal plan for public relations is selection of the trained professionals to create and execute the plan. It is an absolute fallacy to believe "anyone can do public relations."

The resources that can be used in public relations are unlimited. Here is a brief list of some of the vehicles public relations personnel use to reach various audiences:

- Announcements
- Broadcast media (TV and radio)
- Print media (newspapers, magazines, etc.)
- News conferences
- News releases
- Civic, social, and community involvement
- Employee relations
- Speeches
- Interviews
- Photographs

In addition, there are an infinite number of public relations techniques that can be employed to obtain media exposure. Numerous articles and texts provide list after list of ideas and suggestions for generating positive publicity, but many authors forget one basic thing—the planned purpose or strategy for achieving such exposure. Even if your relationship with the media is superb, the use and placement of publicity must support an overall marketing objective. The caution is simply stated: "Make your PR count." Some ideas for making your PR count are included in Exhibit 1. Each of the ideas listed in Exhibit 1 should be placed within the context of an overall marketing strategy.

How Public Relations Can Be Applied

Once the ideas and objectives for your public relations plan have been established and tied into the overall marketing plan, it is time to consider how to apply or execute those ideas. You must first answer some questions:

Exhibit 1   Suggestions for Public Relations Opportunities

- Accomplishments of employees or firm
- Activities involving your company employees
- Anniversary dates
- Appointments of key people
- Awards received by firm or employees
- Celebrities who visit you (obtain their approval)
- Community awards
- Contributions to charities and the local community by the firm or employees
- Displays of all types
- Entertainment appearing at your facility
- Events occurring on your property
- Events of special interest—humorous or creative
- Grand openings of all types
- Groups of interest meeting or eating with you
- Guests of interest (obtain their approval)
- Industry-related events
- Interviews with visitors, guests, etc.
- New management, ownership, employees, etc.
- Openings of all kinds
- Operating changes of major significance to the public
- Organizational changes
- Public service events/activities
- Receipt of certificates, awards, etc.
- Recognition of people, places, things, etc.
- Special displays, features introduced, etc.
- Special events of all types
- Speeches of employees, groups meeting at your facility, etc.

1. What medium can best execute this strategy?
2. Who are the key contacts for this task?
3. Is it necessary to establish or resolidify any personal relationships with media personnel before executing the strategy?
4. Is our approach carefully thought out? What are the potential downside risks?
5. Do we have a delivery package ready for the media?

The **delivery package**—a package for the press containing news items, names of contact persons and their phone numbers, property information, photographs, brochures, and so on—is essential. Although there is no guarantee your copy or materials will be used, it is much more likely that your public relations message will correspond to your intentions if you make a delivery package available. The list in Exhibit 2 will aid you in compiling a package that will be useful to the media.

Exhibit 2   Delivery Package Requirements

- Addresses and phone numbers of key media contacts
- Addresses and phone numbers of key corporation personnel
- Approval procedures and required forms
- Biographies of key personnel
- Briefing sheets on individuals, company, product, etc.
- Brochures, if applicable
- Cancellation procedures and policy
- "Canned" formats, releases, letterheads, logos, symbols, etc.
- Confidentiality statements/procedures
- Contacts list and phone numbers/procedures
- Copy samples and actual copy
- Displays, podiums with logos, etc.
- News conference procedures list
- One person to call and his or her phone number (usually public relations contact)
- Photo inventory of product, people, etc.
- Photo library and selection ready for press
- Previous problems files and checklist
- Previous questions files and checklist
- Price/rate information
- Procedures for distribution
- Promotional package on firm or product
- Request forms—data, photo, product information, etc.
- Scrapbook or clipping files
- Speech copies for distribution

Some public relations opportunities—speeches, press conferences, meetings, interviews, and so on—involve personal contact with media personnel and others. If you are going to employ one of these direct-contact PR methods, you need to prepare the individual(s) who will be making the direct contact with the media. *Thorough preparation is essential for successful direct-contact public relations.* Ground rules and suggestions abound as to how to prepare a speech or other public presentation. Assuming your spokesperson follows the rules and makes a good presentation, there is still one critical mistake that can be made—using the wrong person. Simply stated, be sure you put the right speaker in front of the media. If the talk is on technical matters, be certain that the speaker has total command of the technical terms. If the talk is on corporate strategy, be sure the individual has enough authority within the corporation to be credible. If the talk is on your own product or service, make sure the speaker can relate it to the audience's perspective. The following is a brief list of public speaking do's and don'ts:

Do's

- Carefully organize and allow yourself enough time to prepare.

- Be prepared—write out the talk, memorize it, and keep notes.

- Rewrite, review, and rewrite again.

- Create an outline or plan for your speech and follow it.

- Change postures, positions, intonations, emphasis, etc.

- Use pauses for emphasis.

- Check and double-check the visuals, equipment, room, visibility, etc.

- Speak out clearly and deliver smoothly.

Don'ts

- Don't speak on subjects about which you are not qualified.

- Don't ad lib.

- Don't guesstimate numbers.

- Don't read in a monotone.

- Don't use excessive pauses, either in number or length of time.

- Don't prepare unreadable visuals.

- Don't mumble, slur, laugh to yourself, etc.

- Don't wait to read what you are going to say until the plane ride or cab ride there.

Dealing with the Press. Dealing with the press is one of the most difficult tasks marketing and public relations personnel undertake. It is difficult for many reasons, but most of all because the press is *powerful*. It reaches many consumers with a message in writing, so you must be absolutely certain that the press has your facts correct.

Again, many good articles have been written on public relations and the press, many golden rules laid down, and many do's and don'ts have been listed. The recognition factors that follow represent a composite of a number of such lists. These are not all-inclusive, nor are they intended to be golden rules. They are factors that may keep your public relations efforts on a positive note—on the offensive rather than in a defensive position:

Recognition Factors

1. *Identify your purpose.* What is your purpose or reason for seeking the public relations exposure? If your purpose is to make others aware of your new restaurant theme, be sure that is exactly what you convey—don't let it be lost in a story about your chef's auto collection. Be precise and be sure your intent is communicated.

2. *Identify your target and objectives.* Who is your target? Is it prospective consumers of your product? Is it the local financial community? Is it your employees? What are your objectives? Do you want to boost employee morale? Do you want to increase food sales, beverage sales, room sales, or brand awareness?

Public Relations Checklist

_____ Does a PR plan exist and does it support the current priority areas of marketing?

_____ Do the director of marketing and all staff members understand their responsibilities with respect to the press, PR firm, and other outsiders?

_____ Do key managers have good relations with the local media?

_____ Are press release mailing lists up to date, accurate, and readily available?

_____ Are *fact sheets* readily accessible to all and near the phones?

_____ Are *photo files* up to date and fully stocked? Is there an up-to-date black-and-white photo file?

_____ Are brochures and other collateral material accessible?

_____ Are there definite plans, budgets, reviews, and measurement procedures in place for PR?

_____ Is there a property or product press kit? Is it up to date?

_____ What is the quality of photos and stories, and how are they to be used?

_____ Are all key employees briefed and knowledgeable about the value of public relations? Do they know the procedures to follow for press inquiries?

_____ Are PR network memos kept on file? Where? How often are they looked at or discussed?

_____ When was the last PR audit? What were the results, and were all follow-up steps completed?

Think it out and identify how and where in the media you will best achieve your objectives.

3. *Understand the press's perspective.* You know your purpose and your target; that is your perspective. What is the press's perspective? Identify and understand the press's interests. Determine how you can place your purpose and target within a package that directly meets the interest of the press or other media. Think about what will help increase their circulation.

4. *Tailor your preparation.* Having identified your purpose, your target, and the media's perspective, tailor your preparation to include all three. Be sure to include *everything* that the press will need to convey the story—photos, names, releases. Be sure your story is typed, double-spaced, and in the style the medium is currently using. *Follow the editorial style of your selected medium at all times.*

5. *Know the transmission channels.* Knowing where to send your material means knowing the difference between a news and a feature story. News should be directed to the city desk; feature stories should go to the appropriate editor, such as the entertainment editor or the restaurant editor. Better yet, get to

know the editors who can be of most help to you and cultivate those relationships (but don't wear them out).

6. *Deal with the human element.* People do not like extra work or being pressured, and most cannot afford the time to tell you the ground rules. People basically want the easy way out. This sounds cruel, but it should help you understand how to deal with the human element. Find out the media's deadlines in advance. Do not waste your time or the valuable time of media contacts. Do as much of their work as you can. Remember, if your material is well prepared and you do most of the work for them, your material may be used. If you do not do the work, you can expect nothing to appear. Also remember to be available to respond to any media questions or requests for clarification. If you are unavailable, your material may be scrapped or come out wrong.

You will also need some guidelines for answering questions from media representatives. The keys that follow are not all-inclusive, nor are they original, but they are very practical:

1. *Tell the truth.* The message you want to convey should be pure fact. The media want credible, straightforward, and truthful material and relationships. This simply means your materials should be thorough and honest. It does not mean you need to reveal confidential data or private sources, nor does it mean you should violate confidentialities.

2. *Be responsive.* You may not have all the answers at your fingertips for every question or inquiry. Do not lie or guess; say, "I do not have that information with me; however, I will call you and provide it today." Then get the information fast and provide it accurately.

3. *Provide the facts and follow up.* Supply the key facts in print to lessen the chance of being misquoted on key data. If at all possible, follow up with media personnel by going over the facts or key numbers with them to ensure accuracy. If you do not have a requested statistic, get it and call or send a note to the person who requested it. Be sure accurate numbers reach the media.

4. *Be concise.* People usually get into trouble with the media for what they say, not for what they do not say. Provide the facts in a concise, uneditorialized, and unexaggerated manner. Be precise and accurate. Ranges may be okay, but pulling numbers out of the sky is a disaster.

5. *Build the relationship.* If you follow steps 1 through 4 by being truthful, responsive, factual, and concise, you are on your way to achieving the fifth practical key—building good relationships with media personnel. Hostile attitudes, reactionary statements to sensitive questions, aloofness, or a combative position damages relationships with the press. Work hard at being in control of yourself and your responses, no matter what you think of the media or a particular media representative. After all, someone who dislikes you is not going to be eager to give you space or air time.

Tools of Public Relations. A **press kit** is usually a two-sided folder of high quality, often customized with the firm's logo or other identification markings. Background

Exhibit 3 Sample Press Release

NEWS RELEASE

Hospitality Industry Hall of Honor

Houston, Texas 77204-3902   For Immediate Release

HOSPITALITY INDUSTRY HALL OF HONOR TO SALUTE LEGENDS

HOUSTON -- The Hospitality Industry Hall of Honor will induct industry pioneers Conrad N. Hilton, J. Willard Marriott, Kemmons Wilson and Vernon Stouffer as the initial honorees on Sept. 25, 1996, marking the formal inauguration of the unique Hall of Honor.

Co-chairpersons for the historic ceremony are Kenneth F. Hine, president and CEO of the American Hotel & Motel Association; and William P. Fisher, executive vice president of the National Restaurant Association.

The Hall of Honor will be located in University of Houston's Conrad N. Hilton College of Hotel and Restaurant Management. "The Hall of Honor memorializes industry giants whose immense contributions to the industry and society serve as a powerful inspiration for succeeding generations," Dean Alan T. Stutts said. "Their achievements are shining symbols of the strength of the human spirit."

Dean Stutts noted that the Hall of Honor will provide an appropriate tribute to industry leaders and an inspirational learning experience for those individuals preparing to lead the industry in the future. He said it will contain information and memorabilia related to the life, career and accomplishments of each member. These historic materials will be displayed at the Industry Archives and Library at the Conrad Hilton College.

Dr. Ronald A. Nykiel, the Conrad N. Hilton Distinguished Chair, was named chairman of the Hall of Honor. He said new inductees will be chosen annually through a selection process involving the American Hotel & Motel Association, the National Restaurant Association and other hospitality-industry entities.

# # #

Contact: Shaila Seshadri
(555) 555-1234

materials are normally placed in the left side/pocket, timely news items in the right. Examples of background information might include biographies of key property personnel, property fact sheets, and photographs. Timely news items include the actual **"press release(s)"** (see Exhibit 3). The cover of the kit should not only convey your firm's image, but be of a practical weight, size, and nature to protect photos. Photos should be clearly labeled on the reverse side. Few things are more embarrassing to marketers than to have the wrong photo get picked up with a press release.

Press releases may sometimes be picked up verbatim. Therefore, all releases should be "in form" and grammatically flawless. "In form" means just as you would want a publication to present your story. More often, the press release will be used as background or a resource from which the magazine or newspaper editor or reporter will work to mold an actual "story." Here are seven keys to creating a press release with the proper form:

Key 1: The top right or left corner is almost always used for the name of the "contact" person(s); sometimes the contact person(s) appear at the end of the release. These contacts are the people who are readily available to provide more information. This means they should be knowledgeable enough to speak to the press. Under the names should appear their phone numbers, fax numbers, and addresses.

Key 2: A specific release date should be noted at the top of the page, slightly below the contact information. If the information is for a feature story that can appear at any time or is otherwise not date sensitive, the words "FOR IMMEDIATE RELEASE" should appear there, usually capital letters and sometimes underlined.

Key 3: The headline should be presented in capital letters and underlined (if desired) about one-quarter to one-third down the first page. Considerable effort should go into developing the headline, because it is the "hook" that might catch the editor's eye or make your release stand out from many others seeking the same precious space.

Key 4: The "dateline"—city and state in capital letters followed by the month and day—should be the lead into the actual text of the release. Datelines are important because they tell the reader where and when an event is occurring.

Key 5: The "body" or main part of the release should always be double-spaced. Paragraphs should be short, journalistic, and to the point. Like the headline, the first few sentences or lead is a "hook" that must grab the attention of the reader and address the key questions (who, what, where, when, and why—the five w's).

Key 6: Including a few quotes is almost standard procedure with a press release. Whether the quote is from an internal source (someone employed by the organization issuing the release) or an external source, it is imperative that the individual quoted is aware of and approves of the quote. It is best to also let the individuals being quoted know of the date and time of the release so there are no surprises. When multiple quotes are used, it is usually best to alternate direct quotes (those in quotation marks) and factual non-quoted information.

Key 7: Photographs almost always enhance a story. You cannot always read the minds of those picking up your releases/stories; therefore, if you do not know the specifications, it is usually better to provide black and white photos as well as color photos. Color slides or negatives (assuming the publication uses color) are generally better, but send the actual photo to help the editor see what is on the slide or negative.

Internal Public Relations

The jobs of many people in the hospitality industry are challenging and require long hours. Keeping employees motivated and proud of their jobs is a difficult task. One of the most effective devices for combating these problems is a well-organized internal public relations effort. This does not mean promoting the goods or benefits of the company to the employees. It can take many shapes and forms. An especially effective technique is to promote or provide special recognition of employees, their efforts, or even their interests. "Employee of the Month" awards, posters, photos, and so forth, all work well. Special incentive awards and related public relations also are a valuable tool. Giving cash, prizes, or even novelty awards or plaques to deserving employees will help boost morale. Activities and events employees and managers do together—a bowling club or a joggers' group, for example—will help build a team spirit. Common goals, such as company-wide support of a selected charity, is another type of internal PR device for building unity. Perhaps most important of all is the continual recognition of employees' human dignity, pride, and desire for respect. Make internal public relations one of your key strategies for helping your employees be productive and happy.

How Can Public Relations Be Measured?

You frequently hear this comment: "PR is useless because you can't measure it." This is absolutely false! If a public relations program is well organized, it can be measured in many ways. One way is to measure the number and type of media exposures received. Keep a scrapbook of clippings and a current log of exposures—newspaper stories, magazine articles, mentions on the local television news, and so on. Set goals for the number and type of exposures, then measure actual performance versus targets.

A second measurement method is geared to evaluating the effectiveness of internal PR efforts. Look at questionnaires that assess employee morale, as well as employee turnover rates, breakage, pilferage, etc. If your internal PR is working, certain quantifiable trends should emerge. Do not, however, ignore a more subjective yardstick of your efforts: have you improved the esprit de corps in your organization? Are employees busy and enthusiastic?

Specific public relations activities may be measured by increases in sales. For example, if a major event is promoted through PR, and bar or food volume directly increases as a result of additional customers coming in for the event, you know public relations is working for you.

PR Examples to Think About

Public relations can be a marketing tool used to put you on the offensive, or can be a very effective defensive tool for your firm. The two discussions that follow depict one example of each type of PR.

PR on the Offensive. A large hotel located near a major airport and within a substantial minority population area of the city conceived a public relations offensive to achieve the following goals: (1) improve the morale of its minority employees,

(2) increase food and beverage sales, (3) increase room sales, (4) improve community relations, and (5) overcome a location problem.

How did the hotel achieve these goals? The hotel offered its 24-hour coffee shop from midnight to 6 A.M. as a nightly broadcast facility to the largest Spanish-speaking radio station in the city. Over 50% of the hotel's employees were Spanish-speaking; a larger percentage of the cab drivers in the airport area also spoke Spanish. Cab drivers were offered free coffee and given a chip redeemable for coffee or food each time they brought a "late arrival" guest from the nearby airport to the hotel. This scheme was devised to help address the hotel's problem of being too close to the airport for the cab drivers to get a good fare. Soon the coffee shop became a focal point of community activity as a result of the radio broadcast. Food and beverage sales set records from midnight to 6 A.M., employee morale and attitudes toward the hotel were at all-time highs, local community relations were superior, walk-in/fly-in room sales increased, and the location problem was overcome. The hotel succeeded in drawing closer to the local community and becoming a place its employees were proud of.

PR on the Defensive. Another large urban hotel was the site of a tragic event that could have seriously damaged the hotel's reputation had it not been for a well-thought-out press release. The hotel, also located in an airport area, was targeted for a police raid on a suspected abortion ring. Undesirable elements had been operating out of a number of hotels in the area and a number of deaths had occurred. The hotel volunteered its security personnel (off-duty city police) to help in the raid. The raid was staged and the ring was captured; unfortunately, a woman was found dead. However, instead of the front page reading "Raid Reveals Murder and Bloody Abortion Ring at Hotel," the story appeared on page 3 under the headline "Hotel Security Force Helps Chicago Police Resolve Airport Area Crime Problem." A well-thought-out public relations and press approach can make potentially damaging events less harmful to your business. Think about it!

Publications

The hospitality industry is fortunate to have excellent **trade media** in the form of industry-related publications. These publications are widely read not only by those within the industry, but frequently by travel consumers. Some of the major hospitality industry publications that public relations personnel should be aware of are listed in this section.

Major Hospitality Industry and Trade Publications

Association & Society Manager
825 South Barrington Avenue
Los Angeles, CA 90039

Association Management
1011 16th Street, N.W.
Washington, DC 20036

Association Trends
7204 Clarendon Road
Washington, DC 20014

ASTA Travel News
Travel Communications, Inc.
488 Madison Avenue
New York, NY 10022

Aviation Daily
1156 15th Street, N.W.
Washington, DC 20005

Business Travel News
CMP Publications, Inc.
600 Community Drive
Manhasset, NY 11030

Canadian Hotel and Restaurant
Maclean-Hunter Publishing
   Company, Ltd.
481 University Avenue
Toronto, Ontario
Canada M5W 1A7

Club Management
8730 Big Bend Blvd.
St. Louis, MO 63119

The Cornell Hotel and Restaurant
   Administration Quarterly
School of Hotel Administration
185 Statler Hall
Cornell University
Ithaca, NY 14853

Corporate Meetings & Incentives
747 Third Avenue, 7th Floor
New York, NY 10017

Corporate Travel
A Gralla Publication
1515 Broadway
New York, NY 10036

FIU Hospitality Review
Florida International University
Miami, FL 33181

Food & Service
Texas Restaurant Association
1400 Lavaca
Austin, TX 78701

Food Executive
International Food Services
   Executives Association
508 IBM Building
Fort Wayne, IN 46815

Food Service Director
Restaurant Business, Inc.
355 Park Ave. S.
New York, NY 10010

Hospitality Lodging
Penton/IPC, Inc.
614 Superior Avenue, West
Cleveland, OH 44113

Hospitality Restaurant
Penton/IPC, Inc.
614 Superior Avenue, West
Cleveland, OH 44113

Hotel and Motel Management
Advanstar Communications
7500 Old Oak Blvd.
Cleveland, OH 44130

Hotels
1350 E. Touhy Ave.
Des Plaines, IL 60018

Incentive Marketing
633 Third Avenue
New York, NY 10017

Incentive Travel Manager
825 South Barrington Avenue
Los Angeles, CA 90049

Insurance Conference Planner
695 Summer Street
Stamford, CT 06901

Lodging
American Hotel & Motel
   Association
1201 New York Ave. NW #600
Washington, DC 20005-3931

Lodging and Food-Service News
Hotel Service, Inc.
131 Clarendon Street
Boston, MA 02116

Lodging Hospitality
1100 Superior Ave.
Cleveland, OH 44114-2543

The Meeting Manager
Meeting Professionals International
1950 Stemmons Fwy.
Dallas, TX 75207-3109

Meetings & Conventions
8773 S. Ridgeline Blvd.
Highlands Ranch, CO 80126-2329

Meetings & Expositions Magazine
22 Pine Street
Morristown, NJ 07960

Meetings News
600 Harrison St.
San Francisco, CA 94107

Motel/Motor Inn Journal
Tourist Court Journal, Inc.
306 East Adams
Temple, TX 76501

Nation's Restaurant News
Lebhar-Friedman, Inc.
425 Park Avenue
New York, NY 10022

Promo
47 Old Ridgefield Rd.
Wilton, CT 06897

Resort Management
Box 4169
1509 Madison Avenue
Memphis, TN 38104

Restaurant Business
355 Park Ave. S.
New York, NY 10010

Restaurant Hospitality
1100 Superior Ave.
Cleveland, OH 44114-2543

Restaurants & Institutions
Cahners Publishing Company
275 Washington St.
Newton, MA 02158-1630

Restaurants, USA
National Restaurant Association
1200 17th St. NW
Washington, DC 20036-3097

Sales and Marketing Management
Sales Management, Inc.
633 Third Avenue
New York, NY 10017

Successful Meetings
355 Park Ave. S.
New York, NY 10010

*Tableservice Restaurant Operations
  Report*
National Restaurant Association
One IBM Plaza
Suite 2600
Chicago, IL 60611

*Texas and Southwest Hotel Motel
  Review*
Texas Hotel & Motel Association
8602 Crownhill Boulevard
San Antonio, TX 78209

TravelAge East
TravelAge Mid-America
TravelAge Southeast
TravelAge West
Travel Magazines Division
Official Airlines Guides, Inc.
100 Grant Avenue
San Francisco, CA 94108

Travel Agent
American Traveler, Inc.
2 West 46th Street
New York, NY 10036

Travel Management Daily
An Official Airlines Guide
  Publication, Inc.
888 Seventh Avenue
New York, NY 10106

Travel Master
645 Stewart Avenue
Garden City, NY 11530

Travel Trade
Travel Trade Publishing Company
605 Fifth Avenue
New York, NY 10017

Travel Weekly
Reed Travel Group
500 Plaza Dr.
Secaucus, NJ 07094-3626

Trends in the Hotel Industry
PKF
425 California St., Ste. 1650
San Francisco, CA 94104

World Convention Dates
Hendrickson Publishing Company
79 Washington Street
Hempstead, NY 11550

Worldwide Lodging Industry
Horwath & Horwath International
  & Laventhol & Horwath
919 Third Avenue
New York, NY 10022

Key Terms

delivery package

press kit

press release

public relations

publicity

trade media

REVIEW QUIZ

When you feel you have covered all of the material in this chapter, answer these questions. Choose the *best* answer. Check your answers with the correct ones found on the Review Quiz Answer Key at the end of this book.

1. Which of the following statements about public relations is *false?*

    a. Public relations is a marketing tool.
    b. Public relations can be effective in motivating employees.
    c. Public relations cannot be measured.
    d. Public relations does not directly make sales.

2. If you are making a speech, you should *not:*

    a. create an outline of your speech and follow it.
    b. use pauses for emphasis.
    c. ad lib.
    d. rewrite your speech, review it, and rewrite again if necessary.

3. Which of the following statements about a press release is *true?*

    a. All press releases should be "in form."
    b. The "body" of the release should be single-spaced.
    c. You should not include photographs with a press release.
    d. The headline should appear in capital letters at the bottom of the first page.

4. Public relations can be measured by:

    a. keeping a scrapbook of clippings and a current log of exposures.
    b. increases in sales that are tied to PR events.
    c. using an accounting formula that compares revenue projections to PR expenditures.
    d. a and b.

Chapter Outline

Promotions
    Keys to Successful Promotions
    Types of Promotions
    Methods for Executing Promotions
Internal Promotions
Case Examples

Learning Objectives

1. Explain the keys to successful promotions. (pp. 129–130)

2. Identify the different types of promotions. (pp. 130–133)

3. Describe methods of executing promotions. (pp. 133–136)

4. Describe the benefits of internal promotions, identify the elements that determine a successful internal promotion, and cite case examples of good and bad promotions in the hospitality industry. (pp. 136–139)

─────────────────────────────────────10

Applying Key Marketing
Methodologies: Promotions

PROMOTIONS HAVE BEEN USED WIDELY in many industries for a long time, and they are a very powerful and effective marketing tool for the hospitality industry. Perhaps the earliest promotion ever used in the hospitality industry was the offer of the first free cup of coffee. Since then, promotions have become increasingly sophisticated.

Promotions ─────────────────────────────────────

There are seemingly an infinite number of different **promotions,** with their diversity limited only by the boundaries of people's imaginations. However, the one element common to all promotions is that they are designed to fulfill a marketing need. This need may be to build new business, gain a greater share of existing business, keep business, or gain repeat business. Regardless of the type of promotion, its objective is to support the overall marketing effort.

Just as there are many reasons for promotions, there are many keys to making promotions successful. These keys are discussed in the following section.

Keys to Successful Promotions

There are ten keys to successful promotions:

1. *Purpose.* Why is the promotion needed? Answering this fundamental question is the start of executing a good promotion. Is the promotion necessary to create new business? To stimulate demand in a down period? To take business from a competitor?

2. *Target identification.* Who is the promotion aimed at? Be specific in identifying your target. Is the promotion geared toward potential first-time users of your product or service? Is it geared toward previous users? Are they young or old, male or female, upscale income or low income?

3. *Type match-up.* What is the best type of promotion for the purpose and target identified? There are many types of promotions, and not every one will be compatible with your creative idea or, more important, with your marketing objective. Some key questions to ask are: What is it I want to promote, and to whom? What is the demographic and psychographic profile of my target?

4. *Execution determination.* Once you know the purpose of the promotion, its target, and the type of promotion required, it's time to determine how to carry out the promotion. To do so, you must answer these questions: What is the

best method to reach the target? When is the best time to promote? Where is the best place to promote?

5. *Fulfillment.* Anticipate the needs the promotion will create and be sure you can fulfill them. Ask yourself this critical question: If this promotion works as planned, will I have enough available products or services to meet the demand? If you are promoting a food item, drink, weekend, seat, or space, be sure it is there when your customer arrives to accept your promotional promise. Otherwise, you may well lose that sale or customer for good.

6. *Fallback.* No one is ever completely correct in predicting the response to every promotion. If your promotion is a greater success than expected, you may not be able to fulfill the expectations created by the promotion. To avoid customer dissatisfaction in this situation, plan a *fallback.* It can be a menu-item substitution, an upgraded room, a first-class seat, or something else, *but provide it.* An important key when planning a fallback is to ensure it is of like or better value than the promoted item. Even if you use the "rain check" fallback, consider adding some extra value to that rain check to offset the customer's inconvenience.

7. *Real expectation.* Promote only what you intend to deliver. Never lie, exaggerate, or make false promises. Always remember that the *level of expectation* your promotion creates *must* be fulfilled for your customer to be satisfied.

8. *Communication.* Don't forget to tell everyone at your company exactly what you promoted and how it is to be fulfilled. Be sure you clearly communicate in writing such key items as price, quantity, acceptance procedures for the promotion, dates, times, and other key details. Nothing is more irritating to a consumer than responding to a promotion only to find that no one at your company knows about it.

9. *Measurement.* Why did you go through the entire promotion effort? Establish a goal or goals and measure the results of your effort. Did the promotion do what you wanted it to do? Did it accomplish more or less than expected? If more, will it work as well again? If less, what went wrong?

10. *Recordkeeping.* Write down what you did for the promotion and how it worked. Don't be forced to reinvent the wheel next time. How often have you heard, "What was that promotion we ran so successfully a few years ago?"

Types of Promotions

Many different promotions have been used in the hospitality industry. Most of these can be grouped according to the following types or classifications:

1. *Price.* This is a promotion in which the incentive to purchase is based on price. The price is the main attraction and is featured prominently in the promotional message (see Exhibit 1).

2. *Trial.* This is a promotion designed to get your target to try your product or service. Price is one method that is frequently used to motivate customers to try something.

Exhibit 1   Sample of a Price Promotion

It's 20° in the mountains. It's 80° at the beaches. Fortunately, Dollar will go to any degree to give you a low rate.

IN THE MOUNTAINS

$**42** A Day
must pick up Sun.–Tues.

$**49** a day, must pick up Wed.–Sat.

$**237** a week

OPTIONAL LDW/CDW
$13.99/DAY OR LESS

Plymouth Voyager or comparable model.   *Jeep Cherokee or comparable model.*

(Rates good for Denver and Durango, CO; Idaho Falls, ID; Billings, Bozeman, Kalispell and Missoula, MT; Albuquerque and Taos, NM; St. George, UT; Jackson Hole, WY)

IN FLORIDA

Dodge Colt or comparable model.

$**19** A Day
(economy car)

$**89** a week

OPTIONAL CDW
$12.99/DAY OR LESS

Chrysler LeBaron convertible or comparable model.   *Plymouth Voyager or comparable model.*

$**29** A Day
(minivan or convertible)

$**189** a week

OPTIONAL CDW
$13.99/DAY OR LESS

Certain renter qualifications and blackout periods may apply. Some additional charges may apply. Unlimited mileage may be restricted. Rates available to drivers 25 and over and do not include optional LDW, CDW, SLI, PAI or PEP, fuel, additional driver (where applicable) and applicable taxes and airport access fees, if any. Vehicle must be returned to renting location to avoid drop charges, except in Florida, where vehicle may be returned to any authorized Florida location. Offer good through February 14, 1995, and available at participating locations only. Vehicle availability may be limited. Ask for rate code DEGREE when booking.

Regardless of where you're vacationing this winter, you can always count on Dollar Rent A Car for low rates on the cars you'd really rather drive. So call your travel agent or Dollar today.

1-800-800-4000

D LLAR ®
R E N T A C A R

Dollar features quality products of the Chrysler Corporation and other fine cars.

Courtesy of Dollar Rent a Car

3. *Share.* This is a promotion geared toward taking market share away from the competition through some form of incentive. Lower price, an upgraded product, or another advantage is clearly established over the competition and is the focus of the promotion.

Exhibit 2   Sample of an Introductory Promotion

Hawaii.   25% Off.

Introducing "Mix 7 Rates" from Aston.

Guests spend 7 or more consecutive nights with Aston and save
25% off rack. Any room. Any price category. Any combination adding
up to 7 or more consecutive nights. Choose from 31 Aston Hotels
and Condominium Resorts in Waikiki, Maui, Kauai, Molokai,
and the Big Island of Hawaii. Offer valid 4/17-6/30/95.
For more information and reservations, call 1-800-922-7866.

Relax and enjoy the value.™

Courtesy of Aston Hotels & Resorts

4. *Introductory.* This is a promotion designed to introduce a new product or service to the market. An **introductory promotion** may also be designed to build repeat purchases (see Exhibit 2).

5. *Build.* This is a promotion designed to build repeat business through an increase in the reward or payoff for multiple purchases. Today's frequent flyer and frequent guest promotions are forms of build promotions (see Exhibit 3).

6. *Give-away/sweepstakes.* This is a promotion geared toward getting people to buy your product or service by offering the chance of a monetary award or a give-away item (see Exhibit 4).

7. *Ego/recognition.* This is a promotion designed to appeal to an individual's desire to be valued. These promotions may offer customers special recognition in the forms of first-class upgrades, club-floor upgrades, and complimentary suites.

8. *Tie-ins.* This is a promotion of a product or service that ties into another company's product or service. Usually a tie-in is undertaken when there is a clear benefit to both parties.

Exhibit 3 Sample of a Build Promotion

Northwest WORLDPERKS™ Awards

MILEAGE LEVEL	AUTOMATICALLY ISSUED AWARDS			NUMBER OF DOMESTIC TRAVEL DOCUMENTS**	OPTIONAL PICK-A-PERK™ INTERNATIONAL TRAVEL AWARDS		
	NORTHWEST DOMESTIC TRAVEL AWARD +	CAR RENTAL AWARD +	HOTEL AWARD		NORTHWEST TO HAWAII/MEXICO/CARIBBEAN	NORTHWEST TO EUROPE	NORTHWEST TO THE PACIFIC
20,000 MILES	1st Coach Class Certificate	2 Car Class Upgrade	Purchase 1 Weekend Night Get the 2nd Weekend Night FREE (any rate)	1	1 FREE Roundtrip Companion Ticket	1 One Class OR Roundtrip Upgrade on any Pull Fare	
40,000 MILES	2nd Coach Class Certificate	2 FREE Weekend Days (premium car)	1 FREE Weekend Night	2	1 FREE Roundtrip Economy Class Ticket OR	1 FREE Roundtrip Economy Class Ticket OR	50% Off Companion Ticket – Executive or First Class
60,000 MILES	3rd Coach Class Certificate plus First Class Upgrade	3 FREE Weekend Days (premium car)	2 FREE Weekend Nights	3	2 FREE Roundtrip Economy Class Tickets OR	2 FREE Roundtrip Economy Class Tickets or 1 FREE Roundtrip Executive Class Ticket	1 FREE Roundtrip Economy Class Ticket
80,000 MILES	4th Coach Class Certificate plus First Class Upgrade	1 FREE Week (mid-size car)	3 FREE Weekend Nights	4	2 FREE Roundtrip First Class Tickets OR	2 FREE Roundtrip Executive Class Tickets or 1 FREE Roundtrip First Class Ticket OR	2 FREE Roundtrip Economy Class Tickets or 1 FREE Roundtrip Executive Class Ticket
100,000 MILES	5th Coach Class Certificate plus First Class Upgrade	1 FREE Week (premium car)	4 FREE Nights	5		2 FREE Roundtrip First Class Tickets OR	2 FREE Roundtrip Executive Class Tickets or 1 FREE Roundtrip First Class Ticket
120,000 MILES	6th Coach Class Certificate plus First Class Upgrade	1 FREE Week (luxury car)	5 FREE Nights	6			2 FREE Roundtrip First Class Tickets

* Domestic First Class Upgrades valid on any published fare
NOTE 1) FREE Northwest Domestic Travel Certificates are valid for travel between points in North America (including Alaska and Canada, excluding Hawaii), or between points in the Pacific (excluding Hawaii), or between points in Europe.
2) Car Rental award is valid for National Car Rental OR Thrifty Hotel award is valid at Mandarin Oriental Hotels OR Marriott Hotels OR Radisson Hotels

** Travel Documents include any unexpired Free Flight Plan Travel Certificates, Republic Timesaver tickets or Northwest WORLDPERKS Domestic Travel Certificates

WORLDPERKS PARTNERS	National	Thrifty	MANDARIN ORIENTAL	Marriott	Radisson

Courtesy of Northwest Airlines, Inc.

9. *Cooperative.* This is a promotion similar to a tie-in in which two firms cooperatively promote a product or service for a mutual benefit (see Exhibit 5). The **cooperative promotion** may be undertaken because of the limited budget of each firm, or because the products or services are of more value promoted together. An example of a cooperative promotion would be a fly-and-drive promotion involving an airline and a rent-a-car company.

There are many other types of promotions or variations of the promotions listed above. Some promotions may be intended to build good will, others are designed as paybacks for the use of your product or service, and still others are designed to expand the awareness of your product or service into new market areas or expose new market segments to your product. Always keep in mind your *purpose* for entering into a promotion and the *benefit* you will receive from the promotion.

A word of caution is appropriate at this point. Do not enter into a tie-in, cooperative, or other joint promotion without determining the impact that the promotion will have on your base business, your image, or your overall market. While it is enticing to be offered a low-cost tie-in into someone else's package or promotion, it may not always be beneficial. In fact, it could be detrimental. Look closely at your own image and reputation and make it your rule of thumb not to enter into a joint promotion unless the other parties have an equal or better overall reputation.

Methods for Executing Promotions

One of the key reasons promotions fail is that the wrong method of execution is used. Take the time to determine the best promotion method for reaching your

Exhibit 4   Sample of a Give-Away/Sweepstakes Promotion

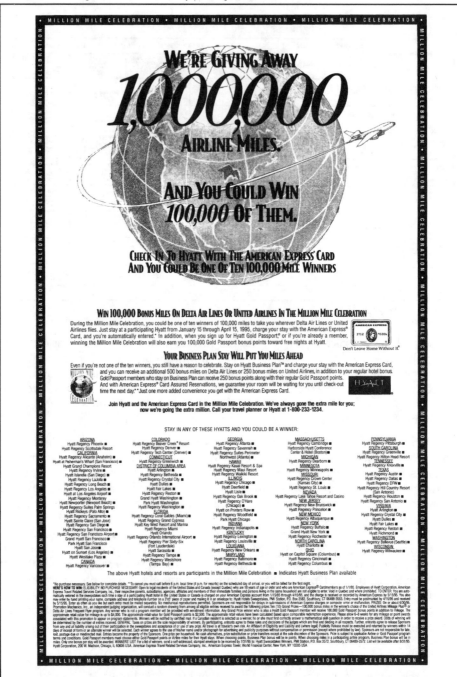

Courtesy of Hyatt and American Express

Exhibit 5   Sample of a Cooperative Promotion

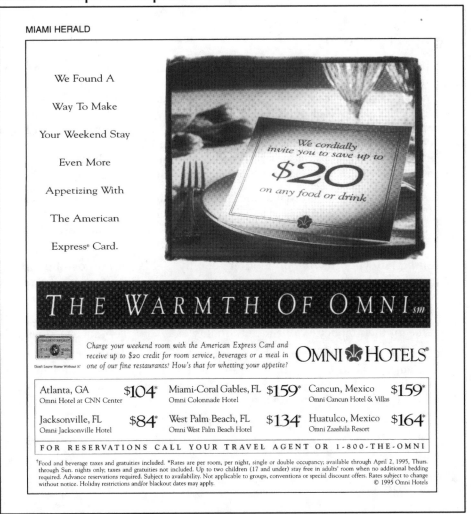

Courtesy of American Express Card and Omni Hotels

target and achieving your purpose. These methods include advertising (outdoor, displays, TV, radio, and print), direct mail, tent cards, publicity, personal selling, handouts, telephone sales, a special benefit to loyal customers or club members in monthly billings, and so forth.

You may promote your purpose and reach your target yourself by directly appealing to the end-users of your product or service, or you may reach your target through appropriate intermediaries such as travel agents, retailers, wholesalers, traffic departments, suppliers, secretaries, tourist organizations, associations, convention bureaus, franchise affiliates, and distributorships. You may use credit-card mailing stuffers, mailing lists, someone else's outlets, and posters and fliers of all types. Just make sure you select the methods that most efficiently and effectively reach your target and accomplish your purpose.

Internal Promotions

Up to this point the chapter has covered some general aspects of promotions. Frequently a major way to increase the revenue and profit yield from your existing customers is to promote to them once they are inside your door. This can be achieved in many ways, but should be done selectively and with a specific purpose or goal in mind. Internal promotions should be created and executed with the same care given external promotions. In fact, there are additional considerations to take into account when promoting internally. Assuming all the keys to successful promotions have been followed, consider these additional items:

- *Compatibility.* Is your internal promotion compatible with how your customers perceive your product or service? Never cheapen the image your loyal customers have of you by using a slapped-together, poorly thought-out, poorly executed promotion.

- *Benefit.* Will your internal promotion not only meet your purpose, but offer a perceivable benefit to the customer? Will it keep the customer as a friend, or will the customer be offended?

- *Value.* Does the internal promotion provide your customers with a perceived value for their money? Value means quality at a fair price—not cheapness.

- *Clutter avoidance.* Will your internal-promotion piece clutter or detract from the table, desk top, wall, or other area where it is presented? Be sure your overall product quality is not cheapened as a result of the physical promotion piece or content of the promotion.

These considerations should be thought out prior to doing any internal promotions of your own or allowing anyone else's promotions to be viewed by your customers.

Case Examples

There are many examples of both good and bad promotions in the hospitality industry. The following sections will present a few case examples of successful and unsuccessful promotions. Look closely at why each promotion succeeded or failed, keeping in mind the keys to successful promotions discussed earlier.

Case Example A: The Great Idea. In a medium-sized New England city, an independent motel owner/operator was trying to compete with a nearby national-chain motel. Overall, this was a good occupancy sector of the market, averaging 80 percent. The chain motel had a slightly better location, but the independent motel had a better physical property. The chain motel was running an 83 percent occupancy, the independent motel a 73 percent occupancy. Mr. Owner/Operator watched that occupancy percentage weekly and was getting frustrated. He came up with what he thought was a logical "great idea," but he didn't research it.

He called a friend who painted signs, and he ordered a large sign with red letters reading "Low Discount Rates—Stay Here," with a large red arrow pointing to his motel's entrance. This "great idea" resulted in Mr. Owner/Operator's occupancy gradually declining to 63 percent and his bottom line sinking even further. In desperation he called in a marketing consultant.

The consultant examined the market and determined that rate was of less significance to consumers than quality of the facility. Mr. Owner/Operator had a high-quality facility; however, his great idea had given his property the image of a cut-rate, low-quality independent motel. The consultant recommended that Mr. Owner/Operator change the name of the motel to "The Lexington Inn," incorporating the name of the city, and that he replace the homemade price-war sign with a permanent high-quality sign made of brick and brass with the motel's new name on it. The consultant also recommended that Mr. Owner/Operator improve the landscaping and lighting, paint the entry façade, install a new awning canopy, and implement a new rate structure $2 above the chain motel's rate structure. The final touch was a promotional slogan on the marquis: "The new Lexington Inn—the finest in town."

The results were dramatic. Occupancy jumped to 83 percent, with a rate averaging $2 higher than the franchise motel and $7.50 higher than a year earlier for the same independent motel. The chain motel's occupancy dropped to 74 percent.

Case Example B: The Simple Idea. Often, the simpler the promotion and the less complicated its execution, the more successful it is. Two national chains have succeeded in getting a large share of the summer family market with very simple promotional concepts. Holiday Inn's "Kids Stay Free" program and Ramada's "Four for One" program have both succeeded. "Kids Stay Free" simply means that children under age 18 accompanying their parents at a Holiday Inn stay free in the same room as their parents. Ramada's "Four for One" program permits four people to stay in the same room for the price of one person.

These promotions are successful for two basic reasons. First, each meets the needs of the summer family market segment by offering a tangible, perceived value. Second, each is straightforward and easy for both the consumer and the operations to understand. Other hotels and motels have tried similar promotions, but have confused consumers with such restrictions as "only children under 12 years," "no extra beds allowed," and "only at the following Inns …." But both Holiday Inn and Ramada have kept it simple for their consumers and their front desk agents. They have offered a plain value and have succeeded.

Case Example C: The Addicting Idea. The fast-food industry is tremendously competitive. Market share and repeat business factors are constantly measured and monitored. Advertising and promotions demand the best creative ideas. A major challenge for fast-food restaurant operators is to increase market share without having **price promotions** put major dents in their restaurants' financial statements. McDonald's creates extremely effective promotions based on a simple concept—give people a reason to come in and come back. McDonald's "Build a Big Mac" promotion, for example, gave customers puzzle pieces of a Big Mac when they made certain purchases. When they put a complete Big Mac together, they

Exhibit 6   Sample of a Payoff Promotion

Courtesy of Premier Cruise Lines and Walt Disney World

won a cash prize. The idea that only one more piece of the puzzle was needed to win up to $100,000 instantly kept people coming back and helped McDonald's build volume during a recessionary period.

Case Example D: The Pay-Off. Pay-off promotions blossomed in the 1980s and continued to be extremely popular in the 1990s (see Exhibit 6). There are many examples of this type of promotion: airline frequent traveler programs such as

United Airline's Mileage Plus, American's AAdvantage, and Continental's One Pass, and hotel frequent guest programs such as Marriott's Honored Guest, Hyatt's Gold Passport, and Stouffer's Club Express. The pay-off works along these lines. A "cost" is figured, such as five percent. This is a marketing expense that is applied to cover the cost of awards. The awards are then equated to points, credits, miles, or other measurements applied on a scale. Achievement of points, etc., on the scale corresponds to award levels or the "pay-off" back to the loyal customer. The pay-off increases with the volume of consumption. For example, customers flying 30,000 miles receive a free first-class round-trip ticket, while those flying 50,000 miles receive two free first-class tickets.

Key Terms

cooperative promotion
introductory promotion
price promotion
promotion
tent card

REVIEW QUIZ

When you feel you have covered all of the material in this chapter, answer these questions. Choose the *best* answer. Check your answers with the correct ones found on the Review Quiz Answer Key at the end of this book.

1. Which of the following is a key to successful promotions?

    a. promoting only what you intend to deliver
    b. maintaining a code of silence at your company regarding the promotion
    c. forgetting about past promotions when preparing a new promotion
    d. not wasting time anticipating the customer needs the promotion will create

2. A build promotion is designed to build repeat business by:

    a. increasing the market share taken away from the competition.
    b. establishing a lower price than the competition's price.
    c. introducing a new product or service to the market.
    d. increasing the reward or payoff for multiple purchases.

3. Which of the following statements about joint promotions is *true?*

    a. You should not enter into a joint promotion unless the other party guarantees the cost-benefits ratio.
    b. Joint promotions always improve your base business.
    c. You should not enter into a joint promotion unless the other party has an equal or better overall reputation.
    d. Joint promotions always improve your overall market.

4. Which of the following should you do when preparing any internal promotion?

    a. Make sure the promotion is compatible with your customers' perception of your product or service.
    b. Make sure the benefits of the promotion aren't directly perceivable.
    c. Make sure the customer will encounter the promotion before he or she is inside your door.
    d. Make sure the promotion piece is not placed on a table.

Chapter Outline

Data Base Marketing
  Data Base Systems
  Keys to Successful Data Base
    Marketing
Sales Through Direct Mail
  Keys to Direct Mail

Learning Objectives

1. Describe the origins of data base
    marketing, explain three key elements
    of data base systems, and summarize
    keys to successful data base marketing.
    (pp. 143–147)

2. Summarize keys to successful direct
    mail. (pp. 147–149)

11

Applying Key Marketing Methodologies: Data Base Marketing

COMMUNICATING YOUR SALES OR PROMOTIONAL MESSAGE is more challenging in a crowded media marketplace. Getting your message directly into your target audiences' hands is what data base marketing is all about. This chapter will discuss why data base marketing has become increasingly popular, the components of a data base system, and keys to selling through direct mail.

Data Base Marketing

In 1884, Montgomery Ward mailed its first catalog. Soon other retailers began using catalogs to reach customers. By 1902 Sears produced over $50 million in catalog sales. America was experiencing an incredible explosion in **direct mail** sales.

No one in the early 1900s could have imagined what would occur in direct mail sales in the second half of the century. In the 1950s, a concept arrived that would further increase direct-mail sales and lead to the birth of **data base marketing**: the credit card. As consumer acceptance and use of credit cards grew, so did the "data" to form a "base" list of prospective customers. Then in the 1970s came a technological development that really allowed data base marketing to take off: the computer. By the 1990s computer technology, optical and electrical scanning devices, and a multitude of software programs and other technological advances propelled data base marketing to the forefront of many businesses' marketing plans. Today, data base marketing is a multibillion dollar business influenced by many factors (see Exhibit 1).

More than technology has contributed to data base marketing's success. Geographic segmentations of the U.S. population (such as by zip code) and more sophisticated demographic information from the U.S. Census Bureau have helped shape the growth of data base marketing. Demographics and psychographics have also played key roles in influencing the acceptance of this marketing tool. With the increasing demands placed on people's personal time, the weakening of the traditional television networks, and the overabundance of product and service offerings, new ways to reach potential customers directly with marketing messages became essential. Shifting and declining brand loyalties also supported the need for direct mail's personal and targeted marketing approach. Getting direct mail messages into the hands of consumers in a cost-effective manner and breaking

Exhibit 1   Influences on the Development and Popularity of Data Base Marketing

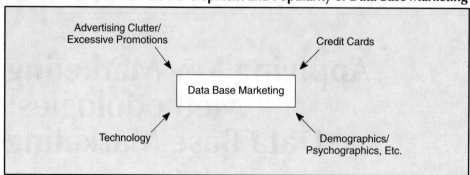

through the advertising clutter with response-generating, creative direct mail pieces are the challenges facing data base marketing today.

Data Base Systems

To make a data base system work, you need three key elements: technology, accurate information, and prioritization.

Technology. Simply defined, data base marketing "technology" is computer hardware and software capable of supporting data base marketing. The degree of technological sophistication you need depends on the complexity of your marketing needs. The more **mailing lists** you use, the more customer data you store, and the greater your frequency and measurement of responses, the greater your technological needs will be.

Accurate Information. A data base is only as good as the integrity of the data it contains. Valid records, including correct addresses, correctly spelled names, most recent purchase activity, and so on, are all essential components of accurate data base information. Clean lists (lists free of invalid or out-of-date information) increase response rates, reduce costs, and improve return on investment. When purchasing lists, always seek to verify the last date the list was cleaned. Also purge (remove) duplicate records—few things turn off a prospect more than two personalized letters arriving on the same day that offer a "once-only" opportunity.

Prioritization. Having a conceptual understanding of which prospects and customers are likeliest to respond to your direct mail will help you improve return rates and increase revenues. In general, people who have recently purchased your product or service are most likely to remember you; they make great first-priority targets for a direct-mail piece urging them to make another purchase (see Exhibit 2). The second likeliest response group would be those who have made multiple or frequent purchases. The third would be those who have spent the greatest amount of total revenue with you historically. The fourth likeliest group to respond is made up of those prospects who reside in areas or purchase from locations similar to those of your best customers. These priority categorizations will help you select

Exhibit 2   Group Priorities for Direct Mail

Group A—Recent Purchasers
Group B—Frequent Purchasers
Group C—Large Purchasers
Group D—Similar Purchasers

likely responders to your direct mail and help you develop realistic response expectations.

Keys to Successful Data Base Marketing

Like all other marketing methodologies, data base marketing requires planning to be on target and successful. Here are ten keys to data base marketing success:

1. *Preplan.* To successfully use any marketing tool, especially a very targeted one like a data base mailing, you need to preplan. Preplanning not only includes developing objectives, return estimates, and a budget, but also should include determining where data base marketing fits and what role it plays within your total marketing effort.

2. *Specify targets.* Unless you are very specific in lining up your target market(s), your direct mail will be wasted. You'll need to specify your audience in terms of size, locale, and make-up (psychographic profile, demographic profile, benefits sought, needs, and so on). Once you have identified this target market, you're ready to take the next critical step.

3. *Select an appropriate message.* Selecting the correct message and presenting it in a manner that will entice your target market to respond will increase your chances of connecting with prospects. For example, if you are mailing to price-sensitive individuals, a strong financial incentive within your product/service offering will probably produce better results than one that offers no discount. On the other hand, if you mail a discounted offer to individuals who are more sensitive to ego and status issues, your chances for success may actually be hurt if your discount is viewed as cheapening the product or service. Selecting the right message to get the job done the first time is better than sending the wrong message and having to start all over again. For one thing, before you can get a corrected message out, someone else might connect with your prospect and eliminate you from the competition.

4. *Predetermine return on investment.* Ask yourself, how much return do I need to generate to cover my basic mailing costs? Then ask, how much more return do I need to achieve an adequate return on investment (ROI)? You should always try to predetermine your ROI and compare your direct-mail ROI with that of the other marketing tools you use.

5. *Maintain creative consistency.* Maintaining creative consistency with your direct mail pieces provides multiple benefits in direct mail marketing. Some of these

---

Ten Keys to Successful Data Base Marketing

1. Preplan
2. Specify targets
3. Select an appropriate message
4. Predetermine return on investment
5. Maintain creative consistency
6. Integrate your mailings with your overall marketing program
7. Use clean lists
8. Know when to mail
9. Repeat your message
10. Track the results

---

benefits include: clearly perceived brand identity, clearly perceived positioning, increased association/recognition from mailing to mailing (when multiple mailings occur), and carry-over brand awareness to other media.

6. *Integrate your mailings with your overall marketing program.* Multiple marketing methodologies working in concert and orchestrated within a total marketing program are much more likely to succeed than hit-or-miss, uncoordinated marketing efforts. Be sure to integrate your data base marketing efforts with the overall marketing program for your product or service offering.

7. *Use clean lists.* Always use "clean" mailing lists. This is the best way to improve ROI and **response rates.** A clean list has a minimal number of duplicated, erroneous, or false addresses.

8. *Know when to mail.* The best way to decide when to mail is to determine when responses are needed. If you need business in December and you know it takes six weeks to get results from a mailing, sending out your direct mail pieces in December or January isn't going to help you. It is always good to prepare to mail sooner than you need to. Build in a "time cushion" to allow for correcting errors, fine tuning or redoing the direct mail piece, and dealing with problems such as delays at the printer. Preparing early makes it more likely that you will be ready to go when your mailing date arrives.

9. *Repeat your message.* Use the power of repetition throughout each direct mail package. The synergy of multiple messages and calls to action can only increase the chance that your prospects will see your message and respond. Use the outside of the envelope, front and back; use the response card or other reply vehicle; use every opportunity in the direct mail piece itself to convey the message. Try to get your message out in like or identical form at least five times somewhere in each direct mail package.

> ## Keys to Direct Mail Success
>
> - Good mailing lists
> - A good direct mail piece
> - Knowing when to mail
> - Knowing when to stop mailing
> - Timely fulfillment

10. *Track the results.* How will you know how well or poorly a direct mailing did if you don't track the results? Tracking results will help you justify future mailings, compare direct mail to other marketing methods, evaluate the effectiveness of the direct mail piece(s), etc.

Always remember to alert all of the departments within your business that will be affected by a direct mail campaign. If you're mailing out a large promotional offer, be sure staff members understand what the offer is, when they can expect customer responses, and what they are supposed to do to fulfill the offer.

Sales Through Direct Mail

If you were to look closely at all of the direct mail pieces you receive in a week, you would be examining the results of great creative energies. Unless you look closely at your direct mail, you might not be aware of all of the things you "may" have won—from cashier's checks, to cars, to lifetime memberships, to your own vacation home. If you're like most people, when you open your charge card or gasoline credit card bill, a handful of fantastic offers "too good to refuse" fall out of the envelope.

Keys to Direct Mail

Selling the products and services of the hospitality industry via direct mail presents special challenges and requires special knowledge. In direct mail sales, you do not have the chance to personally talk to your prospects, as you do in face-to-face or telephone sales. For direct mail to be successful, it must be sent to prospects who have needs that your product or service can meet. Therefore, starting with a good mailing list is vitally important. Then you must develop a good direct mail piece—a communications vehicle that relates prospect needs to your product or service offering. It is also necessary to know when to mail and when to stop mailing. Last but not least, when prospects respond, you must fulfill your direct mail offer promptly and accurately. In the following sections, we will briefly discuss each of these keys to direct-mail success.

Good Lists. Knowing to whom your sales letter or other direct mail piece is going is of primary importance. A simple thing like the correct spelling of a manager's name means a lot if you want your letter read. Lists should constantly be "cleansed" or "purged" of invalid or out-of-date information. Lists should be updated each time a new piece of information becomes available. Verify names, titles, and addresses from your most recent contact with each sales prospect. Constantly strive to be accurate.

The Direct Mail Piece. You can develop checklist upon checklist of do's and don'ts for direct mail promotional literature. There is no single "best" approach. Sometimes a very personal approach is appropriate; at other times, a formal approach should be used. Some general rules for promotional literature are helpful, but if rules are strictly followed, they may inhibit an engaging personal touch. For example, when using a sales letter, one good guideline is to be sure to send an "original" —or at least have it appear to be an original. No one wants to read a "personal" letter that has been photocopied. Also be sure to include the key to any direct mail sales message—relate the prospective customer's needs directly to your product or service. If possible, place your message on one page. Time is important to everyone, and a personal one-page letter has a lot better chance of being read by Ms. Decision-maker than a multi-page direct mail package containing flashy but lengthy promotional pieces.

Knowing When to Mail. Knowing when to mail is important. Consider the example of a large publishing company that just came out with a terrific consumer-oriented book about saving money on federal income taxes. The publisher is excited because this is a super book—new ideas, right price, and so on. So why doesn't the publisher promote it in June and July when the press runs are complete? The answer is timing. People buy books about the federal income tax in October through March, not in June, July, and August. So time of year is sometimes a consideration when you are deciding when to mail. Day of the week is also a consideration. If possible, when mailing to a business address you should time your direct mail piece to arrive on a Tuesday, Wednesday, or Thursday. You know what Mondays are like in a busy office. You also know if your direct mail piece arrives on Friday afternoon it may not even make the reading file. So, think it out—when do you need the business and when is the best time to send that letter?

An example of *not* knowing when to mail is provided by Mr. Go-Getter, an enthusiastic sales manager for a large New York hotel. Mr. Go-Getter compiled a list of prospective customers and prepared a personalized letter for each customer that concluded with, "I'll call you later this week to set up an inspection tour and complimentary luncheon." All 150 letters went out in the 4 P.M. mail on Monday afternoon to ensure delivery on Tuesday. He then caught a 5:30 P.M. flight to Los Angeles for a four-day sales blitz. The moral is simple. Think! Be there when your letter says you will be, and call when you say you will. Otherwise, you will have to start all over again to land that prospective customer, only now you will be battling a credibility problem.

Knowing When to Stop Mailing. Promotional materials and sales letters are expensive; it is estimated that it costs up to $8 to create and send out a letter today. Thus, knowing when to stop mailing makes a lot of "cents." Many mailings may be sequential, with up to four or five pitches to the same mailing list. Be sure you have a system that will eliminate the portion of the list that has already responded "yes" or "no" to an earlier mailing.

Timely Fulfillment. Once you get a positive response, be sure you are in a position to fulfill what you promised on a timely basis. If you offered Mr. and Mrs. Jones a weekend vacation any weekend in May with the proviso that an advance reservation be made, be sure you handle their reservation properly and have their room ready when they arrive. If you fail to fulfill your offer, you may as well eliminate Mr. and Mrs. Jones from your "good" list, along with the names of their friends and neighbors—they won't be responding either.

Key Terms

data base marketing
direct mail
mailing list
response rate

REVIEW QUIZ

When you feel you have covered all of the material in this chapter, answer these questions. Choose the *best* answer. Check your answers with the correct ones found on the Review Quiz Answer Key at the end of this book.

1. Which of the following groups of people is *most* likely to respond to a direct mail offer?

   a. People who reside in areas or purchase from locations similar to those of your best customers.
   b. People who have recently purchased your product or service.
   c. People who have made multiple or frequent purchases.
   d. People who have spent the greatest amount of total revenue with you historically.

2. Which of the following is an example of putting an inappropriate message into your direct mail piece?

   a. Sending a budget, "no-frills" offer to individuals to whom ego and status issues are very important.
   b. Offering a spring-break package to college students that emphasizes value and fun.
   c. Sending a 2-for-1 offer to individuals who are very price sensitive.
   d. Offering a weekend package for senior citizens that emphasizes safety, security, convenience, and value.

3. Why is it important to use a clean mailing list?

   a. A clean list improves the response rate to your mailing.
   b. A clean list improves your return on investment.
   c. A clean list has fewer duplicated or erroneous addresses.
   d. All of the above.

4. Timely fulfillment—one of the keys to successful direct mail—refers to:

   a. producing in a timely way the direct mail pieces you will use in your campaign.
   b. quickly repaying those funds in the marketing budget that you used to create and mail your direct mail piece.
   c. delivering in a timely way what you promised prospects in your direct mail offer.
   d. knowing when to mail out your direct mail piece.

Chapter Outline

Packaging in the Hospitality Industry
    Packaging Benefits
    Packaging Participation
    Types of Packages

Learning Objectives

1. Define "packaging," and explain packaging's benefits to consumers and hospitality firms. (pp. 153–155)

2. Summarize some questions hospitality businesses should ask themselves before participating in a package. (p. 155)

3. List and briefly describe common types of travel packages. (pp. 155–161)

12

Applying Key Marketing Methodologies: Packaging

TODAY MORE THAN EVER, people are buying a complete product or service, such as all-inclusive cruises, weekend accommodations that include a rental car, and so forth. A travel or vacation experience, be it for a single weekend or for several weeks, can also be presented to consumers in a complete "package." Packages may contain every component or just some of the components of the total travel experience. Packaging makes the purchase more attractive to the consumer: it simplifies a multiple purchase and may even offer price advantages. Packaging is an important marketing tool that is becoming increasingly popular in the hospitality industry. In this chapter, we will examine the benefits of packaging, then look at some examples of typical travel packages.

Packaging in the Hospitality Industry

In the hospitality industry, **packaging** can be defined as combining two or more travel products and/or services and offering them to consumers for one price. Packages range from simple "escape weekends" that may include rooms and meals to more elaborate packaging schemes, such as "fly-drive-cruise" packages that include air travel, car rental, the cruise ship cabin rental, meals, entertainment, and other services.

Packaging has become a very useful and widely applied marketing strategy within the hospitality industry. Packaging is more than just a promotion concept; it involves every step of the marketing process, from pricing to identifying customer needs. As travel and the products and services of the hospitality industry continue to grow, the acceptance and need for simplified purchasing will increase. Packaging directly meets that need. While packaging employs the marketing tools of advertising, promotion, and sales, it is also a tool unto itself.

Packaging Benefits

A typical travel package should offer benefits to consumers and to the participating hospitality firms. Consumers should feel that they are benefiting from the package offer by (1) having many travel-related decisions simplified and (2) saving money or otherwise receiving value. While these consumer benefits seem straightforward, providing them presents a substantial challenge to hospitality firms.

What are packaging's benefits to hospitality industry product or service suppliers? There are many potential benefits. A package can:

Exhibit 1   How Packaging Works

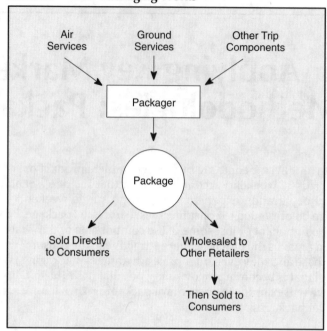

- Increase sales.

- Fill fringe or down periods with sales.

- Make your product easier for consumers to acquire because it is part of another, better-known product.

- Make your product or service appear more attractive than if it were offered on a stand-alone basis.

- Help you achieve economies of scale because your product or service is being offered through many sales channels.

- Gain recognition for your company or build your reputation in a new market.

- Help you introduce a new product or service.

Besides consumers and the participating hospitality firms, who else profits from packages? The person or firm that puts the travel products or services together. Packagers may buy travel products and services, put them together in a package, and sell the package directly to consumers—this is known as **retailing** a package. Packagers may also perform another role—contracting for the travel products and services, packaging them together, and selling the packages to others to sell directly to the public. This is known as **wholesaling** a package (see Exhibit 1).

Regardless of whether a package is offered directly to consumers or whole-saled through other retailers to consumers, it must be attractive to consumers from a marketing perspective as well as a financial one—that is, the package must meet the needs of consumers. These needs are often complex, and defining them requires considerable thought.

Packaging Participation

Not every hospitality industry product or service lends itself to packaging. Also, there are times when participating in a package at a discounted rate can hurt you. Let's consider some questions to ask yourself before you put a package together or participate in someone else's package:

- What benefits will my business receive from participation? More room nights? When? In season? Or in the off-season when I need them most?

- Will my participation in and identification with the package be advantageous or detrimental to my business's image? In other words, am I the Cadillac among Fords or the Ford among Cadillacs?

- What is the downside risk in including my product or service with the package?

- Are my "partners" in this package going to do their part to keep our customers happy?

- Who is handling the details? Will I have enough control over my portion of the package to keep my customers satisfied?

- How will my business be paid for providing its share of the package?

Let's assume that your answers to these questions point to your participating in a package. Perhaps you even want to put one together and reap the benefits of being the packager. Let's also assume you have the financial resources, the key contacts, and the willingness to accept the risks of being a packager. How do you create a package? This question should lead you to think about such marketing issues as: Which market segment is my package going to go after? What are the needs of that market segment? Where do I go to reach that market segment? What kind of pricing structure will that segment respond to? A package must be thought out with all the skill and care you would put into a marketing plan, because a package is just that— a plan to bring your products or services to the market for purchase.

Types of Packages

There are virtually limitless applications of the packaging idea. In the following sections, we will look at some common types of travel packages. Be aware that these packages sometimes overlap; for example, some weekend packages can also be considered special-interest or special-event packages.

All-Inclusive Packages. All-inclusive packages are complete in that they include air services, lodging, **ground services,** car rental, admissions to attractions, taxes and gratuities, and so forth. Examples of all-inclusive packages include the following: "One week for two adults at Walt Disney World via Delta Air Lines" (hotel, car rental, and admissions included), or "Complete three-day Las Vegas Spree—$399"

Exhibit 2   Sample Fly-Drive Package

Courtesy of Auto Europe

(air fare, deluxe rooms, meals, and shows included). All-inclusive packaging lends itself to destination trips, since it simplifies the purchase of the complete trip.

All-inclusive packages may be offered directly to consumers via local newspaper ads; through clubs, churches, or civic organizations; or through retail travel agents. Or, a package wholesaler may supply an all-inclusive package to one or more retail outlets that in turn sell them to consumers. Frequently, price discounts for all-inclusive packages can be arranged as a result of averaging off-season and in-season rates, purchasing hotel rooms or airplane seats in bulk, and so on.

Fly-Drive Packages. Fly-drive packages (see Exhibit 2) are popular and continue to grow in number. In a fly-drive package, air services and auto rental services are combined. For example, one airline's "California Fly-Drive" package included air fare to Los Angeles or San Francisco, a rental car for five days, and return air fare from San Francisco or Los Angeles. The concept was to offer consumers a way to fly to California, drive up or down the coast, and return home—all for $499 per

Exhibit 3   Sample Fly-Cruise Package

Courtesy of Cunard Line Ltd.

person. For many years, air carriers and rent-a-car firms on the east coast have successfully marketed fly-drive packages to Florida. Fly-drives are particularly popular in markets where renting cars is difficult—for instance, in-season in Florida—or where many of the destination's attractions are best seen by automobile.

Fly-Cruise Packages. A variation on the fly-drive package is the fly-cruise package (see Exhibit 3). Originally conceived to eliminate cold days at sea for cruise passengers, the fly-cruise package flies consumers to a warm seaport where they begin the cruise. For example, vacationers from the northeast might fly from Boston to Miami, from where they sail to the Caribbean and back to Miami, then return to Boston by air. Recently, the struggle to maintain long-distance cruising (for instance, transatlantic cruises) has resulted in a fly-cruise variation in which consumers fly first-class one way (say, from the United States to Europe) and then cruise back across the Atlantic. The packaged transatlantic fly-cruise offers the cruise experience consumers seek, while reducing the total cruise time by offering air travel one way.

Weekend Packages. Perhaps the most common and one of the simplest forms of packaging centers on weekend promotions (see Exhibit 4). Convenience and price are important, but the main reason consumers purchase weekend packages is that they offer a much needed getaway or escape. Examples of weekend packages

Exhibit 4   Sample Weekend Package

Courtesy of Wyndham Hotels & Resorts

include "family escape packages" geared to family fun and value (for example, the kids stay free Friday and Saturday nights, or four stay in the room for the price of one); second-honeymoon escape packages (which typically include a deluxe room, champagne, breakfast in bed, and so on); and hundreds of other escape-weekend concepts, from ski packages to sporting-event packages.

Special-Interest Packages. A package can be successfully created to appeal to people's special interests. The concept behind a special-interest package is to combine a basic hospitality service or product (lodging, for example) with a special interest such as boating, golf, tennis, swimming, skiing, or horseback riding. Special-interest packages need not be limited to sport or recreational activity tie-ins, however. They may also relate to history, religious interests, or hobbies.

Examples of successful special-interest packages are weekend "foliage" bus tours of New England to see the changing landscape as fall unfolds. Meals and rooms at quaint New England inns are usually packaged along with the bus tour; the tour usually features photo-taking opportunities at scenic overviews along the highway. Another example of a special-interest package is "Friday Night at the

Exhibit 5   Sample Special-Destination/Attraction Package

Courtesy of Premier Cruise Lines

Races" in which consumers are taken to the race track via motorcoach, with dinner, cocktails on board, and general-admission tickets all included for one price.

Special-Event Packages. Packaging around a special event is another form of package marketing. Each year tens of thousands of people purchase special-event packages to the Super Bowl, Mardi Gras, college football bowl games, major boxing events, the World Series, and many other special events. The event is the reason for the trip; the package provides the easiest method to purchase everything in one step.

Some creative individuals have developed not only special-event packages but even the special event itself. These types of packages include transcontinental balloon flights, nationwide bike races, and weekend dinners or festivals honoring people or places.

Special Destination/Attraction Packages. There are special places that lend themselves to being promoted via a package (see Exhibit 5). These include the Holy Land; the Vatican; Israel; Washington, D.C., and capitals in general; theme parks (Disney World, Six Flags, and so on); Atlantic City and Las Vegas; mountains (the Catskills, for example); beaches (Myrtle Beach, Virginia Beach, Cape Cod); Alaskan cruises; and so on. One of the best examples of a special destination that is packaged for the young (school-aged children) as well as the old (retirees) is Virginia's Colonial Williamsburg Village.

Theme Packages. With a theme package, the packager literally creates the reason for the package. For example, a number of New York City hotels looking for weekend business have created successful packages on the theme of "a weekend in New York, including dinner in Central Park and an evening at the theater." This theme requires

Exhibit 6   Sample Price Package

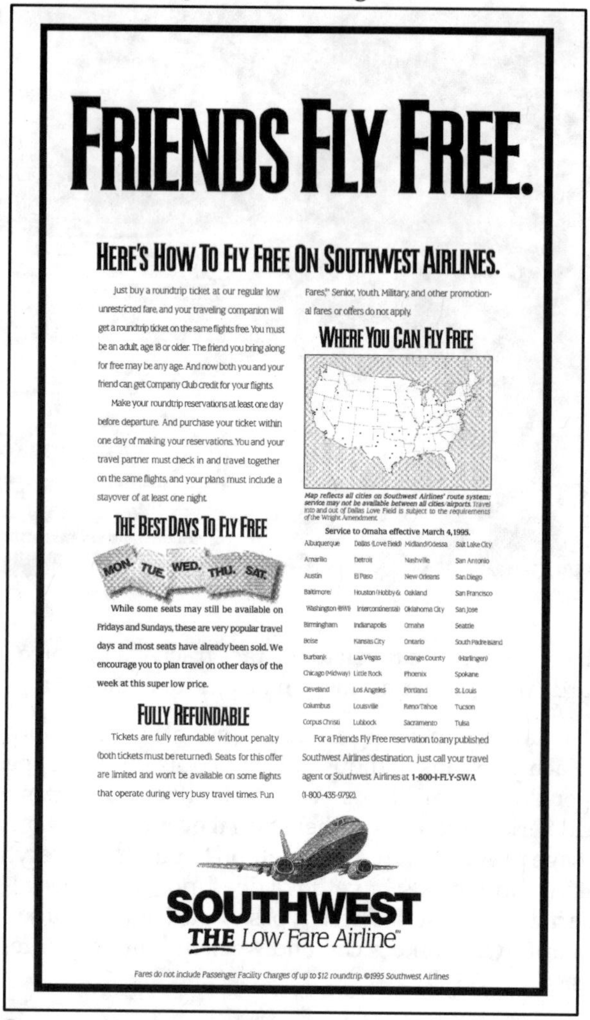

Courtesy of Southwest Airlines

the package to include rooms, theater tickets, and meals; most of the packages also include a buggy ride through Central Park or a limo ride to and from the theater as part of the attraction. Other theme packages have related to art shows, cultural displays at museums, gambling, and even "celebrity weekends," which center around the appearance of a celebrity.

Holiday Packages. "Winter vacation week of 12/28 to 1/5 in sunny Florida via Delta only $469 air fare, room (double occupancy) included" is a frequent type of holiday package promoted on college campuses in the Northeast. Other holiday packages include everything from "Easter in the Holy Land" to "St. Patrick's Day in Dublin" to a week in sunny Spain to witness Pamplona's running of the bulls.

While the reason to travel is the holiday event itself, the packaging of that event with other hospitality industry products and services for one price is the key to making the sale.

"Price" Packages. There are many types of "price" packages (see Exhibit 6). With price packages, the marketing message focuses on value. One successful concept in price packaging is the "give-away," frequently called the "two-for-one" concept, in which the purchaser's spouse or significant other goes along "free." Other typical price-oriented travel packages include weekends at 50% off, a free suite, the second week is free, "two extra days on the Costa del Sol included at no cost," and so on.

Key Terms

ground services   retailing
packaging   wholesaling

REVIEW QUIZ

When you feel you have covered all of the material in this chapter, answer these questions. Choose the *best* answer. Check your answers with the correct ones found on the Review Quiz Answer Key at the end of this book.

1. Combining two or more travel products and/or services together and offering them to consumers for one price is called:

    a. combining.
    b. packaging.
    c. discounting.
    d. consolidating.

2. A package designed to combine air services and auto rental services is called a _____ package.

    a. holiday
    b. special destination/attraction
    c. fly-drive
    d. special-interest

3. Which of the following statements about weekend packages is *true?*

    a. They are one of the simplest forms of packaging.
    b. Their main appeal to consumers is that they offer a much needed getaway or escape.
    c. They are relatively uncommon—few hospitality firms put them together or participate in them.
    d. a and b.

4. If a group of hotels in Miami puts together a "theater weekend in Miami" package that includes rooms, theater tickets, and meals, such a package is called a _____ package.

    a. holiday
    b. theme
    c. fly-drive
    d. none of the above

5. A package marketed primarily on its low cost is called a(n) _____ package.

    a. all-inclusive
    b. theme
    c. special-destination/attraction
    d. price

Chapter Outline

Collateral Materials
    Types of Collateral Material
Employee Motivation
    Employee-of-the-Month Programs
    Employee-Interest Promotions
    Employee Community Service
        Recognition
Clubs
    VIP Clubs
    Secretaries Clubs
    Salesperson Appreciation Clubs
    Meal-of-the-Month Clubs

Learning Objectives

1. Explain eight key points for preparing and presenting collateral materials. (pp. 165–166)

2. Describe several types of collateral materials used in the hospitality industry. (pp. 166–174)

3. Give examples of employee motivational programs that help make a property more marketable, and explain how they are used. (pp. 174–176)

4. Describe the club concept as a marketing tool and give examples of successful uses of the club concept. (pp. 176–178)

13

Applying Key Marketing Methodologies: Collateral Materials and Promotional Support

To market your establishment effectively, you need to use a variety of tools. This chapter examines some very specific types of marketing tools: collateral materials, employee motivation programs, and club concepts.

Collateral materials are printed items such as brochures, maps, guides, flyers, posters, tent cards, etc. They help advertise your property or the services within it.

Employee motivation programs help make your property more marketable by motivating your primary resource—your employees. These programs help make your employees more committed to their jobs and to making sure that the property succeeds.

Club concepts have taken a variety of different forms, but all of them succeed by giving the customer extra recognition. A club concept tells a particular market segment that it is special, and that your property values its business.

Collateral Materials

Collateral materials are the print support materials that help market your product or service. In the hospitality industry, they include brochures, maps, guides, menu inserts, tent cards, photo displays, and posters. The cost of preparing, printing, and distributing collateral materials is easily measured.

It is important to approach the preparation of each collateral piece with the same care you would give your best advertisement or most important sales call. Your collateral materials are always being viewed by your potential market and customers. The same "do's and don'ts" that apply to general promotion pieces apply to collateral materials. There are eight key points to keep in mind when preparing and presenting collateral materials:

1. *Identification of purpose.* Your first step—before you determine whether you need color, what quality of paper **stock** to use, or what shape, size, etc., you should make an item—is to ask yourself what the primary purpose of the piece is and who the intended audience is.

165

2. *Fallacy about quality.* There is a fallacy about quality that states: "If it's four colors and on high-quality stock, it's got to be good." Remember that the true value of a collateral piece is its marketing purpose, not its physical appearance.

3. *Compatibility.* Your collateral materials should reinforce the image you are trying to establish or maintain regarding your product or service. Don't let it contradict that image. If you are running an upscale gourmet restaurant, be sure your materials are compatible with that image. There are times when you might try to improve on your establishment's image by improving the collateral materials. An example might be creating a new brochure that portrays a better image than that currently being portrayed. A word of caution, however: if you allow a new brochure to build a level of expectation beyond what the product can deliver, you could be doing yourself more harm than good.

4. *Consistency.* The single greatest fault with most collateral material is its lack of consistency. Is your collateral material consistent with your other marketing and image-related visual aids? Simple things such as the use of a logo, certain colors, print styles, and so on will help build consistency. You may want your piece of collateral material to stand out, and it should, but not by detracting from your image.

5. *Practical detail.* Does the collateral material accomplish the marketing purpose it was designed to meet? Too often things like picture selection take precedence over clear directions and a useful map. The result may be great photos, but customers who can't find you! Remember to review the materials and be sure every detail is accurate and useful.

6. *Visibility.* If you want customers to pick up and respond to your collateral materials, don't hide them! Check often to see that these materials are where they belong—somewhere where the customer or potential customer can clearly see them and pick them up.

7. *Clutter avoidance.* Be sure you are not a victim of "the more-the-better" syndrome. Yes, it's great to have good information for your hospitality customers, but too much collateral material in one place results in clutter. You may even find that the customer has left you to spend time and money at an external attraction you promoted overzealously.

8. *Keep it clear.* Make sure that the purpose of each piece is clear. Do not overload it with too much copy or detail or it will lose its purpose as a marketing vehicle. A customer or potential customer picks up the material to get a message. Don't bury that message in fine print or, worse, too much print.

Types of Collateral Material

Given these key points, let's look at some specific types of collateral materials employed in the hospitality industry.

Brochures. A brochure is a highly specialized piece of collateral material Its preparation requires careful thought. It is not simply a collection of sexy photos and some copy. A successful, well-prepared promotional brochure for a property should contain the following ten elements:

1. Identification of the property, including its logo

2. Descriptive facts about the property

3. Directions on how to get to the property

4. A map with travel times

5. The property's telephone number(s)

6. The property's address

7. The person or individual to contact for more information (sales director, the catering department, etc.)

8. Amenities within the property (recreational, food and beverage, etc.)

9. Nearby attractions and items of interest to the guests/customers (i.e., shopping, tourist attractions, etc.)

10. Transportation information (limo service, buses, airlines, rail, interstates, rental-car companies, etc.)

Including these ten elements will not necessarily guarantee that your brochure is successful. You must also consider the eight key points to preparing successful collateral material mentioned earlier and, of course, use professional photos, art, design layout, and copy to produce a quality final product.

Directories. There are both large-volume reference directories and pocket-size or briefcase directories. If you produce a directory that you want the traveling consumer to use, be sure that it fits in a briefcase or purse. No one wants to (or will) carry an oversized book. Make it easy to use. Follow a format that is logical—to the customer, not you—and include an index and a key. Put your phone number wherever possible, preferably on every page, as well as on the front and back covers.

If you list your property in someone else's directory, observe the following points:

- Proof everything twice.

- Be careful about being too specific with prices or rates; use ranges (especially if it is an annual directory).

- Check and double check your address, phone and fax numbers, and telex number (if applicable).

- Ask to review the final copy.

- Ask to review the actual placement.

- If a photo of your product or service is used, be sure it is up-to-date, representative, and a sales tool; otherwise, do not use it.

Today there are more than 5,000 different reference directories, ranging from the local yellow pages to *A Directory of Directories,* many of which are available in

CD-ROM format or on-line. In order to determine which directory listings are most helpful to you, you will need to analyze *where* your business is coming from, *how* potential customers find out about you, and *what* type of business you are getting.

Answer the following questions to help determine which directories you should list in for the most exposure of your product or service:

1. Do I currently receive business as a result of a directory listing?

2. Does my competition receive business as a result of a directory listing that I do not receive?

3. Will I receive enough business from a directory listing to offset the cost for the listing? This is especially applicable with respect to fees for computerized directories and CD-ROM distribution.

4. Are there any key directories in which my competitors are listed and I am not?

5. Is my product or service compatible with the directory format (i.e., one line, block ad, a photo ad, etc.)?

While these five practical questions should provide you with some rationale for whether to list in a directory, often trial and measurement will be the best test. If you decide directory listings will be helpful in marketing your product or service, be sure that the content and the **placement** of that listing are well thought out to convey your marketing message. Directory listings often require similar information from all contributors. It is to your advantage to fill in every line in the listing questionnaire. If the directory you select allows leeway, be sure to include the following:

- A landmark reference along with your address—for example, "next to the Metro Station in Crystal City"

- Your phone number

- Any special information that will give potential customers a reason to call you (this reason can be referred to as the "why statement")

Insist that you review the placement of your listing—the actual spot in the directory where your listing will appear—and, most important, that you have an opportunity for a final review of the copy that goes into the directory. Do not scan it—read it word for word and number for number. Once in print in a directory, the listing is widely circulated—errors, wrong phone number, and all. Again, if you must list rates or prices, use a range. Most directories are published annually, and you may not want to commit to specific rates (especially during times of high inflation).

Fact Sheets. A fact sheet is an abbreviated version of a hotel's brochure. It is usually in a one-page, bulleted format. It contains brief descriptive phrases that convey the key information about the property (see Exhibit 1). It is used as a "stuffer" in mailings, as a self-mailer, or (in less expensive form) as a handout for people making inquiries at the property.

Gift Certificates. Another very useful application of collateral materials is the gift certificate. Gift certificates let consumers buy your product or service for someone

Exhibit 1   Hotel Fact Sheet Format

Name	Name of hotel.
Location	Include street address, distance from airport, and attractions.
Physical structure	Design, number of floors, and number of rooms per floor.
Number and type of rooms	Number of guest rooms and description of the bed types and decor of the rooms.
Number and type of suites	Same information for suites as given for standard rooms.
Club floor	If hotel offers a "concierge" level, description of accommodations and services.
Function space	Location and number of meeting rooms, including dimensions and capacity for each (a capacity chart may be used).
Food and beverage outlets	Names and descriptions of each food and beverage outlet, including type of cuisine, seating capacity, price range, and hours of operation.
Recreation	A list of all recreational facilities.
Amenities	A list of all other hotel amenities, such as turndown service, complimentary *Wall Street Journal,* shoe shine, barber/beauty shop, etc.
Parking	Description of facilities and cost.
Transportation	Description of transportation service to the airport and area with accompanying cost. Does hotel provide complimentary van or limousine service?
Secretaries club	If it exists at the hotel, description of the program.
Frequent guest program	If offered by the hotel, a brief description of its advantages and disadvantages in relation to your hotel.

else. Gift certificates can take on many different forms and be promoted in many ways. One example is McDonald's seasonal promotion of books of gift certificates as a Christmas gift. Another example was executed well by a lodging property that sold "gift boxes" containing escape weekend tickets and empty champagne glasses that would be filled on a complimentary basis. Restaurants offer "dinner-for-two" gift certificates with all sorts of variations. These programs have become increasingly popular, fulfilling people's need to give an unusual and much appreciated gift.

Entertainment Pieces. Collateral materials supporting entertainment (see Exhibit 2) come in many shapes, forms, and levels of quality. Most entertainers will supply photos, posters, or **flyers** (a one-page formatted message). Most hospitality properties use these as supplied. This is fine if the quality and the *taste* in the collateral material are compatible with the establishment's image. There are no standard criteria by which to screen entertainment collateral materials; however, there are some steps that can be taken to ensure the materials are compatible with the establishment:

1. Consider developing a standard poster display case.

Exhibit 2   Sample Collateral Materials Supporting Entertainment

Courtesy of Ramada Inc.

2. Ask entertainment groups to supply appropriate photos or posters to fit the display case.

3. Reject all "homemade" posters, signs, and other wall hangings that are of low or mediocre quality.

4. Consider your print advertising as part of the total campaign for the entertainment—make it stand out from the rest.

5. Be sure that the supplied photos, copy, and any related public relations or press releases are in good taste and compatible with your establishment's desired image.

6. Be sure the entertainment itself is representative of how you want your customers to perceive your establishment. Think of your image at all times.

Flyers. Flyers are announcements usually printed for quick distribution to stimulate interest in a special event or promotion. Flyers may be reminders or even an announcement of an event when time does not permit using another method. If you use flyers, take care that they have a professional appearance and are compatible with the other materials used to promote the event. It is important that you control distribution to ensure that potential customers (and not your parking lot) get the message. Flyers are an inexpensive method to reach the local market. Image concerns may make flyers an inappropriate delivery vehicle for some users or messages.

Guest Services/Guestroom Collateral Materials. There are two approaches to guest services collateral materials: the clutter method and the organized approach. The clutter method is best depicted by a hotel room dresser or desk-top full of everything from credit card applications to room service menus, all set up alongside instructions on how to work the TV, save energy, and so forth. The net result is a cluttered guestroom.

There are many ways to organize guest services information. One method is to use a folder with inserts related to the various services (i.e., room service menu, amenities, and so on). The second method is to use a display made of laminated plastic with slots for inserts. Either is acceptable, and both are preferred to the clutter approach. The guestroom materials should reflect some consistency in color and print style, and—most important of all—they should be readable. Often too much is squeezed on an instructions card with print too small to be of help to the guest, resulting in unnecessary calls to your telephone operator. One final note: Be sure a pen or pencil is included with the collateral materials in the room, preferably one imprinted with the name and phone number of your establishment. Guests will not only appreciate it and use it—they'll probably take it!

Lounge Materials. Collateral material promoting a lounge at the property should adhere to the same guidelines as the materials used to promote the property itself. The lounge materials should convey not only the lounge's environment, theme, and so on, but also a marketing message that relates to the needs of the consumer. The message can be "a place to relax," "a place to unwind," "a place to discuss business or pleasure," or whatever.

If there is something special about the lounge, say so in the collateral material. Collateral material promoting the lounge should tell the reader where the lounge is in the property, indicate any dress requirements, and be placed in visible locations throughout the property. Visible places include, but are not limited to:

- The restaurant
- The elevator lobby
- Elevator display panels
- The hotel lobby
- Guestrooms

Collateral materials for the lounge should convey, via photos, the reason to come to the lounge, whether it be relaxation or the promise of intimate conversation. A photo of four walls does not sell or motivate consumers. People visit lounges to get away from their rooms, seek companionship, or relax. Be sure your collateral materials communicate that your lounge meets these needs.

Maps. A good map will indicate a clear way to reach your establishment. It will also identify landmarks, key roads, and distance or travel time. Use the distance or travel time indicator that is most advantageous to you. If you are three miles from the airport, but it takes 25 minutes to travel the distance, indicate three miles. If you are nine miles from the airport, but only 15 minutes via the expressway, indicate 15 minutes. If you can get your establishment listed on other maps, do so—it is additional exposure for you. Rent-a-car company maps, chamber of commerce materials, Realtor maps, bank maps, on-line direction services, and sight-seeing maps are but a few of the opportunities available to get your establishment noticed.

Menu Specials. Advertisements for special food or beverage promotions are a frequently used type of collateral material. These promotions take many forms, ranging from the photocopied menu clip-on to multicolored menus and tabletop displays. Regardless of the formality of the collateral piece, its objective is to increase sales by getting guests to opt for the special. Potential customers can perceive these promotions as adding "value." The promotion can be on a regularly scheduled day of the week, week of the month, or month of the year. If you use the material as part of an ongoing program, you can more easily implement and control the promotion and measure its effectiveness. Many restaurant chains use this type of collateral sales material. These restaurants regularly promote a number of items as specials, using collateral material clipped to menus. Although the specials frequently change, the clip-on material should be well prepared with quality that is comparable to the menu's quality.

You can design menu specials to achieve many objectives. The purpose may be to increase volume by offering a relatively low-priced special, or it may be to build "trial" (new business) by offering a low-priced special to attract new clientele. You may also design specials to increase profits by promoting low-cost items that provide a higher profit margin, such as pasta dishes. Other specials may be designed to build volume for a specific item, increase beverage sales, increase the average check amounts through dessert promotions, etc. Menu specials can help you meet your objectives if you:

- Clearly identify the purpose and the result expected

- Conscientiously and methodically measure your results

- Carefully plan your collateral promotion piece

Finally, remember to tell the servers, hosts, and hostesses about the special and *how* to promote it to customers. A server who answers, "I don't know" when your customer asks about a special is not going to make a sale.

Meeting Facilities Brochures. If you decide to prepare a brochure about the meeting facilities in your establishment, be sure to include the items of interest to meeting planners. This means every detail, not just photos. Details may include:

- Room sizes/dimensions

- Ceiling heights

- Seating capacity, referencing different setups (theater style, classroom, U-shaped, etc.)

- Audiovisual equipment

- Display capacities (maximum width and height of entries)

- Sketches or diagrams of the rooms

- Breakout room and additional conference room information

- Adjoining banquet facilities

- Meeting and meal setups

- Special features (acoustics, tables, technical capabilities, etc.)

- Service procedures and policies, focusing on the human aspect rather than the physical facility

- Rates and discounts

- Location of the facilities

- Proximity to transportation (subways, airports, etc.)

- Group transportation services

- Other property amenities that will help sell meetings

- Telephone number and name of the person to contact

Make the meeting-facilities brochure easy to read and responsive to the meeting planner's needs. Include the banquet menu and any other related collateral materials as support information for the meeting planner.

The meeting-facilities brochure should answer every question a potential customer might ask about the physical facility and services available. Include a "things-to-do" section or attachment to help sell your facility. This section or attachment should mention nearby or in-house shopping, entertainment, cultural attractions, recreational attractions, etc.

Most important of all, be certain that there is a telephone number and person to call. If that person is not available, be sure that the person answering the telephone is completely prepared to answer questions or that the appropriate salesperson can quickly contact the potential customer. Finally, be certain that there is an adequate stock of all materials on hand to supply potential customers. If volume merits it, consider a CD-ROM version of the information; it is more likely to be retained by the requesting individual or organization.

Rate Cards. Perhaps the single most debatable piece of collateral material today is the rate card. Rates change frequently and are often discounted or tailored for special types of business (for instance, corporate clients, airline crews, families). If rate cards are used, plan to replace them frequently and design them to allow flexibility in selling. The best rate cards:

- Use price ranges

- Clearly define special rate programs and qualifying rules

- Clearly state dates for which the rates are in effect

- Define any special policies

Printing your rates may not always legally compel you, but it certainly builds expectations among your potential customers about what your products and services cost. Always have a disclaimer, such as "rates subject to change." But, more important, strive to have the correct, current rate clearly defined for your customer. Likewise, be sure every employee who has contact with potential customers knows the current rate policy and procedures, and has the current rate card accessible at all times.

Recreational Facilities Guide. Attractions, be they within the hospitality facility or in nearby areas, are an asset to promote. Internal collateral materials can promote attractions that help satisfy guests and attract repeat visitors. Reference materials for nearby local attractions can especially benefit a property that lacks internal amenities or facilities. The caution here is to avoid the clutter of having many different collateral pieces that vary in quality. Also, discard out-of-date brochures. Cooperative programs between lodging facilities and nearby attractions (in which program participants refer to one another) can work very well to increase the exposure and perceived value of all program participants. Give careful thought to consistency and image before you enter into such cooperative promotions.

Shopping Guides. Shopping ranks consistently high on the list of needs expressed by leisure travelers. Collateral materials pointing out nearby or special shopping areas can thus add another perceived value to the hospitality property. Getting your establishment identified within a local shopper's guide as a reference point or map point can provide additional marketing exposure.

Tent Cards. Tent cards are another popular form of collateral material. They can promote everything from a restaurant within a hotel to a drink or dessert special within the restaurant. Tent cards come in all shapes, sizes, and forms. Some practical considerations are:

1. Use all sides of the tent card.

2. Design it in a practical manner to rest on a table or a desk.

3. Make it look attractive.

4. Avoid the temptation to use a "totally unique" tent card—it will usually be costly to produce, difficult to use, and constantly in need of replacement.

5. Be sure that size and placement of the tent card are consistent with the purpose or message on the card.

6. Monitor and measure the results of each tent card promotion to determine its real value to you.

7. Avoid clutter or promotions that cheapen your overall product or service offering.

Employee Motivation

Customers are often impressed when an establishment recognizes good employee performance. You can keep your customers informed and motivate your employees through a number of in-house marketing methods. As a labor-intensive industry, motivated employees with good service attitudes are very often the keys to a successful operation. Ensuring employee motivation is a very difficult task in the services business. In-house materials that help employee morale are important and have a direct impact on the sale of your product or service. Do not ignore strategies for improving employee motivation; such strategies are key marketing tools. Some examples are included in the following sections.

Employee-of-the-Month Programs

One of the more successful applications of motivational principles in the hospitality industry has been "employee-of-the-month" programs. The visual execution of these programs is important; often, a photo poster is prominently displayed in a high-traffic employee area.

An even more meaningful—and potentially more beneficial—method is to establish a permanent display case for such a poster, thereby allowing your guests to also see this recognition award. This placement method provides even further recognition for the employee and fosters additional feelings of goodwill among both employees and guests. A successful employee-of-the-month program requires a well-planned program of support, frequently including external public relations and some form of reward for the recognized employees. Selection criteria, fairness in judgment, and the involvement of other employees as judges or award presenters are keys to success in making these employee-recognition programs work. Management's involvement in these programs and respect for the employees and their achievements are also critical factors.

Employee-Interest Promotions

Employee-interest promotions help motivate employees and increase the marketing exposures for your establishment. An employee-interest promotion begins by identifying a hobby or a special interest of an employee. One example is that of a chef whose hobby is driving race cars. The hotel where he worked successfully placed a number of human interest stories in the media about the "fastest chef in town," featuring the employee and his hobby. Management then displayed the news clippings and photos of the chef and his autos in a number of high-traffic employee areas within the property. Employee-interest promotion possibilities are limitless, but they should be used sparingly or their internal value may dissipate.

Employee Community Service Recognition

Another effective employee program is recognizing employees' efforts in their local communities. Many employees do volunteer work, make special efforts on behalf of charities, or make unique contributions to their communities. Identifying and providing public recognition for these employees and their service efforts benefits both your establishment and the employees. These are "win-win" promotions. Examples include employees who walk, run, or rock for contributions to charity; employees who perform volunteer work for people who are sick, disabled, or

Exhibit 3   Sample VIP Club Card

Courtesy of Hertz

elderly; and employees who help save lives as volunteer fire fighters or rescue-squad personnel.

Clubs

Clubs for specific consumer groups are another marketing device that can work for you. Regardless of your sector of the hospitality industry, you can create a "club" concept to promote business. A few examples follow.

VIP Clubs

Just as employee recognition programs identify employees who are important to you, VIP clubs recognize segments of customers who are "very important people" to you. Examples of such concepts are numerous and include: Hertz #1 Club; Hertz Platinum Service; the various airline frequent-traveler clubs such as United's Red Carpet Club, Delta's Crown Room Club, and American's Admiral's Club. The lodging sector also uses a variety of VIP concepts and promotions (see Exhibit 3).

Today's VIP-club concepts are sophisticated and require a variety of skills, such as building direct-mail lists, publishing special magazines, and completing merchandising programs. VIP clubs can also exist *within* a lodging or food and beverage facility. It can be a concept as simple as designating upgraded rooms or floors for VIPs or sectioning off an area of the dining room for VIPs. Recognition, appreciation, and appeal to the repeat user are the motivators behind such VIP club concepts. Key factors for a VIP club concept include the following:

- Recognition of frequent users of the product or service
- Perceivable benefits to membership
- Special services
- Exclusive items or services for members only
- Membership symbols (membership cards, wall plaques, etc.)
- Emphasis on taking problems out of the travel experience
- Simplifying the product or service purchase

Secretaries Clubs

Secretaries are important intermediaries in the hospitality industry. A secretary is often in direct contact with the customer and, more important, is often a decision-maker. Hotels have been leaders in recognizing this and developing special-appreciation club concepts. For example, one such club concept created by a hotel chain offers incentive awards to secretaries in appreciation for various levels of business directed to their establishments. The concept is well thought out and exemplifies how to organize a productive secretaries program. Here's a sketch of how it works.

The establishment assigns an individual to identify secretaries who are providing reservations on a regular basis. A list is developed, and those secretaries are invited to join the "club." The club provides:

- A quarterly appreciation luncheon
- Flowers on each secretary's birthday
- Free weekends for certain volumes of room nights
- Free trips for even larger volumes

While this is an oversimplified explanation, the concept is "business is appreciated and, more important, so are you." It's no wonder that the chains' highest percentage of repeat business comes from its secretaries clubs. (It is always good practice to determine the client company's policy with respect to any such incentive reward program.)

The building of lists, enrolling of members, personal letters, gestures of appreciation, incentive gifts, and all other aspects of a secretaries club are designed to build repeat business through loyal intermediaries and friends.

Salesperson Appreciation Clubs

Special club or VIP concepts are particularly applicable to the commercial transient salesperson. These individuals form the loyal core or base for many hospitality establishments as a result of a heavy, consistent travel pattern. Building loyalty to your product or service with this market segment can be very beneficial. The club or VIP concept for salespersons assumes many different forms; however, these forms have as a common premise the recognition that it is desirable to keep this particular customer's brand loyalty. Special rates, rooms, first-drink-free promotions, every tenth room free, free coffee and breakfast, and even free car washes have been offered as part of the special treatment for salespersons.

Meal-of-the-Month Clubs

Building a loyal or regular following in today's food and beverage market is increasingly difficult because of the many new concepts and the increase in competition. One method of ensuring a regular following is to develop a meal-of-the-month or some other dining-out club. Meal-of-the-month clubs can have a number of different appeals, ranging from price and value to a variety of themes to entertainment tie-ins. Regardless of the method selected, the idea is to use the club to build a core of regulars.

Key Terms

collateral materials
flyer
placement
stock

REVIEW QUIZ

When you feel you have covered all of the material in this chapter, answer these questions. Choose the *best* answer. Check your answers with the correct ones found on the Review Quiz Answer Key at the end of this book.

1. Which of the following is *not* a key point for preparing and presenting collateral materials?

    a. compatibility
    b. clutter avoidance
    c. cocooning
    d. fallacy about quality

2. The first step in preparing and presenting collateral material is:

    a. determining compatibility.
    b. ensuring consistency.
    c. including practical detail.
    d. identifying the primary purpose.

3. The best way to avoid clutter when providing guest services/guestroom collateral materials in guestrooms is to:

    a. use a folder with inserts related to the various services.
    b. put all guest services information on the guestroom desk top.
    c. personally hand guest services information to guests at check-in.
    d. put each piece of guest services information in a different spot in the guestroom.

4. A promotion that features a property employee and his or her hobby is called a(n):

    a. secretaries club.
    b. employee-interest promotion.
    c. employee-of-the-month program.
    d. property sports team.

5. Special services, membership symbols, and recognition of frequent users are key factors of what marketing tool?

    a. VIP clubs
    b. employee-of-the-month promotions
    c. meal-of-the-month clubs
    d. all of the above

Chapter Outline

Hotel Rates
    Standard Rates
    Other Rates
    Ranges
    Rate Strategies
    Rate Comparisons
Airfares
    Carrier Strategies
Rental Car Rates
    Rental Car Strategies
Cruise Ship Rates

Learning Objectives

1. Explain the different types of room rates charged by hotels. (pp. 181–183)

2. Describe ranges of rates set by hotels, identify the purpose of rate strategies, and give examples of strategies based on the grid-positioning concept. (pp. 184–186)

3. Describe air carriers' rates and the factors affecting rate strategies. (pp. 187–188)

4. Explain types of rental car rates and the factors affecting rate strategies. (pp. 188–190)

5. Describe cruise ship rates. (p. 190)

Applying Key Marketing Methodologies: Understanding Rates and Fares

A RATE IS THE PRICE that is established for a service. The hospitality industry applies different rates for its services. Rates may vary for virtually every day of the week, every market segment, and every event one can think of—or create. In fact, rate is one of today's most powerful marketing tools, and consumer-attracting terminology such as "discount," "special offer," "trial," and "preferred" abounds in marketing and promotions.

One purpose of this chapter is to explain and show the relationships between various types of rates used in the hospitality industry. This chapter also discusses the concept of ranges of rates and describes some of the rate-setting strategies used by hotels, air carriers, rental car firms, and cruise lines. It also emphasizes the importance of rate management.

One key to any discussion of rates is a clear and consistent use of terminology. This is especially important to consumers, whose patience with the wording of fine-print **restrictions** placed on special offers is just about exhausted. Many professionals in the industry use rate terminology inexactly, causing confusion and undermining their own credibility. Definitions of rate-related terminology should be specific and consistent; however, rate categories and associated terms or conditions are in constant flux, even within a single hospitality business enterprise.

Hotel Rates

In hotels, standard rates are applied in common situations as noted in this section. Additional types of rates that apply in market-specific situations are also discussed.

Standard Rates

Standard hotel rates include corporate, rack, preferred, super-saver, weekend, summer, and club-level.

Corporate. In today's marketplace, the **corporate rate** is a competitive rate used to attract frequent business travelers. Depending on the quality of a hotel and its location in relation to its top competitors in the marketplace, the hotel's corporate rate should be the same as or rather close to those of its four major competitors. If an established property has the clearly superior location and product, the hotel can be the rate leader in the market. But if a hotel is new or not yet established, its corporate rate might be lower than the competition's rate in order to bring in trial business.

As hotel managers plan a hotel's rate strategy, the corporate rate should be established first. Management should strive to ensure that the corporate rate that is advertised in all automated reservations systems, on-line services, and directory listings is the most competitive corporate rate or range of rates offered. The hotel's range for its corporate rate should be based on room type, location, or other selected criteria.

Rack. A hotel's highest rate category is called its rack rate. Rack rate should be used as a positioning rate. Rack rates provide the consumer and travel intermediary with a perception of the quality level of the hotel in relationship to its competition and all other hotels in a given market. Rack rates are the standard from which other rates are discounted. In general, the broadest range is desirable for rack rates, beginning with a property's least desirable room category (at its full, non-discounted price) and topping out with its best rooms priced slightly above its nearest competitors. This broad range creates the perception of the hotel as the best hotel in the marketplace and allows for revenue maximization through controlled sale and inventory of the lowest-priced non-discounted rooms. These lowest-priced non-discounted rooms should be advertised in automated systems, directories, and on-line services and entered in the central reservations system.

Preferred. Also known as a preferred corporate rate, a **preferred rate** is a specific amount charged to a volume consumer of rooms. Preferred rates are lower than corporate rates. There may be—and should be—many different preferred rates. Usually, the higher the room volume that a company consumes, the lower the preferred rate the company is charged.

Because a hotel may have many different corporate rates, preferred rates should be referred to by the name of the company or organization to which each rate has been provided, such as the "IBM rate," the "3M rate," or the "Nestlé rate."

Super-Saver. The **super-saver** is a rate that should be lower than the corporate rate and used for rate resistors (people seeking lower rates) or as a discounted promotional rate to attract guests when conditions merit. The super-saver can and should be used to fill empty rooms during valley periods or days. Like rack rates, super-savers help maximize revenue by filling what would otherwise be empty (zero-revenue) rooms. This rate also should be used to win business over from the competition.

The super-saver rate can be changed as needed. It can be offered to any market segment and is usually capacity-controlled—that is, applied to a limited number of rooms in the inventory. It is the responsibility of the general manager to close off this category daily or hourly if necessary.

Weekend. Weekend rates are those in effect for weekends, meaning Friday/ Saturday/ Sunday. These are flat room rates (that is, the rates do not vary depending on the number of guests staying in the room). Depending on the market and local events, this room category can be closed off for any day or period. For instance, a manager may wish to close this category on Sundays in a high Sunday-arrival market, which may be the case for football weekends or other events. Weekend rates should be promotionally oriented: they should be set at fixed amounts of $49, $59, $69, $79, or $89 (and so forth), which lend themselves to being advertised effectively.

Summer. Usually in effect from Memorial Day to Labor Day, summer rates are promoted to attract summer vacationers. These vacationers usually belong to a specific market: families. Summer rates can be either flat room rates or person rates (that is, rates that vary with the number of guests staying in the room). The rates are flexible and capacity-controlled, based on local market conditions. The category can be open or closed at the discretion of the hotel. Because it is a promotional rate, the summer rate type should be of the $49, $59, $69, $79, or $89 (and so forth) variety.

Club-Level. This rate is assigned to rooms located on the club floors, executive floors, or concierge-attended areas. This is a premium rate that is higher than the rack or corporate rates for the same room type on a non-club-level floor. To vie with other hotels that also have club or tower floors, a hotel's rate should be competitive, but in line with the hotel's total positioning strategy.

Other Rates

The following additional rates apply to very specific markets:

- *Package plans* provide rates for a room plus other items, such as meals, amenities, or a car.

- *Contracted rates* apply to rooms contracted for a period of more than 30 days. These may be airline crew rooms, relocation rooms, or training rooms (if not preferred rate rooms or another category).

- *Seasonal rates* incorporate premiums added or subtracted based on the desirability of the locale due to climate. These rates are usually set for in-season or peak periods, out-of-season or off-peak periods, and "shoulder" periods (the periods between peak and off-peak seasons).

- *Group rates* are based on volume or length of stay.

- *Suite rates* vary. At the lower end, a hotel can be competitive; at the upper end, the property can strive for top dollar and positioning as the best hotel.

- *Government rates* are based on the market, competition, and need for business from government-sector employees.

- *Retirees or military personnel* are often given a lower rate. This rate is applied to a limited capacity or number of rooms allocated for these market segments.

Exhibit 1   Hotel Room Rate Categories

	Standard Room	Superior Room	Deluxe Room
Rack	$125	$135	$145
Club-Level	135	145	165
Corporate	95*	105	115
Corporate Club	115	125	135
Super-Saver	89†		

*Rate published in airline terminals and directories.
†Rate which is managed and controlled by hotel and is used to sell empty rooms in "valley" or down periods.

Ranges

Ranges of rates should be used in the following rate categories: corporate, rack, club-level, and any other category for which there is not a flat room rate. Ranges should be broad to allow for selling up or down within the range. As mentioned earlier in the discussion of the corporate rate, a hotel should publicize the low end of the range (for example, "$99 and up") in the automated reservations system, directories, and other listings in cases where the listing space does not allow the hotel to offer the full range. Ranges may relate to various criteria, such as room types, locations, and views (see Exhibit 1).

Rate Strategies

A hotel's managers must oversee and control the property's rate categories. Management must know when to open or close these categories and must effectively control or limit the number of rooms in each rate category. Managers must also understand how to take full advantage of rate ranges. They must know how to establish rates to meet current market segments' needs, as well as how to use these rates to solicit increased business from additional, desirable markets. Effective rate strategies can help managers accomplish such goals.

Examples. The following examples of rate strategies are based on the grid-positioning concept. A property's position on the grid is a function of both the strength of its market and the position of its product within the market. This grid position helps determine what actions should be taken with respect to rate strategies (see Exhibit 2).

Strategy 1: Strong Market/Strong Product

- Maximize rates in periods of strong demand (sell up and/or raise rates).
- Stay ahead of the competition in servicing accounts.
- Use the hotel's quality to win over business in valley periods at competitive rates.
- Move business to days or periods of lower demand.

Exhibit 2   Competitive/Market Positioning Grid

		MARKET		
		Strong	Moderate	Weak
COMPETITIVE POSITIONING	Strong	1 Strong Market Strong Product	2 Moderate Market Strong Product	3 Weak Market Strong Product
	Average	4 Strong Market Average Product	5 Moderate Market Average Product	6 Weak Market Average Product
	Weak	7 Strong Market Weak Product	8 Moderate Market Weak Product	9 Weak Market Weak Product

Strategy 2: Moderate Market/Strong Product

- Strive for market share via competitive pricing.
- Capture better (rate) market segments for the future.
- Use product strength to sell up.
- Don't price the hotel out of the market.

Strategy 3: Weak Market/Strong Product

- Go after repeat business by building loyalty. (Also, "Love thy intermediary.")
- Build the base—shrink the empties. As you build your base of rooms sold, it allows you to begin selling the remaining rooms at higher prices. Go for *all* the business!
- Use several different pricing strategies that relate specifically to different market segments.

Strategy 4: Strong Market/Average Product

- Price slightly below competitors to gain market share.
- Go after the value-oriented market—that is, the segments that are more price sensitive but that still want a high-quality facility.

- Be sure the hotel's product is sold and perceived as an acceptable alternative: not as the most expensive, but as the best.

- Capture a corporate or preferred "base"—then sell up.

Strategy 5: Moderate Market/Average Product

- Go after market share with lead promotions and rates.

- Distinguish the hotel's product in the minds of a specific market segment, and *own* that segment.

- Price the product to the public as number two, but concentrate heavily on selling corporate and super-saver rates (as a better value by stressing price).

- Give a reason to come back—provide an incentive such as "an upgrade to club floor on your next visit."

Strategy 6: Weak Market/Average Product

- Go after competitors—take advantage of their weaknesses. Win over their business via pricing.

- Go after all market segments by using short-term promotions.

- Create new market segments or reasons to stay (such as local festivals or special events, and so on).

- Shrink the product or rooms base. Seek contracted rooms such as for airline crews that provide revenue and reduce the number of rooms available in the inventory, allowing you to sell remaining rooms at a higher price.

Strategy 7: Strong Market/Weak Product

- Maximize rate on high demand days.

- Promote relatively lower rates on weak demand days.

- Consider upgrading your product and raising rates.

In positions 8 and 9, rate strategy will be of little or no value, as the combination of weak product and lack of demand suggests selling the hotel. In position 8, if the market is expected to move from moderate to strong, consider upgrading the product and following position 7 strategies.

Rate Comparisons

You can keep track of your competitors' rates by reviewing their advertisements, calling their toll-free numbers, looking up their published rates on automated systems, and talking to your customers to determine if your rates are in line. One of the benefits of knowing the competition's rates is that this information enables a manager to assess his or her rate strategy and implement new strategies if required. Exhibit 3 is an example of a weekly intelligence sheet format, and Exhibit 4 shows a similar format filled in. Many hotel managers regularly chart information

Exhibit 3   Sample Weekly Intelligence Sheet Format

RATES 800 Tel. No.	Competitor I	Competitor II	Competitor III	Competitor IV	Your Hospitality Hotel
Rack	$ –$	$ –$	$ –$	$ –$	$ –$
Corporate	$	$	$	$	$ –$ –$
Corporate Club	$	$	$	$	$ –$ –$
Super-Saver	$	$	$	$	$ –$
Hotel Direct Tel. No.					
Rack	$ –$	$ –$	$ –$	$ –$	$ –$
Corporate	$	$	$	$	$ –$ –$
Corporate Club	$	$	$	$	$ –$ –$
Super-Saver	$	$	$	$	$
Weekend	$	$	$	$	$

Questions

1. Are we competitively priced?
2. What are the publicized rates in airline terminals?
3. Are we positioning our hotel correctly?
4. What actions should be taken immediately?

about their competitors' rates on a sheet such as this so that they can effectively develop rate strategies.

Airfares

The principles of rate strategy for air carriers are not very different from those for hotels. Where hotels deal with occupied rooms, average rates, and rooms revenue, airlines deal with load factors (occupied seats), average revenue per passenger mile, and passenger revenues. Instead of the term "rate," airlines use the terms "fare" or "tariff." There is general consistency among airlines in their use of symbols and definitions, although frequently the fine-print **disclaimers** and restrictions vary by carrier. Exhibit 5 is a list of the various fares and related symbols used for classes of airline service.

Carrier Strategies

The large number of fares shown in Exhibit 5 suggests the broad spectrum of rate strategies that air carriers use to achieve market share. These strategies range from offering all first-class services to offering all deep-discount services, with virtually every variation in between. Some carriers select a strategy for competitive reasons,

Exhibit 4   Sample Filled In Weekly Intelligence Sheet

	Competitor I	Competitor II	Competitor III	Competitor IV	Hospitality Hotel
General					
Rack	$100 –$125	$105 –$135	$110 –$140	$115 –$155	*$100 –$165
Corporate	$ 95	$ 95	$101	$103	*$ 98 –$103 –$108
Corporate Club	$105	$115	$120	$122	$118 –$123 –$128
Super-Saver	$ 85	$ 89	$ 95	$ 99	$ 88
Corporate*					
City I	$ 79	$100	$120	$135	*$ 98 –$108 –$128
City II	$115	$118	$119	$130	*$115 –$125 –$135
City III	$ 86	$ 95	$105	$105	*$ 95 –$105 –$115
City IV	$ 89	$ 98	$ 99	N/A	$ 99 –$104 –$109
Corporate*					
City V	$ 92	$ 91	$ 81	N/A	*$ 79 –$ 89 –$ 99†
City VI	$ 79	$ 86	N/A	N/A	*$ 85 –$ 95 –$105†

*Publicized rate in airline terminals.
†Not best product—Here we have better hotels with which to compete.

others because of their market position or even based on the hour of departure per flight.

In essence, revenue management for airlines is similar to that for hotels or any other business. The bottom line on the revenue side is to maximize revenue per flight—in other words, to get the highest yield (of revenue) out of each seat or each flight. How this yield is achieved—whether by selling many seats at lower prices or fewer seats at higher prices—is fairly well defined as the selected marketing strategy of the carrier.

Other factors that affect airlines' strategies and have counterparts in hotels are labor costs, fleet and size of aircraft (analogous to the size of a hotel), and route structure (analogous to hotel location). Then there is the consumer: the consumer who is loyal to a brand or carrier responds to the price and level or quality of service based on his or her changing needs. An air traveler on a business expense account may be willing to pay for an upgrade, while that same person traveling with his or her family may consider price to override upgrade desires. When airfare wars break out, the consumer benefits. The airline that "wins" is usually the carrier with deeper pockets (which can absorb more losses). The loser is the less financially stable carrier.

Rental Car Rates

How rental car rates are presented often depends on who is applying the rates as well as the day(s), rental period, and time of the year during which a car is rented. The following is a general overview of the types of rental car rates and the factors affecting the rates.

Exhibit 5   Airline Service Fares and Related Symbols

A	First class discounted
B	Coach/economy discounted
Bn	Controlled inventory or limited number of seats available—night coach rate (usually after 9, 10, or 11 P.M., depending on carrier)
C	Business class: a class of service and related fare between first class and coach, aimed at the international business traveler
Cn	Night or off-peak (peak travel hours/days) business class
D	Business class discounted
F	First class service, usually the highest fare (generally synonymous with P below)
Fn	Night/off-peak coach in first class compartment (a lower-than-usual first class fare that allows seating in first class)
H	Coach economy discounted
J	Business class premium
K	Thrift: usually capacity-controlled or offered in off-peak hours; a fare lower than coach
L	Thrift discounted
M	Coach economy discounted
P	First class premium
Q	Coach economy discounted
Qn	Night coach economy discounted
R	Supersonic
S	Standard class
T	Coach economy discounted
U	No reservation services/baggage check limitations
V	Thrift discounted
Vn	Night thrift discounted
Y	Coach economy
Yn	Night/off-peak coach in other than first class compartment

- *Weekday.* Usually applied Monday through Thursday, this rate generally is a premium rate (except in the case of a weekend destination location, for which a weekend rate may be the premium rate).

- *Weekend.* This rate is usually in effect for Friday, Saturday, and Sunday. (Many define it as noon on Thursday through noon on Monday.) In most locations, a substantially discounted rate is offered on weekends.

- *Daily.* Usually one of the highest rate categories, this rate is applied if the car is rented for a 12- or 24-hour period only. (Hourly rates, if offered, are usually at a premium over daily.)

- *2-, 3-, 4-, or 5-day.* Rental firms often offer some form of discounted rate based on the number of days (12- or 24-hour periods) for which a car is rented.

- *Weekly.* This rate is discounted based on a 5-, 6-, or 7-day rental.

- *Monthly.* This discounted rate is applied to long-term rentals.

- *Corporate.* This rate is usually a 10 or 20 percent (or deeper) discount, based on a company's levels of use.

- *Preferred corporate.* Rental firms may offer even deeper discounts to corporations that are frequent users. Discounts of 30 percent and even more are common.

- *Class of car.* Rental rates vary based on the type of auto—the generally used classes are luxury, standard, compact, and subcompact. (One problem with using this rating is that not all firms' definitions of each car type are the same.)

- *Other rates.* Holiday specials, seasonal rates (in Florida, for example), and event-related rates (such as for the Super Bowl) can also be developed and offered.

Rental Car Strategies

With all the variations available in rental periods, classes of cars, special rates, and upgrades, rental car strategies are plentiful. Some firms rent luxury-class vehicles at standard-class rates or at fixed rates—"Lincolns at $59.95," for example. Others opt for straight price sells only—"$29 a day." Still others may use service as their marketing pitch—"No lines. We'll meet you at the baggage claim with your rental car."

There are charge-per-mile and free-unlimited-mileage marketing options as well. These strategies depend on competition and other variables such as fuel costs, days used, distance traveled, and other factors.

The location(s) and number of rental points is a strong factor in brand selection. As is true with airlines and hotels, brand loyalty in the rental car industry is a function of price and service in meeting challenging and changing consumer needs. Just as occupied seats or occupied rooms are critical to revenue production for airlines and hotels, rented units per day for rental car firms are also critical. Whether the break-even point is achieved through volume, price, or a combination of both factors, the strategies include the same components: rate setting, rate management, and maximization of revenue.

Cruise Ship Rates

Cruise rate options and strategies depend largely on the itineraries and configuration of the specific ship. In general, cruises are priced according to the number of days/nights—for example, "5 days/4 nights." The rate is usually inclusive—that is, it includes 3 meals per day. In addition, the rate will vary based on a particular ship's cabin or room layout. Generally, the higher-level cabins or rooms with outside views will command maximum rates, while lower-deck, inside cabins will be the least expensive.

Key Terms

corporate rate
disclaimer
preferred rate

restrictions
super-saver

REVIEW QUIZ

When you feel you have covered all of the material in this chapter, answer these questions. Choose the *best* answer. Check your answers with the correct ones found on the Review Quiz Answer Key at the end of this book.

1. A hotel's rack rate should be used as a(n) _____ rate.

    a. intermediate
    b. non-ranged
    c. valley-period
    d. positioning

2. Ranges of rates for hotel rooms should be:

    a. narrow.
    b. broad.
    c. based on the hotel's retiree market.
    d. based on the hotel's government market.

3. Which of the following is one action within the rate strategy for a hotel that offers a strong product in a strong market?

    a. Move business to days or periods of lower demand.
    b. Move business to days or periods of higher demand.
    c. Lower the hotel's rate.
    d. Keep rates the same.

Chapter Outline

Pricing Techniques
    Technique 1: Offering a Price Range
    Technique 2: Selling Up
    Technique 3: Selling Down
    Technique 4: Focusing on Revenue
       and Profit per Unit
    Technique 5: Using the Inflation
       Rate-Plus Factor
    Technique 6: Using Intuitive Judgment
       and Flexible Breakeven Analysis
    Technique 7: Rate Pyramiding
    Technique 8: Analyzing Market
       Segments

Learning Objectives

1. Define "pricing," and explain the importance of offering consumers price ranges and choices in hospitality products and services. (pp. 193–195)

2. Explain the concept of selling up and some general circumstances under which the technique may be applied. (pp. 195–196)

3. Describe the cost-plus theory and its application in selling down. (pp. 196–197)

4. Compare the technique of focusing on revenue and profit per unit to that of emphasizing average checks/rates/percentages. (p. 197)

5. Summarize the use of the inflation rate-plus factor. (pp. 197–198)

6. Explain the importance of making intuitive judgments, and outline the concepts and steps for conducting a breakeven analysis. (pp. 198–199)

7. Describe the uses of rate pyramiding. (pp. 199–200)

8. Explain how analyzing market segments can help maximize revenue for a hospitality operation. (pp. 200–201)

15

Applying Key Marketing Methodologies: Pricing Strategies

THE GAMUT OF MARKETING TACTICS extends beyond generating revenue through sales, advertising, public relations, promotions, direct mail, and packaging. The ultimate generator of revenue and profit is pricing. Pricing is the application of rates in a selective manner to generate sales.

Once you have a base of business for your hospitality product or service, the challenge becomes how to maximize revenues and profits, build beyond the base, and gain every possible benefit from your marketing efforts. The keys to achieving success are a creative mind, a practical perspective, and a willingness to work hard at implementing ideas. Inherent in these three characteristics is a willingness to listen to new ideas and, when necessary, to discard traditional beliefs and measures of hospitality industry success.

Pricing Techniques

Pricing can be used to maximize revenue and profit. The eight techniques described in this chapter offer a broad selection of effective tools that you can use to better focus and maximize your marketing efforts.

Technique 1: Offering a Price Range

For years, Marriott and Hilton have done an outstanding job of offering a price range for their rooms. They give the consumer a choice of rates from which to select. This multi-rate structure permits the consumer to select a rate from within a range. For instance, a reservations agent might state, "We have rooms available from $119 to $159." A price-conscious consumer can ask for the $119 room. A consumer who is not interested in the cheapest rate might ask for a room at $129. Guests who are not concerned at all with rate (perhaps individual travelers on unrestricted expense accounts) may well opt for rooms at $149 or $159. Using a price range allows a hotel to sell essentially the same room at different rates.

Offering a range is the basic starting point in increasing revenue per room. A trained reservations agent can attempt to "sell up"—that is, attempt to persuade the guest to select a room at a rate above the minimum. For example, a reservations agent might say, "We still have rooms available at $139 and $149" and the guest might take one of these rates. The hotel may well have sold the same room for $119 had the reservations agent not sold up. If the guest resists and says, "Don't you have any rooms at the $119 rate?" the agent could respond, "Let me check ... yes, I can make a room available to you that evening for $119."

Other chains (for instance, Holiday Inns) have believed that publicizing and honoring a fixed rate for single and double rooms is the strongest promise they could make to the consumer.

The following example looks at Holiday Inns and determines the impact of selling up by using a price range instead of stating the fixed rates. (For illustrative purposes, this first example makes broad assumptions that are *not* intended to represent actual financial results. This example is used solely to point out the potential advantages in using ranges of rates from which consumers can select.)

Example: Holiday Inns—Price Ranges. With over 300,000 rooms, Holiday Inn Worldwide is one of the world's largest hotel chains. This example assumes that the chain's occupancy averages 70 percent, resulting in 210,000 rooms that are occupied on a nightly basis. There will be a number of nights during the year for which occupancy is 100 percent. Let's conservatively assume that selling up can occur in half of the locations only 50 times (nights) during the year. The 210,000 occupied rooms per night thus is reduced to 105,000, multiplied by 50 nights on which rooms can be sold up. Therefore:

105,000 eligible rooms × 50 potential sell-up nights = 5,250,000 sell-up room nights

What if, rather than stating a fixed single and double rate, Holiday Inn chose to go to price ranges and trained its front desk personnel to sell up? Assume this selling-up process resulted in only $1.50 more in rate on the average room per night. Multiply $1.50 by 5,250,000 room nights. The result would mean an additional $7,875,000 each year in Holiday Inn room revenue. Moreover, this money essentially drops to the bottom line; assuming Holiday Inn has a profit ratio of four percent of total revenue, sales would have to increase by $197 million to generate the same amount of profit.

Offering a price range is a simple technique that maximizes profits through marketing. The technique offers the consumer a choice of rates and human nature sees to it that the low rate is not always selected. There are many methods by which to establish price ranges; for example, hotels may vary rates based on room amenities, location, view, floor, furnishings, and so forth. The important point is to offer the choice and benefit for the customer's selection.

Even if the rate range is narrow ($72–$78), you can still realize the benefits by ensuring that the low end of the range is equivalent to the fixed rate you normally would request. This helps eliminate the risk in using ranges, because the low end of the range is identical to the fixed published rate, and both are equally available and accessible to the consumer.

The way to maintain a firm promise to the consumer and still have the ability to offer a price range can be shown using Holiday Inns in another example.

Example: Holiday Inns—Consumer Choices. Perhaps because the chain believed in the value of the promise of charging its stated rate but recognized the need to maximize room revenues, Holiday Inns changed its approach to room rates in the 1980s and began offering consumers a selection of rooms and rates.

Holiday Inns' approach was to do away with the traditional single- and double-room classifications and stated rate. The chain decided to offer customers three choices: "special" (priced at the low end of the rate range), "standard" (priced in the middle of the rate range), and "king leisure" (the top-price rooms, all containing a king-size bed). The hotels now had some ability to maximize room revenue through the consumer's selection of accommodation.

This approach to categorizing the rooms also relates to the different needs and desires of different market segments. The "special" category appeals to older clientele, retirees, or those on restricted expense allowances; the "standard" appeals to the broader spectrum of the market; and the "king leisure" attracts executive travelers, weekenders, escape-weekend couples, and those whose height requires a larger bed. While most Holiday Inn rooms fell into the "standard" category, this approach still offered the consumer a choice of rooms and the operator the ability to offer a price range.

Technique 2: Selling Up

Making money is seldom easy. It frequently requires hard work, sound research, and good timing. The hard work includes keeping records, analyzing data, plotting trends, identifying the right timing, and doing your homework. All of these tasks play an important role in the technique called **selling up.** As stated earlier, selling up is seeking to obtain a higher price for a room, selling a higher profit margin item, or simply seeking a premium price when demand favors the seller. Selling up has many applications; it can mean promoting a higher-priced item on a menu or offering a higher-priced vacation. The example that follows may include some ideas that can help you make money by selling up.

Example: The Well-Trained Food Server. Dimitri owned an upscale restaurant and always managed to show better profit margins and higher check averages than his competitors. His technique for achieving this exceptional performance was called "recognition, recommendation, and results," or the "3 R's."

Dimitri trained his food service staff to recognize regular customers and those trying to impress others. He instructed his personnel first to ask which entrées interested the customer the most. Depending on the response, the food server was then to take one of three courses of action:

- If the choice of entrée was a high-priced, high-profit item, the food server was to agree with the customer's selection by saying, "An excellent choice this evening—we have had many compliments on that."

- If the choice was a mid-priced item with a relatively low profit margin, the food server's response was simply, "That is a superb dish; however, tonight I would highly recommend [name of the same entrée as in the first action above]." If customer resistance or indecision was noted due to the price of the recommendation, an interjection was then appropriate: "May I also recommend [name of an alternate mid-priced item with a high profit margin]? It is really outstanding this evening."

- The third approach was reserved for the potential high spender who just could not make up his or her mind. It was called the "Dimitri recommendation." In this situation, the food server was instructed to say, "Please take your time to make your selection. I'll be right back." Then Dimitri would appear, introduce himself, welcome his guests, and, of course, provide his personal recommendation for the menu item with the highest profit margin. Who could resist the owner's recommendation? The recognition of the opportunity to sell up and the use of the recommendation resulted in the third "R": results.

Technique 3: Selling Down

More and more travelers today are seeking the "best" value—which often translates into the best price or lowest rate. "Selling down" works to address the price-oriented guest or "rate resistor." The premise is that by using a rate range and quoting a rate in the mid to upper portion of the range, you can sell down to accommodate the rate resistor. For example:

> *Guest:* "What are your rates for Tuesday?"
>
> *Agent:* "We have rooms available at $139, $149, and $159."
>
> *Guest:* "That's too much. Don't you have any lower rates?"
>
> *Agent:* "Let me check. Yes, I do have a few rooms available that night at our lowest rate of $119."

The premise behind selling down is that revenue in excess of cost is desirable, even if average rate or profit margins decline. Knowing periods of weak demand for your product or service and knowing your fixed costs are essential elements in successfully applying this technique.

The **cost-plus theory** simply states that revenue in excess of the cost of the unused product or service (an airline seat, hotel room, bus seat, etc.) is desirable. The following example shows how the cost-plus theory can be put to work.

Example: Cost-Plus Theory. A 200-room budget motel owner charted his occupancy pattern and analyzed his costs per room. He discovered that for four months a year, his property never exceeded 50 percent occupancy. He further learned that his average fixed cost per room (that is, the cost to him whether the room was occupied or not) was $6. He then calculated the incremental or variable costs (costs that are incurred only when a room is occupied, such as linen laundry and utilities) at $4 per room. His total costs therefore were $10 per occupied room. The motel's single-room rate was $32 to $38 per night.

The owner recognized that for four months of the year, half his rooms were empty and costing him $6 per night. Applying the cost-plus theory, he solicited business for the four-month period with a special program. *New* customers who stayed in his motel during the slack period were offered single rooms for $20 a night, if they stayed three to six nights; $18 a night, if they stayed seven to ten nights; and $15 per night, if they stayed 11 or more nights.

The results were dramatic—occupancy went up to 68 percent for the four-month period. His average daily rate and his profit ratio went down, but his actual profits went up. Furthermore, when the program ended, the owner was able to retain more than 40 percent of the newcomers as regular repeat guests at the standard rates. He was not only covering his costs and earning excess revenues during his slow period, he was also converting trial business into repeat business.

Technique 4: Focusing on Revenue and Profit per Unit

In the previous example, the motel owner's competitors may have turned away low-rate rooms business because it diluted the average rate. If that were the case, what actually occurred was that they lost an opportunity to generate revenue. Such an overemphasis on average checks, rate, or percentages can become counter-productive. Unless your product or service is in constant strong demand and in a strong market area, focusing instead on revenue and profit *per unit* is a technique that can help you.

The revenue and profit per unit technique maximizes total revenues and total profits per unit. In the case of a lodging facility, the unit may be the available or occupied room. In the case of a food service facility, the unit may be a seat. Focusing on revenue and profit per unit is critical where the unused unit (room, airline seat, bus seat, and so on) is a perishable item. This means that once the night is over or the plane has left or the bus has pulled out, the fixed costs per unit remain, but the opportunity to generate per-unit revenue is gone, and zero revenue and less overall profit are the results.

For example, assume that a hotel has fixed costs of $20 per room per night and an average daily rate of $89. An empty room not only produces no revenue, it costs $20. Therefore, it makes sense to sell rooms that would otherwise go unused at a discount, even though the discount reduces the ADR. Selling unused rooms in this hotel for, say, $49 results in a lower ADR, but in greater total revenue and profit.

Technique 5: Using the Inflation Rate-Plus Factor

For many years a large national chain that relied on royalty revenue from room sales was concerned about its franchisees' lack of aggressiveness in raising rates. Many of the franchisees were absentee owners, some were looking for tax write-offs, and others lacked business sense.

The chain published a directory twice a year and solicited new rates prior to printing the new directory. An analysis of the return cards from the franchisees revealed that a large group consistently raised their rates five percent every six months. Another smaller group raised their room rates only for the January direc-tory and indicated "no change" for the June directory. When the inflation rate was very low, the chain's concern was not very intense; however, in one 12-month period, the inflation rate jumped over 12 percent and the ramifications started to become apparent. The buying power of the royalty revenue and fees based on rooms revenue began to shrink dramatically. The costs for media, personnel, sup-plies, and so on were increasing at double the rate of the inflow of incremental royalty fees. The company realized it needed to take action.

Using the **inflation rate-plus factor,** the chain began an intensive program to educate its franchisees that their rates should increase in proportion to the inflation rate factor for costs associated with their facilities. The *plus* concept suggested that increasing rates beyond the inflation rate factor (where demand allowed) would enhance the profit margin.

This program worked well, but timing was another factor. The chain needed the franchisees to provide rate changes 90 days in advance of directory publication, and these rates were in effect for six months. Even if the franchisees were conscientious and raised their rates, by the time the directory was published, three percent was lost to inflation (based on the 12 percent inflation factor). Also, by the time the directory rates were replaced six months later, an additional six percent would have been lost to inflation.

To help alleviate this problem, the chain's management invested in an alternate printing schedule and directory format that cut the 90-day lead time to 30 days. In addition, the chain went from publishing two directories per year to four. Publication costs went up, but were more than covered by the increase in the incremental royalty revenues being received.

Technique 6: Using Intuitive Judgment and Flexible Breakeven Analysis

Establishing the most effective price to charge for your product or service is based on many factors. The local market and competition will, in all likelihood, prove to be dominant factors in influencing a pricing decision. However, the local market conditions and your need to break even need not overly restrict your judgment or creativity in establishing a pricing strategy. Frequently, the most important factors in selecting the optimum rate or pricing strategy will come from your own intuitive judgment about what will work best for the product or service in view of the local market and competition.

Once the market has been analyzed and the competition profiled, a breakeven analysis is another tool to assist in selecting the optimum pricing strategy. A breakeven analysis is a look at the relationship between total sales and total expenses for an establishment, be it a lodging facility, airplane, or restaurant. Often depicted on a simple graph, the analysis demonstrates the effects of changing the levels of total sales in terms of dollars or volumes. The vertical (Y) axis represents revenue. The horizontal (X) axis represents volume in units sold, which can be expressed as occupancy, occupied seats, and so on.

Total costs at the various levels of volume are plotted with a straight line that crosses the Y-axis at the level of fixed costs. In the simplest terms, total costs are a combination of fixed costs (costs that are incurred whether sales occur or not) and variable costs (costs that are incurred only when sales are made). Therefore, at zero sales, total costs equal fixed costs ($18,000 in Exhibit 1); at any level of sales beyond zero, total costs equal fixed costs plus the number of units sold times the variable cost per unit. Total revenue is also entered as a straight line starting at zero on both axes (since, unlike fixed costs that are incurred regardless of sales, revenue is only received as sales are made; that is, zero units sold means zero revenue). The point at which these lines cross represents the breakeven point, the point at which sales are adequate to cover costs. Any point above the total cost line represents profits; any point below the total cost line represents losses. In the sample shown in Exhibit 1, the breakeven point can be stated either in dollar volume ($24,000) or in unit volume (2,400 units).

Exhibit 1 Sample Breakeven Chart

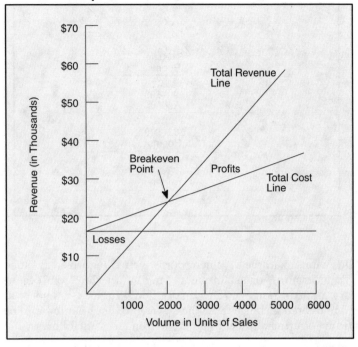

Breakeven charts are useful tools, although they are not always precise. There are also two mathematical equations that can be used to calculate the breakeven points for units or sales.

The breakeven point in units is determined by first subtracting the variable cost per unit from the selling price per unit. The result is then divided into the total fixed costs:

$$\text{Breakeven point in units} = \frac{\text{Total fixed costs}}{\text{Selling price per unit} - \text{variable cost per unit}}$$

To determine the breakeven point in sales, multiply the breakeven point in units by the selling price:

$$\text{Breakeven point in sales} = \text{Breakeven point in units} \times \text{Selling price}$$

With the tools of the basic breakeven chart and the unit and sales equations, you can use the flexible breakeven analysis to establish profit objectives and the required sales revenue to meet these objectives.

Technique 7: Rate Pyramiding

This technique is a hybrid of Technique 1, offering a price range, and Technique 2, selling up. **Rate pyramiding** is segmenting or identifying the product or service by different characteristics or descriptions. The distinctions may be like those in the

Exhibit 2   Rate Pyramid

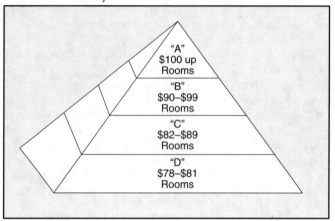

earlier Holiday Inns example in which rooms were categorized as "special," "standard," or "king leisure," or as simple as "mountain view" or "ocean view." For each category, a rate or range of rates is specified. When customers inquire about a room, they are offered a choice from the "pyramid" (see Exhibit 2). The technique then goes from "offering a price range" to "selling up," as follows:

> *Front desk clerk:* "Welcome to the Clifton Hotel, Mr. Jones."
>
> *Mr. Jones:* "What are your rates?"
>
> *Front desk clerk:* "Our rates range from $78 for an economy room, from $82 for a standard room, from $90 for a deluxe room, and $100 and up for a suite."
>
> *Mr. Jones:* "I'd like an economy room, please."
>
> *Front desk clerk:* "Mr. Jones, we only have an $80 economy room available; however, we do have a very nice $82 standard room that I think you would like. It is in a better location and has a better view of the city."

If Mr. Jones opts for the $82 standard room, he has been "pyramided" up $4 from the $78 economy room he wanted. If he opts for the $80 economy room, he has still been sold up $2. Many people will not ask for an economy room simply because they do not want the cheapest room; usually they do not want the most expensive, either. By offering a pyramid rate structure, you capitalize on this tendency and can directly affect your revenue potential.

Technique 8: Analyzing Market Segments

Another way to view pricing or revenue generation is by the type of business. The mix or types of guests in a facility are not all the same in terms of their needs, desires, and level of expenditures. On one hand, kids may stay free, eat hot dogs, or not eat on your premises at all. On the other hand, a man attending a group meeting may eat a banquet meal, drink in your bar, and buy gifts for his children and spouse in your gift shop. Given a choice of to whom you should sell your room, the decision becomes clearer.

Marriott has been a leader in food and beverage sales in its hotels. While it is true that Marriott creates restaurant concepts that appeal to the local market, it is also true that Marriott's mix of business is heavily oriented toward groups, executives, and corporate meetings. The result of this orientation is that it produces higher revenues throughout the properties.

You do not have to be as sophisticated as Marriott to analyze your market segments and go after the revenue producers. For example, take the case of a local restaurant called Nick's. The restaurant appeals to a broad spectrum of consumers, ranging from families, to office workers, to couples dining out. Nick's faced a choice—a local office supply company wanted to book the banquet room for Friday evening for 15 people for a sales award dinner. At the same time, the River City boys baseball champions requested the room for 23 boys and 2 adult coaches for a dinner.

Nick's selected the office supply company with only 15 people instead of the baseball champions with the party of 25. The restaurant's analysis revealed that while both groups selected the same item (at the same cost) from the banquet menu, the office supply group was expected to purchase enough alcoholic beverages to more than offset the reduced food revenue from 10 fewer people. The message is simple: Whether you're Marriott or Nick's, go after the high-volume/high-profit producers.

Key Terms

cost-plus theory
inflation rate-plus factor
rate pyramiding
selling up

REVIEW QUIZ

When you feel you have covered all of the material in this chapter, answer these questions. Choose the *best* answer. Check your answers with the correct ones found on the Review Quiz Answer Key at the end of this book.

1. When a hotel offers ranges of prices for its rooms:

   a. its operating costs generally go down.
   b. consumers lose choices.
   c. the operator gains more opportunities to sell up.
   d. a and c.

2. Focusing on revenue and profit per unit is critical where the unused unit is:

   a. a perishable item.
   b. a non-perishable item.
   c. an inflation-driven item.
   d. a fee-based service.

3. The breakeven point in sales can be calculated by:

   a. multiplying the breakeven point in units by the selling price.
   b. dividing the selling price by the breakeven point in units.
   c. dividing total fixed costs by the selling price.
   d. dividing the selling price by total fixed costs.

Chapter Outline

Market Mix
    Example: The Church Convention
Pricing
    Example: The Park, the Plaza, and the
      Palace
Yield Management
Revenue Maximization in Practice

Learning Objectives

1. Describe how market mix is used to maximize revenue. (pp. 205–207)

2. Give examples of how pricing strategies are used to maximize revenue. (pp. 207–208)

3. Describe how yield management is used to maximize revenue. (pp. 208–210)

4. Identify objectives, strategies, and key tactics of revenue maximization. (pp. 210–212)

Applying Key Marketing Methodologies: Revenue Maximization

REVENUE MAXIMIZATION consists of the total management of revenue production. It involves the selection and use of marketing tools to bring in the desired market mix. It also involves researching your market and competition and developing correct pricing for each market segment. And it requires the application of yield management to set rates according to changes in demand and supply patterns. The smooth management of all three processes results in **revenue maximization:**

Market Mix + Pricing + Yield Management = Revenue Maximization

Market Mix

Market mix is the combination of different guest categories that a hotel tries to attract. Before you can manage yield (defined later in the chapter) or set prices, you need to determine the targeted market mix that provides you maximum revenue and profit potential. Research has shown that there are different levels of rate resistance and different on-premises incremental spending patterns for different segments of the market. For example, executives on unrestricted expense accounts or attending corporate group meetings are likely to pay higher room rates and spend more in high-profit areas (the bar, gift shops, etc.) than government employees or those on restricted expense accounts. The same spending differences can be found among leisure travelers. For example, incentive groups usually produce higher revenues than individuals traveling with small children (see Exhibit 1).

Guidelines for determining marketing priorities and sales objectives may be as simple as targeting only certain market segments in the high-potential categories or as complex as tracking and modeling revenue and profitability by industry category. The principle is the same: seek the highest revenue-producing market segments with the greatest overall profit potential. An example of the use of the "market mix" principle to maximize revenue is discussed in the following section.

Example: The Church Convention

Two 400-room hotels in the same market, both having rack rates of $150, know their city is likely to sell out during a large three-day church convention. Hotel A believes a rate of $130 for a double room and $110 for a single is acceptable, projecting

Exhibit 1   Revenue and Profit Segmentation

Market Segments with High Revenue/Profit Potential

- Executives with unrestricted expense accounts
- Corporate group-meeting attendees
- Selected association group-meeting attendees

Market Segments with Medium Revenue/Profit Potential

- Couples without children, business travel
- Couples without children, pleasure travel
- Selected association group-meeting attendees

Market Segments with Low Revenue/Profit Potential

- Executives/business travelers with restricted expense accounts
- Rooms-only weekenders
- Families with children
- Government, military, and education market segments

---

that 60 percent of its rooms will achieve double occupancy, or a rate of $130. Hotel A likes the idea of selling out during the convention, and it commits to a church group nine months out. Hotel A revenue projection is as follows:

$$3 \text{ days} \times (400 \text{ rooms} \times 60\%) \times \$130 \text{ per room} \quad = \quad \$93,600$$
$$3 \text{ days} \times (400 \text{ rooms} \times 40\%) \times \$110 \text{ per person} \quad = \quad \$52,800$$
$$\text{Total Room Revenue:} \qquad\qquad\qquad\qquad\qquad \$146,400$$

Historic trends have shown that this particular church group will not generate much in-house food and beverage revenue. Let's assume in-house food and beverage revenue (all food, as this is a non-alcohol group) has been estimated at a per diem of $15 or:

$$240 \text{ rooms} \times 2 \text{ people} \times 3 \text{ days} \times \$15 \quad = \quad \$21,600$$
$$160 \text{ rooms} \times 1 \text{ person} \times 3 \text{ days} \times \$15 \quad = \quad \$7,200$$
$$\text{Total Food \& Beverage Revenue:} \qquad\qquad \$28,800$$

Thus, Hotel A estimates that this church group will generate total revenue of $175,200. Let's look at how the other 400-room hotel approaches the same week of the church convention.

Hotel B reviews the same research and knows it too can sell out. However, Hotel B believes in revenue maximization. It knows that 200 of its rooms that particular week, like most other weeks, are projected to be occupied with executives at the average corporate and concierge level rates of $140. The sales department has a commitment from a small corporate group for 50 rooms per day over the three-day period, at $105 per room plus meal functions. Since Hotel A and two other competitors usually sell their rooms to individual executive travelers and/or high-rate incentive groups and have committed 50 percent of their rooms to the church group convention, Hotel B believes it will capture another 100 rooms at the full corporate rate of $135. Finally, knowing a citywide sellout will occur, it believes it can get the full rack rate of $150 for 25 rooms and can sell its remaining rooms to church-group overflow guests at $110 at the last moment, thereby having a room revenue mix as follows:

$$200 \text{ rooms} \times 3 \text{ nights} \times \$140 = \$84,000$$
$$50 \text{ rooms} \times 3 \text{ nights} \times \$105 = \$15,750$$
$$100 \text{ rooms} \times 3 \text{ nights} \times \$135 = \$40,500$$
$$25 \text{ rooms} \times 3 \text{ nights} \times \$150 = \$11,250$$
$$25 \text{ rooms} \times 3 \text{ nights} \times \$110 = \$8,250$$
$$\text{Total Room Revenue:} \qquad \$159,750$$

Hotel B knows that its executive-segment guests spend an average of $28 on food and $7 on beverages and that the small corporate group has committed to a food and beverage budget of $50 per person per day, including its cocktail reception. Food and beverage revenue is therefore estimated to be as follows:

$$325 \text{ people} \times \$35 \times 3 \text{ days} = \$34,125$$
$$50 \text{ people} \times \$50 \times 3 \text{ days} = \$7,500$$
$$25 \text{ people} \times \$15 \times 3 \text{ days} = \$1,125$$
$$\text{Total Food \& Beverage Revenue:} \quad \$42,750$$

As you can see, Hotel B, by opting not to seek a sellout nine months in advance and by not participating in the church convention business, has a total revenue of $202,500, far in excess of Hotel A's $175,200.

There are many more examples that clearly demonstrate how managing the market mix maximizes revenue, and which demonstrate the importance of planning ahead, knowing your competition, and understanding the real value of your market segments.

Pricing

Another component of revenue maximization is pricing. As one of the key elements in revenue maximization, pricing involves setting rates using strategy and flexibility.

Have you ever wondered what might be the "best" hotel in a city you have never traveled to, or how you would find out which hotel is the best? You might look at a directory of hotels or a publication like *Hotel & Travel Index,* scan the listing looking for the highest rates, and assume that the hotel with the highest rack rate listed must be the best. What if you saw that that same "best" hotel had a corporate or weekend rate that was competitive with the corporate or weekend rate of a hotel with a lower rack rate? You might conclude that the "best" hotel also has the best deal, or that the other hotel has a high corporate or weekend rate in comparison to its own rack rate. Let's look at a rate example in the following section.

Example: The Park, the Plaza, and the Palace

The Park, the Plaza, and the Palace are hotels located in the same city. The Park has a listed rack rate of $150 to $170, the Plaza has a listed rack rate of $145 to $175, and the Palace has a listed rack rate of $155 to $200.

You might assume that the Palace must be the best hotel in town—its rooms cost up to $200, and its minimum rack rate is $5 more than the Park's minimum rack rate and $10 more than the Plaza's minimum rack rate. You call the three hotels' reservations departments and find out that the Park's *corporate rate* is $138, the Plaza's corporate rate is $135, and the Palace's corporate rate is $138 to $153. The Palace also tells you it has rooms available at $138 the night you desire to stay. The Palace wins both the pricing perception strategy and value strategy in this case—you could have a $200 room at the Palace versus a $170 or $175 room at the Park or Plaza.

Using the same city and same hotels, let's compare weekend pricing strategies. This particular city runs about 50 percent occupancy on weekends. The motels and "middle tier" hotels charge anywhere from $49 to $79 for a weekend room. Our three upscale competitors have taken a different approach, seeking to maximize revenue and maintain their position as the "best." The Park states weekend rates of $109 and complimentary continental breakfast for two in its all-day restaurant. The Plaza advertises the same rate and complimentary continental breakfast for two in its all-day restaurant. The Palace advertises somewhat differently, with three weekend packages: (1) a room only, at $109 (plus continental breakfast in the lobby lounge); (2) a concierge-level king room with in-room continental breakfast for two at $119; and (3) a suite (based on availability) with a king bed, welcoming champagne or beverage, and an in-room complete breakfast for two at $129. The Palace is offering the same price/value as its competitors in package one, and an option for privacy and prestige in packages two and three. With a hotel that has a concierge level, suites, and empty rooms, why not upsell, keep your positioning, and yet remain price-competitive in your own segment of the market? The Palace understands the psychology of the market. For those seeking privacy and prestige, a $10 or even $20 premium will bring many takers. Not having these options simply eliminates the opportunity to upsell or meet the needs of a portion of the weekend market. Think about the consumer perception strategy: Would you say your hotel has a "weekend room rate of $109 and two coupons for breakfast in the all-day restaurant," or would you say either "we have a concierge-level king room and breakfast in the room for $119," or "we have a suite and breakfast served in the room for $129"? Using your empty suites and concierge- or club-level rooms to upsell and keep your image and value perception is not only a good pricing strategy—it is a revenue maximization strategy.

Yield Management

Yield management is a tool used to increase revenue by establishing prices based on supply and demand and the competitive dynamics of the market. In essence, when demand is strong and trending toward exceeding supply, prices are increased. Conversely, when demand is trending downward and supply exceeds demand, prices are decreased. The objective is to achieve the maximum yield given the supply and demand scenario. The **yield** measurement is a comparison of actual revenue achieved to the theoretical total potential revenue. The definition and calculation of the total potential revenue often varies by chain or hotel.

The principle of yield management can be applied to demand trends that have been determined hourly, daily, weekly, or even months or years in advance. For example, rates can be raised for a period when future demand is forecasted to be strong, and rates can be lowered during weak demand periods in order to bring in room revenue by taking market share.

Instead of measuring occupancy or rate, the focus in yield management is on *revenue per room*, not unlike revenue per rental in the rental car industry or revenue per passenger in the airline industry. Although the term "yield management" originated in the airline industry, hotels and resorts were applying the principle of yield management long before there were airlines. Historically, resort managers knew that "in season," the property would sell out because demand was so strong. Accordingly, many resorts charged only their highest rates when they were in season. Thus, one component of yield management—the relationship of rate to demand—was in practice.

In fact, to a large degree, the forecasting element of yield management was also in place—if you desired a room next "season," you were going to be quoted an "in-season" rate. And some resorts would use rate categories, selling their water-view rooms for the higher rates or their beach-front rooms for a premium, with in-season versus off-season rates for both. So before the first jet airplane ever took off, another component of yield management—variable rates/pricing—was being practiced. Granted, the hospitality industry was still focusing on occupancy and average rate as their performance measures when the "yield management" concept emerged in the airline industry and spread into the hospitality and rent-a-car industries.

The application of yield management in the hospitality industry blossomed in the mid-1980s. By the late 1980s, the concept of a multi-dimensional model incorporating market mix, pricing strategies, and yield management proved to be a better methodology for maximizing revenue than a single principle or application. Yield management had matured from a measuring tool for judging performance to a science and methodology unto itself. Regardless of the school of thought, yield management was a tool for the 1990s that would continue to emerge in virtually every major hotel chain in the hospitality industry as a standard procedure.

In the hospitality industry, management of **room categories,** discounts, and length of stay all help determine yield. Components of yield management also include variables such as the **booking pace** for groups (the rate at which the group's room block is filling up) and the transient sales trend/forecast (the rate at which individual reservations are being made). These factors, plus cancellations and other influences, help shape the actual forecast. The forecast then suggests the strategy for rate quotes and availability. This total interactive process is the product of yield management.

While hotel chains and major hotels and resorts guard their specific yield management procedures, some of the key yield management premises and components are as follows:

1. *Use rate ranges.* A **rate range** allows you to sell up or down.

2. *Develop "room categories" (for example, deluxe, standard, and views).* Room categories allow you to **close** or **open** room categories in order to increase either rates or occupancy.

3. *Maintain rack rate positioning.* Set your published rack rates high enough to allow yourself the flexibility to discount when needed and to "max out" when demand is strong.

4. *Develop rate categories.* Have rate categories for as many valid reasons or segments as you can identify. This allows you to meet everyone's needs within your own rate-range parameters.

5. *Establish guidelines.* Be sure you have clear and enforceable rate-control guidelines in place in all areas where rates are provided—reservations, sales, front desk, catering, etc. Make sure your signals for closing or opening up rates are understood by all. Better yet, automate the rate categories.

6. *Conduct a review meeting daily.* A daily review meeting allows you to check to make sure that all assumptions regarding demand (and supply) are correct and that everyone understands the current status for the day, week, month, and the future months.

7. *Contact the Central Reservations Office (CRO) daily.* This allows you to determine if all changes to your rate strategy have been communicated to all shifts and are clearly in place.

These seven keys will help ensure that yield management works for you.

Revenue Maximization in Practice

To maximize your hotel's revenue, you must first understand market mix, pricing, and yield management. But you must also be able to implement these concepts. The objectives and strategies in the following checklists will help you put revenue maximization into practice.

Objectives

- Select the optimum market-mix targets.
- Develop pricing strategies and related rate ranges.
- Plan for the sale of all empty rooms.
- Aim to sell all rooms at the maximum rates demand will allow.
- Control and manage the type and nature of group business and transient business.
- Provide for hourly, daily, weekly, monthly, quarterly, and yearly management of room rates, room reservations, room sales, and catering functions.

Strategies

- Adjust your corporate rates to be competitive with your top four competitors.

- Tell everyone about your new rates. Communicate!

- Establish rack rates—both top-end and low-end rates—to increase revenue. Publish the low-end rate.

- Shop your competitors *daily* via direct calls to their hotels. Call your competitors' "800" numbers or call through the airline terminals.

- Publish your corporate rate and list it wherever you can (at airline terminals, in directories, and so on).

- Establish a super-saver rate and appropriate room allocations, timing, etc.

- Establish a task force to implement your rate strategy and provide: (1) ongoing training, (2) daily management responsibility, (3) checks and balances, and (4) measurement.

- Price your product appropriately. *This is your most important management responsibility.*

While the objectives and strategies just listed are overall steps to revenue maximization, there are many tactical steps that must be taken on a daily, weekly, and monthly basis to ensure that the goal of revenue maximization is achieved. These key tactics are as follows:

Key Tactics

- Develop a 365-day calendar that clearly states the selling tactic (up or down) for each day.

- Be sure all room rates are available during low occupancy periods (no "closed out" rate categories).

- Be sure discounted room rates are not available during forecasted high-occupancy periods.

- Consider implementing a "minimum stay" requirement for extremely high-demand periods (for example, during citywide sellouts).

- Hold a review meeting each morning to be sure everyone in sales, reservations, catering, convention services, and the front-desk area are all informed of the day's revenue maximization game plan:

  — Review the prior day's revenue performance and compare it to budget and forecast.

  — Review the month-to-date revenue and year-to-date results.

  — Review your competitive intelligence (rate surveys, groups booked, etc.).

  — Review the day's, week's, and month's occupancy forecasts.

  — Review the group room blocks and related trends (cut-offs, pace, etc.) and make adjustments.

  — Review future valley periods and/or peaks in demand.

  — Review the impact of all new business from all sources in the forecast.

— Make appropriate adjustments to the rate strategy for that day, that week, the month ahead, and any period in the future that will be affected by changes in the demand pattern.

•   Communicate daily with the Central Reservations Office (CRO) to ensure that all the property-level rate changes the CRO desires have been implemented.

•   Daily communicate any rate strategy changes to all other selling functions (the Regional Sales Offices, contracted agents, automated systems, representatives, and so on).

Following these tactics will result in effective management of market mix, the best selection of pricing strategies, the highest yield, and—ultimately—the maximum revenue.

Key Terms

booking pace
close
open
revenue maximization
room category
yield

REVIEW QUIZ

When you feel you have covered all of the material in this chapter, answer these questions. Choose the *best* answer. Check your answers with the correct ones found on the Review Quiz Answer Key at the end of this book.

Multiple Choice

1. Before you can manage yield or set prices, you need to:

    a. ensure that yield will exceed revenue.
    b. determine the targeted market mix that provides maximum revenue and profit potential.
    c. define pricing strategies that will determine the annual rate-resistance level.
    d. set on-premise incremental spending patterns for different market segments.

2. "Booking pace" is the:

    a. speed at which a front desk agent checks in guests.
    b. frequency of return guests' visits.
    c. rate at which a group's room block is filling up.
    d. frequency of a hotel's yield investment.

3. An objective of revenue maximization is to:

    a. control and manage the type and nature of group business and transient business.
    b. select market mix targets based on the lowest corporate rate.
    c. select market mix targets based on the highest corporate rate.
    d. sell all rooms at the corporate rate when demand is high.

Chapter Outline

The Marketing Plan
    Marketing Plan Outline and
      Instructions
    Competitive/Market Positioning Grid
Work Plan Example

Learning Objectives

1. List the elements of a marketing plan and summarize steps for putting one together. (pp. 215–222)

2. Describe and use the competitive/market positioning grid. (pp. 222–223)

17

The Total Hotel/Unit Marketing Plan

YOUR HOTEL'S MARKETING PLAN is its blueprint for gaining market share and financial success. Completing this plan requires detailed analyses of your product, market, and competition. A carefully crafted marketing plan is a useful working document. Once completed, it should be periodically reviewed, assessed, and—when appropriate—adjusted to take changing situations and circumstances into account.

This chapter provides instructions, sample forms, and an actual workable marketing plan for an individual hotel or unit. The chapter's purpose is to walk you through the complete process of preparing an annual marketing plan.

The Marketing Plan

One of the best ways to begin creating a marketing plan is to establish a timetable for completion of key plan components. Here is an example:

Marketing Plan Timetable

July 15	Instructions issued
September 1	Completion of mission statement
	Objectives and strategies
	Competitive/market analysis
September 15	Preliminary expense budget summary
	Completion of preliminary advertising plan
October 1	Final detailed budget
	Completed advertising plan
November 15	Summary work plan by segment
	First-quarter chronological plan
January 15	Second-quarter chronological plan
April 15	Third-quarter chronological plan
July 15	Fourth-quarter chronological plan

Marketing Plan Outline and Instructions

The first step in creating a marketing plan is to set forth all the items and information required to produce a complete plan. In the pages that follow, an actual outline

Exhibit 1　Sample Statement of Objectives and Strategies

OBJECTIVE 1: BUSINESS MIX

Increase the group segment from 35 percent to 40 percent of the hotel's business mix.

Strategies

- Raise group room allotment to 250 rooms Monday to Thursday nights.
- Raise sales goal for staff.
- Increase number of sales trips to New York and Washington, D.C.
- Increase advertising and direct mail to corporate group meetings planners.

OBJECTIVE 2: PRICING PHILOSOPHY

Become the price leader in the city, maintaining a $10 margin over the competition. Achieve an AT of $82.

Strategies

- Increase rates $2 every two months or as needed to maintain the number 1 position.
- Conduct a monthly rate survey.
- Maintain a $60 average rate for packages June to September; $64 October to December.
- Raise suite prices 10 percent in January.
- Do not book groups below $50 average rate on weekends without approval of general manager.

---

of a marketing plan is reproduced. Included are step-by-step instructions and definitions of what is to be completed and presented.

MARKETING PLAN

OUTLINE AND INSTRUCTIONS

I.　Mission Statement—due September 1

Provide a concise mission statement for your hotel that includes the following:

a.　Desired position and perception in the marketplace

b.　Targeted **business mix** (transient percentage versus group percentage)

c.　Overall revenue goals such as revpar (revenue per available room), ADR (average daily rate), occupancy, gross operating profit, and other measures significant to your hotel

II.　Objectives and Strategies—due September 1

Using brief statements, list the key objectives (what you wish to achieve, quantified by dollar amounts or percentages if volume-related) that, when achieved, will result in the fulfillment of the mission statement. For each objective, list the strategies or action steps you will implement to achieve the objective. (See Exhibit 1 for a sample excerpt from a list of objectives and strategies.) Objectives should address, but not be limited to:

a.　*Business Mix.* Identify the objective and strategies planned to achieve the group/transient business mix goal you have set.

Exhibit 2   Sample Rate Survey

	Hospitality Hotel	Hilton	Marriott	Holiday Inn	Sheraton	Radisson
Single Rack Rate	105/115/125	95/105/115	89/99/119	79/89	85/95/105	89/99
Corporate Rate	95/105 S/D	85/95 S/D	80/90 S/D	69/79 S/D	75/85 S/D	79/89 S/D
Preferred Corporate Rate	85/95 S/D	80/90 S/D	75/85 S/D	65/75 S/D	70/80 S/D	74/84 S/D
Secretary's	85/95 S/D	80/90 S/D	75/85 S/D	NA	70/80 S/D	NA
Club Level Executive Room Tech. Room	$20 Extra	$15 Extra	$15 Extra	NA	$15 Extra	NA
Government Rate	$72	$68	$65	$60	$60	$60
Weekend Room Only	$79	$69	$69	$59	$59	$59
Weekend Package Room/Breakfast for 2	$85	$75	$75	NA	NA	NA
Suite Range	$175–$375	$160–$380	$175–$425	$125/$150	$150/$175	$125/$175

b. *Pricing Philosophy.* State your objective pertaining to room rate and positioning. List strategies for achieving your targeted average daily rate. Include a competitive rate survey (such as the example in Exhibit 2) in the appendix to the marketing plan.

c. *Transient Market.* State your objective for weekday/weekend transient rooms mix. List major strategies planned to achieve desired results. List major strategies for travel industry sales and corporate transient sales.

d. *Group Market.* State your objectives for group business as they pertain to group room nights, rate, and revenue. List your strategies. Include a summary of your group room-night targets by market segment (including travel industry sales) in the appendix, using the Group Rooms Market Mix form shown in Exhibit 3. Also include a list of sales staff market assignments.

e. *Low Occupancy Periods.* Provide specific strategies aimed at solving low occupancy periods, be they weekends, summer, off-season, holiday, etc. Include results expected.

f. *Community Awareness.* List strategies planned to increase your hotel's visibility and enhance its reputation in the marketplace. In the appendix, include a list of professional and civic organization memberships maintained by the management staff.

III. **Competitive/Market Analysis—due September 1**

In this section of the marketing plan, give a very brief overview of market conditions and trends, then identify your hotel's position in the marketplace as it relates to your competitors. Be concise.

Exhibit 3   Group Rooms Market Mix Form

Market	**19xx Total**		**19xx Total**		**19xx Total**		**19xx Total**		**19xx Total**	
	Total	%	Total	%	Total	%	Total	%	Total	%
Corporate										
State/Regional Association										
National Association										
Travel Agent										
Motor Coach										
Sports										
Government										
Total (%)		100		100		100		100		100

Group Rooms Market Mix (trends and forecast)   Hotel: _____   No: _____

a. *Economic Conditions.* Describe how the prevailing local economic conditions will affect your transient and group business. Information should include average occupancy for the marketplace during the past 12 months (if available).

b. *Opportunities/Concerns.* List any known or anticipated changes in your marketplace that would positively or negatively affect your hotel during this plan year.

c. *Business Trends.* Briefly describe any trends exhibited during the past $2\frac{1}{2}$ years with regard to transient demands (weekday and weekend), business mix, and valley periods. Complete the Group Rooms Market Mix form (Exhibit 3) for this past period and include it in the appendix.

Exhibit 4   Competitive/Market Positioning Grid

		MARKET		
		Strong	Moderate	Weak
	Strong	1	2	3
COMPETITIVE POSITIONING	Moderate	4	5	6
	Weak	7	8	9

   d. *Product and Competitive Analysis.* Complete a fact sheet on your hotel and your three major competitors. Market your strengths and develop strategies to overcome your property's weaknesses.

   e. *Competitive/Market Positioning Grid.* Using the form shown in Exhibit 4, denote your hotel's position by placing an "X" in the most appropriate box. Do the same for your three major competitors on separate grids. (This form is discussed later in the chapter.)

IV. Appendix—due September 1

   a. *Marketing Budget Estimates.* Using the summary form shown in Exhibit 5, outline your actual expenses for the past year, your estimated expenses for the current year, and your projections for the plan year ahead.

   b. *Room Rate Survey.* Complete a rate survey of your competitors using the sample format shown in Exhibit 2.

   c. *Business Mix Trends.* Record the desired transient rooms mix versus group market mix by month for future measurement against actual performance.

   d. *Transient Market Segment Prioritization.* List all transient market segments you will address in the plan year and prioritize them according to their profitability to your hotel.

   e. *Group Market Segment Prioritization.* List all group market segments you will address in the plan year and prioritize them according to their profitability to your hotel (see Exhibit 6).

Exhibit 5   Marketing Expense Budget Form

Marketing Expense Budget Summary and Estimate			

Hotel: _____ No. _____

Account	Last Year	Current Year	Plan Year
Direct Sales (Includes Travel, Telephone, Dues/Subscriptions, Professional Fees, Entertainment)	$_____/____%	$_____/____%	$_____/____%
Public Relations (Includes Professional Fees for Public Relations Only)	$_____/____%	$_____/____%	$_____/____%
Sales Promotions (Includes Direct Mail and Postage)	$_____/____%	$_____/____%	$_____/____%
Collateral Materials (Includes Costs for Photo Shoots, Brochures, and Other Sales Collateral)	$_____/____%	$_____/____%	$_____/____%
Payroll (Includes Salaries, Wages, and Benefits)	$_____/____%	$_____/____%	$_____/____%
Office Supplies	$_____/____%	$_____/____%	$_____/____%
Miscellaneous	$_____/____%	$_____/____%	$_____/____%

Advertising

a. National Media and Production:	$_____	/____%
b. Local Media and Production:	$_____	/____%
c. White/Yellow Pages Listings:	$_____	/____%
(a.b.c.) Sub-Total:	$_____	/____%

Total:	$_____	/____%

   f. *Sales Staff Market Assignments.* List how market solicitation responsibilities have been assigned within the sales department (see Exhibit 7).

V. Preliminary Budget and Advertising Plan—due September 15

A first cut at the budget and advertising plan should be completed by mid-September.

VI. Final Detailed Budget and Advertising Plan—due October 1

Final budget and advertising plan should be agreed to in order to allow optimum time to prepare advertising and purchase media.

Exhibit 6   Group Market Segment Prioritization

	HOSPITALITY HOTEL	
Segment A	**Segment B**	**Segment C**
Local corporate	National associations	Fraternities/sororities
State associations	Motorcoach tours	Military reunions
Corporate transient (RSVP)	Sports teams	Social rooms
Weekend packages	Relocation/long-term stays	Airline crews
	Government	Special events
	Travel agents	

Exhibit 7   Market Assignments and Goals

	HOSPITALITY HOTEL
Sales Manager:	Jim Smith
Primary markets:	Washington, D.C. national associations
Primary accounts:	All major associations
Secondary markets:	Government groups; Baltimore corporations
Secondary accounts:	IBM; Ernst & Whinney; Star Shipping Lines; Baltimore Port Authority
Geographic area:	Washington, D.C.; Maryland; Virginia (Washington NSO)
Room nights:	250 per week
Outside calls:	8 per week
Steam leads:	1 per week
In-house entertainment:	3 per week

Note: Use this format, but include *all* salespeople on one or two pages.

VII. Summary Work Plan by Segment—due November 15

Using brief statements, for each market—including travel industry sales and corporate transient sales—outline your specific planned activities under the categories of:

a. Direct sales and promotions (familiarization trips, trade shows, etc.)

b. Direct mail (local and regional only)

c. Advertising

d. Public relations

Exhibit 8   Sample Chronological Work Plan

HOSPITALITY HOTEL, HEAVENLY, MARYLAND
JULY 199X

Week One: Monday, June 27–Friday, July 1

Association sales calls in Washington, D.C. (two days)	J. Smith
Summertime government rate mailer to Annapolis	M. Patton
Local sales calls in Towson with G.M.	B. Wallace
Begin to prepare for August corporate phone blitz	D. Carney

Week Two: Monday, July 4–Friday, July 8

Attend Meeting World in New York City	P. Johnson
RSVP Quarterly Newsletter mailed	B. Wallace
Research reunion leads from VFW magazine	J. Smith
Update DVSAE list	M. Patton

Week Three: Monday, July 11–Friday, July 15

Sales calls on state associations (two days)	M. Patton
Brainstorming session on marketing plan	All staff
Deliver mailer for wedding rooms to local country clubs	B. Wallace
Attend counselor selling class in Houston	J. Smith

Week Four: Monday, July 18–Friday, July 22

Local sales calls in Reistertown	B. Wallace
Follow-up calls to summertime government rate mailer	M. Patton
Sales calls in Philadelphia (two days)	P. Johnson
Finalize lists for August phone blitz	D. Carney

Activities are to be tied to a targeted month and assigned to a salesperson. On-going activities are not to be listed. All work plans are to follow the sample format.

VIII. Quarterly Chronological Plans (first quarter due November 15)

The **chronological work plan** for January–March will be due by November 15. Activities should be listed in the date order by month (see the sample in Exhibit 8). The chronological plan for April–June is due January 15.

Competitive/Market Positioning Grid

A property's operating success is a major factor in determining an appropriate future action plan for that property. The operating success of a lodging facility is a function of both the potential of the market sector in which it is located and its competitive positioning within that market sector.

In order to develop an action plan, use the grid shown earlier in Exhibit 4 to relate the market sector potential to an estimate of the competitive position of each property within its market sector. The horizontal axis of the grid denotes the potential of the market sector, while the vertical axis represents the competitive position of the specific property within that market sector. Ranking on both axes ranges from strong to weak. Competitive position is a function of both quantitative and qualitative considerations, such as the following:

- Amount and quality of competition

- Competitive advantages dealing with location, access, image, facilities, size, rate, etc.

- Ability to meet the needs of available market segments

Fill out these grids for each property. If your property or any of your competitors are renovating or undergoing changes that will affect your positioning during the plan year, complete another grid for the future positioning. Obviously, there is a meaning to the position on the grid where a particular property is placed. A hotel in position 1, 2, or 3 is the best show in town, or there is no discernable difference between the number 1 and number 2 competitors. A hotel in position 4, 5, or 6 is not number 1 or number 2 in town. It is of average quality. A hotel in position 7, 8, or 9 is of relatively poor quality when compared to its competition. This hotel is in a discernibly disadvantageous position.

For each hotel, complete four positioning grids, one for each of the four major markets:

- Business Travel—Group

- Business Travel—Transient

- Leisure Travel—Weekend

- Leisure Travel—Vacation

Consider your property's position for each of these consumer targets. For example, a number 1 position means you have the best hotel in a strong market; that is, you have the best hotel in (for example) an 80 percent occupancy market. A number 3 position means you have a weak market—say, an occupancy market of 40 percent.

To use the grid shown in Exhibit 4, denote your hotel's position on the grid by placing an "X" in the most appropriate box. Do the same on separate forms for each of your three major competitors. Once this is done, you can develop and use strategies that are appropriate for your positioning.

Work Plan Example

The following is an example of a work plan for group business from the corporate market.

Action Plans

	Responsibility	Due Date
Direct Sales and Promotions		
1. Schedule sales solicitation trips to call on key accounts in:		
New York	Smith	Jan./Sept.
Dallas/Fort Worth	Carney	February

Action Plans *(continued)*

		Responsibility	Due Date
	Detroit	Patton	March
	Boston	Patton	April
	St. Louis	Wallace	May
	Kansas City	Carney	June
	Minneapolis	Marshall	September
	San Francisco/San Jose	Smith	October
2.	Attend national corporate business-related meetings for:		
	Meeting Planners International	Smith	June/Dec.
	Dialogue in Dallas	Carney	February
	Dialogue in Chicago	Smith	June
	Dialogue in New York	Smith	September
	Meeting World in New York	Smith	July
	Participate in Midwest Business Travel Association Annual Meeting	Patton	May
3.	Participate in the following blitzes:		
	Boston	Patton	April
	St. Louis	Wallace	May
	Minneapolis	Marshall	September
	San Francisco/San Jose	Smith	October
	Host a Friends-of-the-Family account appreciation function	Staff	May
	St. Louis corporate executives fam trip	Wallace	March

Direct Mail

1.	Include all Illinois corporate clients in quarterly activity schedule mailing	Staff	December March June September December
2.	Schedule a mailing to all corporate accounts promoting our "meetings package" to generate business for July, August, November, and December	Staff	April October
3.	Develop a meetings brochure and mail to Chicago-area corporate accounts not currently on file	Wallace	March

Advertising (local/regional media only)

Heavy emphasis to be placed on advertising to the corporate group market. The following publications have been selected for local/regional placement:	Carney	Ongoing

Chicago Tribune/Business Section

Crains Chicago Business

Action Plans *(continued)*

		Responsibility	Due Date

Public Relations

		Responsibility	Due Date
1.	Releases to St. Louis media on Corporate Executives Fam trip	Carney	March
2.	Releases to trade publications on meetings package	Carney Carney	April October
3.	Releases to local media on Friends-of-the-Family party	Carney	May
4.	General releases on newsworthy events relating to corporate meetings in the hotel	Carney	Ongoing

Key Terms

business mix
chronological work plan

REVIEW QUIZ

When you feel you have covered all of the material in this chapter, answer these questions. Choose the *best* answer. Check your answers with the correct ones found on the Review Quiz Answer Key at the end of this book.

Multiple Choice

1. Completing the marketing plan requires detailed analysis of:

   a. your product.
   b. your market.
   c. your competition.
   d. all of the above.

2. In a marketing plan, key objectives should:

   a. be quantified by dollar amounts or percentages when the objectives are volume-related.
   b. detail how to achieve strategies or action steps associated with the plan.
   c. not address pricing philosophy because of possible antitrust violations.
   d. describe a property's position in the marketplace in relation to its competitors.

3. The competitive/market analysis should:

   a. give a very brief overview of market conditions and trends.
   b. present marketing budget estimates.
   c. list and prioritize the desired transient and group market segments.
   d. list strategies to enhance a hotel's reputation in the marketplace.

4. Competitive position is a function of:

   a. the amount and quality of competition.
   b. your hotel's location, facilities, rates, and so forth.
   c. a property's ability to meet the needs of available market segments.
   d. all of the above.

Chapter Outline

Zero-Base Budgeting
Research and Required Information
    Market Segmentation, Needs
       Identification, and Measurement of
       Customer Perceptions
    Facts About the Competition
    External Facts
    Internal Facts
    Other Hospitality Industry Sector
       Applications
Marketing Plan
    Analysis of Research and Information
    Objectives
    Marketing Program
    Marketing Appropriations
    Sales Goals
    Action Programs
    Communication of Assigned
       Responsibilities
    Monitoring of Action Program

Learning Objectives

1. Define zero-base budgeting, identify the four major types of information required to complete a marketing plan, and summarize how this information is obtained. (pp. 229–236)

2. Describe the structure of a marketing plan and summarize tips for putting one together. (pp. 236–241)

18

The Total Corporate/ Multi-Unit Marketing Plan

Y OU CANNOT DEVELOP an effective marketing plan without knowing your consumers and knowing which marketing tools to use to sell to consumers. The purpose of this chapter is to provide you with an outline for your marketing plan that ties together the research and application phases of marketing.

The issues and strategies addressed in this chapter can be applied, with some modification, to all sectors of the hospitality industry.

With few exceptions, there are rarely sufficient financial resources to support all of the programs and tools a marketer desires. Many marketers approach their marketing plans in a traditional fashion—they sit down with last year's plan and apply additional dollars, or cut out certain programs as a result of budgetary constraints. Those who do approach a marketing plan in this way ignore the basic premise of marketing—researching and knowing your consumer. They may feel comfortable "ball-parking" marketing budget allocations because they have become familiar with their guest markets over time.

To develop a truly effective marketing plan and make the best use of financial resources, you need to know your consumers' needs *today*. You also need to know in which direction their needs are moving. You must know the consumer's habits, preferences, and perceptions of your products or services as well as how consumers perceive your **competition.** You must know your problem areas, whether they be markets, cities, specific properties, or people. Finally, you must identify your strengths and related opportunities. Don't commit one marketing dollar until you have exhaustive knowledge of all these areas. For planning purposes, begin with the zero-base budgeting concept.

Zero-Base Budgeting

Zero-base budgeting is a broad concept that can help you prioritize where you want to spend your limited resources. With zero-base budgeting, no expenditure is justified just because it was made last year. Every expense is re-analyzed and justified annually to determine if it will yield better results than spending the same amount in another way.

One note of caution: frequently there are vital expenses that *must* be maintained at certain minimum levels. For example, a property with a sales force or reservation system must retain certain expenses that relate to those functions and should use extreme caution in applying zero-base budgeting. Some marketers subdivide the marketing budget into a "vital core" of expenses and "all other" categories, and apply the concept only to the "all other" category. Some consider this a violation of the principle of zero-base budgeting, while to others it is simply common sense. You are the best qualified to determine which approach is more applicable for your property.

Research and Required Information

The first step in developing a complete marketing plan is to research and gather required information. Required research and information can be divided into four major areas:

- Market segmentation, needs identification, and measurement of customer perceptions
- Facts about your competition
- External facts
- Internal facts

Market Segmentation, Needs Identification, and Measurement of Customer Perceptions

You may already know a great deal about your market and its segments, based on internal customer-origin analysis, your customer data base, or external marketing information you purchased. To update your knowledge and make the most of your marketing expenditures, use the following nine-step process:

1. Identify the geographic markets that yield the greatest number of travelers (both business and pleasure) to the areas in which your facilities are located.

2. Using the major geographic markets identified in step 1 for research sampling, determine the proper segmentation of the total market. Some common market segments in the lodging industry are:

   - Individuals attending a group meeting or convention
   - Individuals traveling for business with a relatively unrestricted expense account
   - Individuals traveling for business with a restricted expense account
   - Individual pleasure travelers without children
   - Families traveling for pleasure
   - Couples or families interested only in the essentials of lodging (no-frills)
   - Couples or families seeking to avoid the service, tipping, high costs, semi-rigidity, etc., of hotels, motels, and resorts
   - Banquet and local restaurant customers

   Common intermediary market segments include:

   - Meeting planners

- Travel agents

- Traffic departments of major corporations

- Secretaries

- VIP clubs

- Wholesalers

- Airlines

- Car rental companies

- Reservations services

3. During the segmentation process, *roughly* determine the demographic characteristics of each segment, including the segment's approximate size and trend. With respect to "trend," you should be looking for which direction each segment is heading—is the segment increasing or decreasing as a percentage of your business? Is the segment itself growing or declining? (Research techniques are available to more accurately and specifically determine the demographics, but the costs of extensive research may outweigh its value. An approximate demographic definition should be adequate.) Then select appropriate media to promote your product or service to these segments.

4. Evaluate the trends in each of the demographic segments you want to reach. A national probability sample will give you a fairly accurate assessment of these trends. When you add the results of this sampling technique to your in-house demographic data, you can project meaningful trends for your targeted segments. These will probably be sufficient for your initial efforts in **marketing planning.**

5. Decide which segments you want to pursue and which you do not want to pursue. In making these decisions, consider such facts as:

- Suitability of your existing facilities to meet the needs of these segments

- Each segment's trend—is it growing or shrinking?

- The profitability of the segment

For the most part, such decisions will not change your marketing approach. However, for certain segments peripheral to your current business mix, these decisions will be very important, and you will need more information. Defer the marketing decision on whether to pursue the peripheral segments until you get a better idea of the suitability of your property to the defined needs of these segments. (Step 7 helps determine your property's suitability.)

6. Identify in detail the specific needs of each of the segments you hope to reach. Determine what factors, products, or services are most and least important to customers in each segment. Trained interviewers can glean this information from focus groups. (Step 9 helps further measure customer perceptions through focus groups.) A **focus group** is a small representative sample of your customer base and/or potential customer base. The group is subjected to a

structured interview or series of questions; responses are then analyzed to glean marketing information.

7. Analyze how well your existing products/services meet the needs of each segment. Does your property fall short in providing the products or services required by each segment? Can your existing facilities and services be adapted to meet the needs of each segment? Remember to be objective when analyzing your facilities, products, and services. **Customer perceptions** of your facilities and services often differ from yours. At this point, you may eliminate additional segments from your potential market if your facilities don't meet the needs of those segments. (Note: Even though your property may not fulfill the exact needs of a segment, your property may still do so better than any competitor. This will be determined in step 9. If so, you still may want to pursue that segment.)

8. Identify all major companies that serve your total market. To do this, you will have to analyze the companies based in your market, the type of offices they have (i.e., corporate headquarters, regional offices, district offices, and so on), and their major suppliers/visitors and where they come from (their origin points).

9. Conduct focus group interviews with customers from each **market segment** to measure their perceptions of both your products/services and those of all competitors serving the lodging industry. This should be done in several steps:

   • Determine which properties are preferred by customers in the segment. What property characteristics do customers in that segment prefer? How do segment customers perceive each property? Which properties relate best to customers in the segment and why?

   • Determine customer perceptions of other (non-preferred) properties. What characteristics are seen as positive and negative?

   • Determine how each property is perceived to meet the most important need of the segment (as identified in step 6).

   Make sure your property is considered equally with other competitors. You want an objective measurement of how customers in different market segments view each of their lodging options.

   The perceptions customers have of each lodging competitor are the result of the quality of the property's facilities and operations, and also of its advertising and promotion schemes. Likewise, the solutions to making any changes in your image will lie equally in operations, facilities, and marketing.

   The information obtained through research may not be entirely new to you. However, information on how you compare to your competition will probably be more objective than you have obtained before and, therefore, should be more useful to you. For example: Where does your property have a real advantage over your competition? What are your property's weak spots? What are your competitors' weak spots? Into which new segments can you expand your market? Which segments (if any) absolutely don't want your products or services?

With the nine-step process, you have identified the following information:

- Your market's segments, as classified by needs plus rough demographics.

- The size of each market segment and its growth trends—which segments are growing and which are shrinking.

- The specific needs of each segment and the relative importance of these needs.

- An objective measurement of how well your firm and product or service is perceived to fulfill these needs in relation to your competition.

- An identification of which lodging companies best relate to each segment and why.

With this information you will be able to more accurately position your property in the marketplace.

Facts About the Competition

You may tend to dismiss the effects of competition on your business. However, when you ignore the competition, you may overlook several variables that affect marketing planning. Focusing solely on your present strengths is also short-sighted in situations involving increased competition, especially in a given market segment.

Although you regard all the things you do as important, consumers may not always agree with you. They see you as a bed, a courteous (or discourteous) employee, a smoothly handled (or fouled-up) reservation, and so on. They often have different priorities than you. Furthermore, consumers in different segments have different priorities. Price, service level, and an overall good experience (lodging, food and beverage, and service) are extremely important. It is important to know how you stack up against your competitors in these areas.

To evaluate your competition, you need the following information: market share data, competitive marketing strategies and practices, and occupancy detail by city.

Market Share Data. Market share data provides a long-range overview of how your property is faring in relation to your major competitors. Often, accurate figures on the size of the total market are unavailable; however, you can get a fairly useful measurement by comparing your own figures (i.e., occupancy and rate figures) against the total of all your major competitors or against a smaller select group of competitors. This can be accomplished on a local, regional, and national level by subscribing to and participating in various industry services such as Smith Travel Data Research, by reviewing market reports issued by industry accounting firms, and by contacting convention and visitors bureaus for information.

Competitive Marketing Strategies and Practices. Be aware of your competitors' current marketing programs when formulating your own marketing strategies. The most effective way to get information about your competitors' marketing programs is to clip all of their advertising from magazines and newspapers for a period of several months. A clipping service can do this for you, or your advertising agency may be able to help.

It is also useful to get a fix on other media and methods used for competitors' marketing activities, including:

- Radio and TV
- Outdoor and airport advertising
- Direct mail
- Direct solicitation
- Travel agent solicitation
- Publicity
- Sales promotion

This information will be more difficult to obtain, but there may be ways to learn more about these areas. Most advertising agencies subscribe to syndicated services that supply this data. You may also obtain market information on your own from advertising sales representatives and other individuals who work for the various media outlets (magazines, radio stations, etc.).

The information you gather about competitors' marketing programs doesn't have to be precise or detailed. Try to get enough information to answer the following questions:

- What segments are your competitors pursuing?
- What are their strategies in terms of image-building?
- What media or marketing methods are they using?
- How successful do their marketing programs seem to be?

After gathering this information over a period of time, you will be able to detect shifts in competitive marketing strategies.

Occupancy Detail by City. Compare your property's occupancy data and trends to those of each competitive hotel or motel in your major metropolitan area. Occupancy data should include all major competitors, including hotels and motels that meet recreational and family travel needs as well as business-oriented hotels.

External Facts

External data on market and industry trends and travel patterns will be useful when you are ready to develop your own marketing strategies.

Trends in the Overall Travel and Lodging Market. Look for a broad overview of major segment trends, such as signs of growth or decline in pleasure travel versus business travel and/or any other information you can obtain regarding growth trends of the other market segments. This information will be very general, but will help you determine a marketing **strategy.**

Feeder City Data. Feeder city data can be very beneficial when you plan advertising, and may already be available to you. It must be included in the total marketing program. **Feeder cities** are the cities from where your business originates. Convention and visitors bureaus, airport authorities, and rental car agencies are just a few of the sources you can explore for this data. There may be differences in feeder city data for pleasure and for business travel. You must consider both markets.

It may seem overly ambitious to try to gather information in this category. Nonetheless, it may prove beneficial to gather information regarding when certain types of group customers historically have met, when certain industries put their sales people on the road, and other similar information. Concentrate on areas that may help determine specific strategies that can plug holes in your sales patterns.

Internal Facts

Marketing Expenditures. Look at your marketing costs objectively. Marketing cost should be defined as "that amount necessary to procure the sale." Using this definition, include as part of your marketing costs all the following expenses and reductions to income:

- Salesperson salaries and administrative expenses
- Advertising expenditures
- Public relations expenditures
- Travel relations expenditures
- Coupon discounts
- Reservation systems expenses
- Credit card fees you pay to credit card companies
- Others

This definition may not conform to a uniform system of accounts, but it will give you a clearer picture of your actual marketing costs. When you combine an overview of expenditures with a trend analysis, you should be able to more objectively determine the proper allocation of funds needed to carry out the marketing strategies you develop.

Trends in Your Mix of Business. Measure trends in your property's room sales in the following segments:

- Family and pleasure
- Commercial (salespeople, trade, etc.)
- Executives
- Groups (corporate and association)

This information—for a single hotel, on a geographical area basis, or chainwide—will tell you what is really happening when sales go up or down. You need to know how effective your efforts are in building business in a particular segment.

When you have a decrease in sales, you need to know in what segment the problem lies so that you may take immediate, focused corrective action.

In short, trends in room sales are your monitoring system—the indicator of what is happening and how effective you are in your marketing planning and execution.

Other Hospitality Industry Sector Applications

The marketing planning process outlined in this chapter can be directly applied, with some tailoring, to other hospitality industry sectors. The four major types of research and information required apply to restaurant chains, airlines, car rental firms, cruise companies, and any other major entity serving the away-from-home market. The steps and questions listed within each research phase are, to some extent, applicable to your market and product or service. How you apply these, answer the questions, and analyze the data is up to you. The better your effort, the better your marketing and competitive edge.

Marketing Plan

Now that you have examined the first part of the total marketing plan structure, asked the right questions, and obtained factual answers, you can start the actual marketing plan. The following outline displays the next phase of the total marketing plan.

MARKETING PLAN STRUCTURE

- Analysis of research and information
- Objectives
- Marketing program
- Marketing appropriations (the marketing budget)
- Sales goals
- Action programs
- Communication of assigned responsibilities
- Monitoring of action program

In the marketing plan, you analyze what you have learned about your business, and translate it into **action programs.** By combining all of your research into one document, you force yourself to see:

- How (and whether) everything you are doing actually fits together
- Whether it is logical and sound
- Whether, in total, it is possible to accomplish with the manpower and money available.

You also clearly establish guidelines for handling day-to-day matters in a manner consistent with your longer range objectives.

Analysis of Research and Information

The questions below identify specific areas to target in the marketing program. Information needed to answer the questions will come from the market segmentation, needs identification, and customer perceptions research discussed earlier.

Customer Needs, Preferences, and Perceptions

1. Which market segments relate best to your products or services?

2. In which areas of need are your products or services perceived to be strong by current market segments? In which areas are they weak?

3. In which areas of need do your strengths (as perceived by the segment) correspond to the first priority needs of the segment?

4. In each weak area(as perceived by the market segment), are there operational factors that contribute to the perceived weakness, or is it purely an image or awareness problem?

5. In each market segment with which you presently best identify, who are your major competitors and what are their major strengths and weaknesses (as perceived by the segment)?

6. Are your main markets presently within the segments that best identify with your product or service? Are there any areas of need in which your competition is perceived as doing a superior job?

7. Which market segments relate least to your product or service? Is this a result of your past marketing programs being focused in other directions, or does it stem from an inaccurate or inadequate awareness of the product or service itself?

8. In each market segment where you see an opportunity to broaden your market, who are your major competitors and what are their major strengths and weaknesses (as perceived by the segment)?

Competitive Trends

1. How has your property fared against competitive lodging chains in recent years?

2. What are the primary marketing directions of your major competitors?

3. What are the major competitive threats facing your property now and in the near future?

Immediate Problems

What are the immediate problems that must be corrected this year? The following list suggests examples of problems that must be addressed immediately:

- Sales problems at a specific property
- Declining business volumes in particular market segments
- Quality and service problems
- Pricing problems

- New competitive lodging facilities that are expected to have an adverse effect on a particular market or property

- Existing marketing strategies that are unsuccessful

Long-Range Major Problems

What are the major marketing problems you face that must be solved to achieve greater success over the next five years? For example:

- Change of image required

- Industry-wide declining business volumes in particular market segments

- Increasing success of a particular competitor (in hotel facility design, in quality and service, in marketing, in overall results, or in combinations of these items)

- Changes in preferences and needs of a particular market segment

- Pricing

- Adverse trends or yields in marketing expenditures

Opportunities and Alternatives

1. What are the major weaknesses of your competitors that you could exploit more fully?

2. What unsatisfied needs have been identified in your present market segments? Is it possible to provide a service or product that will satisfy this need?

3. What market segments peripheral to your current marketing thrust offer opportunities for you to broaden your market?

Objectives

What are the overall objectives of your marketing program? These objectives should be determined on the basis of your research and information analysis. Objectives should correspond to the following areas:

- Identification of customer preferences and the desire to change customers' perceptions of your product or service

- Changes in marketing direction desired after comparing your present markets with shifts in the total market

- Defensive or offensive marketing moves dictated by competitive successes and new competitive directions

- Immediate problem-solving

- Long-range problem-solving

- Taking advantage of opportunities open to your property

In order to make the marketing program as effective as possible, restrict the number of marketing objectives to the major items of the highest priority. The whole purpose of marketing planning is to "separate the wheat from the chaff" and to focus on those areas that will yield the greatest results. Attempting to focus on everything will result in more work, greater expenditures, minimal results, and frustration for all. By separating priority from non-priority objectives, you can achieve positive results; hence, it is desirable to limit the number of objectives you establish.

Marketing Program

This section suggests an approach to developing your total marketing program for the next several years, with emphasis on the first year. This section, like the whole marketing plan, should be updated each year.

Overall Strategy. First, state the proposition. That is, define, in general terms, what you are trying to provide and sell to your markets. The proposition should be the promise that can be made to have the strongest appeal to the customers' self-interests. It should be based on the information gathered during the research steps of this marketing planning process. It must be truthful, possible to achieve, and unique. It must clearly distinguish you over the competition.

You may need a different proposition for each market segment. If so, make sure there are no inconsistencies between the propositions.

Next, clarify the platform. Your marketing platform is the list of benefits to the customer and advantages over the competition that your property provides. Spell out, item by item, all the claims you plan to make to your customers. This is not another general statement; it is the detail that supports the proposition. Your promotion and advertising will be based on the platform.

Media Strategy. Use your established objectives to identify precise target markets at which to aim the media. Establish specific advertising, public relations, and direct mail programs, and clearly determine the intent of the program, media selection, dates, and dollars for each.

Each of the advertising, public relations, and direct mail programs should be compared with previous media programs. Program changes should be made on the basis of how the new program will achieve the desired objectives and results better than did the old program. Also, compare your media programs to those of your competitors and address any obvious deficiencies.

Selling Strategy. Specific strategies should be developed for sales and promotion to associations, commercial groups, single commercial travelers, travel agents, and other market segments. Development of selling strategies must be accomplished at two levels:

- *Corporate level.* Identify activities that will be carried out by your national sales departments' marketing staffs. Also identify overall sales strategies to be implemented by individual or regional sales teams (where applicable).

- *Property level.* Develop specific sales targets and strategies for each property. (Again, identify a few major strategies rather than attempting all the possible ways of building sales.)

Compare these sales strategies with competitors' sales programs and correct any obvious deficiencies. Strategies should also be compared with previous strategies to determine if there are sufficient differences to achieve your desired changes.

You must also identify new staffing requirements and the difference in cost from the preceding programs.

Operations Changes. Identify the changes in operations or procedures required to achieve the desired marketing objectives and establish timing costs.

Marketing Appropriations

Amount. Determine how much funding is needed to achieve the agreed-upon marketing objectives and supporting programs. What is the difference between the amount needed and available funds? Ultimately, a final amount should be determined. Keep in mind if incremental funding is used, there should be an expected offset in incremental revenue.

Allocation. Determine the allocation of available funds among the various functions of marketing: advertising, publicity, sales force, travel agents' commissions, discount coupons, pre-opening campaigns, and research. Use the zero-base budgeting, wherein all expenditures must be fully analyzed and their justifications verified each year. This approach may help in re-allocating resources from year to year into areas where they will do the most good.

Since there will rarely be sufficient funds available to execute all the programs needed, available funds should be apportioned, according to costs and benefits.

Justification. The justification for the marketing budget is the research and analysis you conduct. If you have approached the marketing planning process in an analytical and pragmatic way, then you will have a strong argument for your budget. If management does not allocate sufficient funds to achieve the necessary results, or if these funds are not efficiently spent, then you must accept something less than the desired objectives.

Sales Goals

Sales goals can be both macro and micro in nature, but they should always be quantified. You may be looking at a sales increase measured in dollars, or you may want to increase your sales percentage as measured against the entire chain's average. The following is a list of questions that can help you identify sales goals:

1. What is the total sales goal for all properties (as a group)? This may be expressed as revenue or in terms of a percentage increase.

2. What is the revenue-per-available-room goal?

3. What is the average occupancy goal for all properties?

4. What is the average room rate goal for all properties?

5. What are the goals for room sales in each major business segment? Determine the percent for each segment.

Exhibit 1   Marketing Program Organization Chart

Item	Target Date	Approved Expenditure	Responsibility
Media Plan			
Selling Plan			

Family and pleasure _____ %

Commercial (sales/trade) _____ %

Executive _____ %

Groups (corporate and associations) _____ %

6. How much additional sales will be generated this year (over last year) for the increase in marketing expenditures over those of last year? Estimate the increase in dollars.

Action Programs

List, in chronological order, all the specific strategies that were allocated available marketing funds. Identify specific target dates, responsibility, and budgeted-approved expenditures. Exhibit 1 shows one way of organizing this information.

Communication of Assigned Responsibilities

Proper steps must be taken to ensure that the most important aspects of this plan, particularly the action program, are clearly communicated to those individuals responsible for program implementation.

Monitoring of Action Program

To properly monitor progress on the action program, institute an adequate follow-up process. The chapter appendix presents a simple worksheet to help you allocate the marketing budget by expenditure and by market segment. The worksheet can be modified and applied at the individual-property level.

The first attempt at completing a marketing planning process of this nature is always the most difficult. Updating and scheduling periodic research will provide you with an ongoing flow of relevant and applicable information. You must be careful to make sound judgments at stages before the research is completed. However, depending on management's judgment, knowledge, and expertise, some of the data may have immediate application and be beneficial to your marketing programs.

Key Terms

action program

competition

customer needs

customer perceptions

feeder city

focus group

market segment

marketing planning

objectives

strategy

zero-base budgeting

Chapter Appendix

	MARKET SEGMENTS											
	Pleasure						Business					
	Int'l	Resort	Family	Singles	Weekend		Other	Group		Execu-tives	Commercial		Other
					Family Escape	Children's Escape		Comp.	Assoc.		Exp. Acct.	Per Diem	
National Advertising Consumer Trade Sports Directories Yellow Pages Airport Display												
Local Advertising												
Production Advertisements & Commercials Agency Fees Agency Travel												
National Public Relations Fees Expenses T.V. Participations												
National Direct Mail Mailings Listings												
Brochures												
Research (Advertising & Marketing)												
Projects/Internal Promotion/Mini Markets												
Advertising Administration												
Local Public Relations												
Local Tie-Ins & Contests												
Direct Selling Local Sales Departments National Sales Departments Special Intermediary												
Trade Shows (Exhibitions)												
Familiarization Trips												
Promotional Parties												
Department												
TOTAL												

REVIEW QUIZ

When you feel you have covered all of the material in this chapter, answer these questions. Choose the *best* answer. Check your answers with the correct ones found on the Review Quiz Answer Key at the end of this book.

Multiple Choice

1. The four areas of information required to complete a marketing plan are:

    a. market segmentation, media selections, budgets, and facts about the competition.
    b. market segmentation, zero-base budgeting concepts, intermediary facts, and occupancy details.
    c. market segmentation, facts about competitors, external facts, and internal facts.
    d. external facts, internal facts, demographics, and market strategies.

2. To determine which market segments your property should or should not pursue, consider:

    a. how profitable the segment is.
    b. how suitable your existing facilities are for that segment.
    c. the segment's trend for growth or decline.
    d. all of the above.

3. A marketing plan helps you analyze what you have learned about your business and translate it into:

    a. action programs.
    b. research questions.
    c. competitive intelligence.
    d. sales.

Chapter Outline

Revenue and Profit Production Ideas
Methods to Distinguish Your Property
Ten Keys to Positive Consumer Reaction
Five Steps to More Competitive Marketing

Learning Objectives

1. Describe several revenue and profit production ideas. (pp. 247–250)

2. Explain how to distinguish an establishment from its competitors. (pp. 250–253)

3. Give ten examples of how to secure positive consumer reaction. (pp. 253–255)

4. Explain five steps you can take to have more competitive marketing. (pp. 255–256)

Practical Steps to Maximize Marketing

Y̲OU DON'T HAVE TO USE sophisticated techniques to produce effective marketing results. There are many practical steps to increasing revenues and profits that include marketing and capitalizing on what already exists within your hotel, restaurant, or customer base. This chapter will identify several revenue and profit production ideas for properties. We will also discuss methods that will distinguish your establishment from its competition. The reaction your customers have to you will be based in large part on how you treat them; this chapter will discuss ten traits that will help customers have a positive reaction to your establishment. Finally, this chapter will guide you through five quick steps that you can take to make your establishment more competitive.

Revenue and Profit Production Ideas

Some of the following ideas may prove useful in bringing additional revenues to your property.

Merchandise and Earn Money. One sure-fire way to bring in additional revenue is to take advantage of your *in-house profit centers*. These centers are ideal spots to offer additional merchandise and services for sale. Two major steps in recognizing the potential of *in-house profit centers* are to:

• View your establishment as a place through which consumers pass

• Recognize that even the smallest service you can provide—and from which you can profit—will help you meet some need of the consumer

A hotel traditionally has revenue and profit centers in the major areas of rooms and food and beverage; some also have banquet sales and gift shops. View each area as a profit center with target markets, sales goals, and profit margin objectives. Try to identify other profit centers within the property. Are there game rooms, lobby displays (space leased from the hotel for display purposes), a health club, a barber/beauty shop, or a lobby bar? Does the property have an infrequently used storage room that should be cleaned out and used to generate revenue and profit? Would a coin-operated copy center be useful? How about secretarial services? Laundromat? Book stand? Wall-art display sales? Do restaurant restrooms lend themselves to vending for necessity items? Examine all these possibilities as well as other opportunities at your establishment that can generate the maximum amount of revenue and profit per room. Apply your creative marketing ability to "sell that guest" when he or she is on your premises.

Restaurants frequently have an old display case with mints, gum, and cigars visible through dirty glass. This is sometimes their only method of increasing revenue through sales at the cashier's stand. However, much more can be done to generate small amounts of additional revenue and profit out of a customer who is already purchasing. Ask yourself the following questions: Are the items in the display case presented in an attractive manner to encourage sales? Are there one or two desserts or specialty items that can be packaged and sold to the departing customer? Are there any items that appeal to children? (Even if children are not your clientele, many parents will buy on a whim.) Would a dessert cart improve the merchandising and volume of dessert sales? Do you have enough customers and space to put in a gift shop?

The answers to these questions will help you maximize merchandising with items that *fulfill the customer's needs* while he or she is in "your house." Make sure you monitor sales and set goals for each profit-making opportunity.

Reduce Guilt and Earn Money. Research has shown that humans have guilt complexes. You can help your guests resolve feelings of guilt and earn money for yourself at the same time. For a long time, the telephone company, postal service, and greeting card companies have suggested, "How nice it would be to call home," or "Aren't you rotten for not thinking of Grandma and sending her a card or a letter?" So, why shouldn't hospitality establishments—through marketing—simply say, "Remember your spouse and children: try our gift stand."

One large hotel chain with mostly male guests tripled its gift-shop sales by tapping into the guilt of businessmen away from home. The chain stocked its gift shops with items for women and children that fit into a suitcase or travel bag, and redistributed its shelf space from 80 percent men's items to 80 percent women's and children's items. Sales of these items, such as jewelry and sturdy high-markup children's toys, helped the male guests feel better by reducing their guilt about being away from home. For the hotel, it meant sizable additional revenues and profits. In addition, the female guests found the women's items attractive and also made purchases from the gift shop. The merchandising was skillful, and the marketing message was subtle. The in-room material simply stated, "We have a well-stocked gift shop, including a fine selection of women's and children's items. It is open from 6 A.M. to 1 A.M." Not coincidentally, the gift shop remained open 30 minutes after the bar and lounge closed. The gift shop was located between the bar and the elevator. A small poster-picture of a child with a tear in his eye was visible through the glass window of the gift shop. The caption, "Did You Remember Me, Daddy?" was clearly visible even to the blurry eye. The period one hour before the gift shop closed was the period of highest volume revenue and profit for gift-shop sales.

Make a Kid Happy and Earn Money. Do you have electronic games or a game room? A game room may make not only children happy, but their parents as well by providing something for the children to do. This revenue- and profit-generating opportunity can be marketed through in-room merchandising. One entrepreneurial hotel owner goes one step further by providing a free game token to all children. Other hotels put electronic games in the guestrooms that are hooked up to the establishment's in-room movie system. They then charge by the hour for the use of them.

Invest $0 and Earn Money. If you have the space, there are many ways to invest nothing but still make money. Consider the game room as one opportunity. You can make a deal with a reliable distributor to set up your game room in the space you provide and collect a percentage of the profits. The same concept applies to vending, although the percentages may be lower. Earlier we mentioned dressing up your property with a display of artwork or glassware. Other possibilities include flower carts, plant displays, and paperback racks. You can collect a percentage of the sales of these items as well. By setting up deals with these types of outside businesses or vendors, you may be able to meet the needs of your customers, enhance your property, and generate additional revenues and profits with little or no investment!

Stay Healthy and Earn Money. Keeping in shape has become a major psychological goal of our population. Take advantage of this fact. If your property has the space (one large room, a rooftop, or a parking-lot perimeter), consider the possibilities of an exercise room, sauna, or jogging course. Some hotels charge guests for using these amenities, but even if you don't charge guests for using, say, your exercise room, that does not mean you cannot earn money through promotions and tie-ins to these health-oriented amenities. In-room materials can promote a "health cocktail of the month" or a "special high-protein dinner." One hotel's promotion program lays out the jogging course and tells the guest to pick up his or her "time card" which, when given to the hostess in the lounge, will give them their second health cocktail free. In addition, the hotel has three menu items (good profit margins on all three) promoted as the "lo-cal," "high-pro," and "dieter's delight." The results have been excellent—guests are satisfied because their needs are being recognized, and the hotel is realizing increased beverage sales and food profits.

Redirect Your Cash Flow and Earn Money. You can improve your earnings and simplify your banking by improving your cash management program. Avoid keeping cash on the premises—for one thing, it's hazardous. Checking accounts *cost* money (for checks, fees, services, etc.)—they don't *earn* money. Savings accounts and NOW accounts (interest-bearing checking accounts) earn money but *can* lose to inflation, if inflation is high. Most people cannot tie up their cash flow in long-term savings certificates. So what other options are available? Money market funds are one place to look. Interest rates generally exceed most local rates offered by savings and loans institutions, and liquidity (the ability to use your cash when needed) is the same as a checking account. Most money market funds also provide free checks. Consider this approach: Use a NOW account (where allowed) for general disbursements, and use a money market fund to channel your cash on a regular basis. Consider the results to your bottom line shown in Exhibit 1. (A list of the money market funds and prevailing rates is published daily in the *Wall Street Journal* and other newspapers. Money market funds also represent a good resting place for advance deposits—why not earn interest on someone else's money?)

Exhibit 1   Financial Management: Comparison of Types of Accounts

Type of Account	On $1,000,000 in Average Cash Flow Available for Investment	On $100,000 in Average Cash Flow Available for Investment
Standard checking account	Costs you money	Costs you money
Savings account/NOW checking account	Earns 4–6% interest	Earns 4–6% interest
Certificates of deposit	Earns 7–16% interest (Ties up your cash)	Earns 7–16% interest (Ties up your cash)
Money market fund	Earns 5–15% interest or $75,000–$150,000	Earns 5–15% or $5,000–$15,000

Increase Productivity and Earn Money. Improving the productivity of your sales-people can increase your profits. There are two opposite approaches to increasing your salespeople's productivity. Approach one is a "see-what-happens" approach called "Let Someone Go" or "Don't Fill It." It often applies when there is a sizable staff involved. Someone leaves your sales staff or is released by you. You then need to evaluate what happens to your overall sales (and, more important, your overall profits) if you do not fill the position. A number of things can happen, such as a decrease in costs per sale, an increase in productivity per remaining salesperson, or the worst—a decline in sales which is greater than the total cost of the person who left the operation.

Approach two, called "Bring Someone In," adds a salesperson to the staff but sets a reasonable production target that the salesperson has to meet; this target may equal total costs for the new salesperson times nine or ten, or some other specific dollar amount in sales.

A variation on the "Bring-Someone-In" approach is to offer an attractive in-centive to travel agents producing a specific multiple of the incentive cost in sales for your product or service. The advantage to this alternative is that you have no additional overhead, yet you have effectively extended your sales force. One hotel chain offered an expensive sports car to the travel agency that produced the great-est sales increase over a base figure (four times the recovery cost of the car). The results were dramatic—agency sales quadrupled and the winning firm produced enough additional sales to pay for a fleet of vehicles!

Methods to Distinguish Your Property

Increasing revenue and profits from your operations may involve more than applying a marketing strategy. Frequently you may need to make operational, physical, or attitudinal changes. Let's briefly look at some ideas that may help you distinguish your operations, products, or services.

There are a number of marketing methods that can add to the *marketing attrac-tiveness* of what you offer. The following suggestions may not work for all, but they might help you think of other ideas to improve the marketability of your hospitality product or service.

Make Something Perfect. Offering a good selection (in price and variety) in your food and beverage operation or restaurant will help you meet broad customer needs. However, you should also identify at least two items that you can offer to perfection. You should be able to build a reputation as the best place to have the items. These "signature items" can help you attract repeat visitors. The perfection of an item can be measured in any of the following characteristics:

- Quality
- Preparation
- Presentation
- Promotion
- Perception as a real value

A signature item may be a specialty dish, main entrée, or unique dessert. For a signature item to be successful it must have broad appeal and be consistently perfect. *Consistency* in the preparation and presentation of a signature item is critical.

Do Something Unique. If you can find something unique to offer guests in your establishment, your guests will not only purchase it—they'll talk about it to their friends and acquaintances. Find some way to make some of your services or products stand out from your competition. This method of distinguishing your operation can take on many forms. For example, one Midwest hotel's restaurant/lounge offers a unique "English Bloody Mary." The drink is served in a large, frosted, bowl-shaped glass, dressed with a salt coating, and garnished with a celery stick and parsley. In addition, a four-ounce cold beer chaser is set next to the mildly spicy drink. Tent cards advertise this unique beverage and well-trained servers encourage guests to buy it. The pricing is two-tiered: $2.25 for the English Bloody Mary and the first beer chaser; refills of the four-ounce chaser, which are served by alert and well-trained servers carrying small 16-ounce frosted pitchers of cold brew, are priced at $1.50. Needless to say, many patrons end up spending six or seven dollars on their English Bloody Mary, because they buy many four-ounce chasers to go with their one large, well-presented specialty drink. This beverage offering has developed its own following, thus encouraging repeat business. It is also an excellent trial item for the new patron. The result is higher profits, more volume, and a unique identity for the restaurant.

The Up-Front Signals. What is first perceived is believed. Applying this phrase can help you market your products/services and add revenue to your bottom line. A hotel in the western United States has taken this "up-front signals" method to heart and to the bank—here's how.

The hotel (we'll call it Classic Hotel) was a first-class hotel, but it was more than 40 years old. The owners were concerned about competition from a new Hilton high-rise with a magnificent black-glass exterior. The new Hilton looked good—it had marketability from the outside appearance; however, the older hotel's service levels and quality were better. How could the older facility distinguish itself and retain its status? It needed to give an immediate "up-front" perception to potential customers that was equal to or better than the "black-glass special" without spending millions. A consultant came up with a practical and inexpensive "up-front signal." He suggested that the owners of the older brownish stone building add a door-to-street gold-colored canopy and an appropriately plush sidewalk covering. The consultant also suggested a few additional investments. One was to add the word "The" before the hotel's name on the canopy in script writing: *The* Classic Hotel. Next, he helped the owners recruit a local college basketball player (over six feet, four inches tall) to work in a luxurious doorman's suit and top hat (also gold and brown) from 4 P.M. to 9 P.M. Finally, to recover these investments, he suggested that the older hotel *raise its rates* slightly above the new Hilton's. The owners agreed. Here are the results.

First, the canopy and tall doorman were the most visible sights when coming down Main Street. So eye-alluring were the canopy and doorman that the "black-glass special" just faded into the skyscape. First-class guests coming to this western city received only one reply when they asked about the best place to stay—"The Classic Hotel is the classiest place in town, and it is only one or two dollars more a night than the Hilton." (This same concept has worked well for a number of restaurants trying to upgrade their images.)

Inside Signals. Improving the marketability of your product or service to the consumer doesn't have to involve the outside wrapper or packaging. There are a number of highly visible interior areas where simply changing the lighting or adding a mirror can work wonders. For example, a major luxury hotel chain discovered it had an operational problem: occasionally its elevators gave slow service during high-occupancy periods. In addition, the windows at the end of the corridors where the elevators were looked out onto the hotel's heating and ventilation equipment. It was physically impossible to add elevators. The solution to keeping the guests occupied during their wait was very simple. The hotel installed full-length mirrors on the walls near the elevators. The mirrors provided a perfect distraction for the guests, who could look at themselves and check their appearance. With this simple ploy the hotel diverted attention from a potential annoyance and enhanced the appearance of its interior. Complaints virtually ceased and the idea was soon adopted by other hotels in the chain with similar elevator problems. The guests' dissatisfaction turned into satisfaction when they viewed themselves in those wonderful mirrors by the elevators!

Another general manager knew his guestrooms were not due for refurbishing but that their appearance was not competitive with the guestrooms of other properties. His approach was to compensate through substitution. He decided to set aside about 20 percent of his rooms for female travelers, and another large percentage for men only. In the rooms for women, he added a fresh flower in a clearly visible bureau-top vase, new- and softer-color towels, new shower curtains of a different color, a skirt hanger, and a new double dead-bolt lock. In the rooms for men, he placed a current issue of *Sports Illustrated, Time, Newsweek,* or *U.S. News,* the latest edition of a newspaper, and a complimentary pen and pencil set. While the hotel incurred small costs, it regained guest satisfaction and business stayed.

The hotel's slightly worn rooms remained competitive. In essence, his inside signals were compensating for the aging-guestrooms problem.

The "Can-of-Paint" Technique. The least expensive way to change the appearance of something old or dirty is to paint it. The "can-of-paint" technique can work for you! Walk around the outside of your property. Look for the most visible aging signals. It may be a dirt-stained wall near the lobby entrance, striping on the parking lot surface, or deteriorating signs. Invest in a "can of paint"—it's a signal to consumers that you have changed from dirty or old to fresh, clean, and well kept.

Ten Keys to Positive Consumer Reaction

There are signals or keys that can help bring new consumers to you and then bring them back as repeat visitors. Let's look at ten keys for repeat business, greater marketability, and improving the consumer's perception of the product or service you offer.

Key 1: The Fresh and New Signal. "Fresh" and "new" are positive signs to most consumers. Whether it be the can of paint or the replacement of tablecloths, napkins, towels, uniforms, or menus, you need signals that clearly convey that your product or service is fresh or new. Take a good look at your facility or operation and identify what you can do to provide the strongest "fresh and new" signal to your market.

Key 2: The Neat and Clean Test. Your product or service need not be brand new to convey positive signals. Cleanliness is another very strong desire on the part of the lodger, diner, and traveler. Rooms (especially bathrooms), lounges, restaurant floors, and even airline seats should pass your cleanliness inspection. Even new facilities will lose out if they are sloppy or dirty. Guests rank cleanliness consistently high when they are surveyed about hotels, restaurants, and public travel-oriented facilities. Check out your establishment:

- Are the lounges cleaned before and after meeting breaks or large volumes of traffic?

- Are the carpets clean and vacuumed?

- Is everyone a member of the "paper patrol"? (This means that if discarded paper is on the floor or room-service trays are in the hallways, do all staff members—including you—understand it is their job to pick it up or move it from the consumer's view?)

Key 3: Efficiency. For many travelers, time is of the essence. Fast check-in and check-out and an impression of efficiency at the front desk are essential to ensure a positive customer reaction. While it is important that front-desk personnel display warm, friendly attitudes, pleasant faces are no substitute for efficiency to the busy executive. Your employees can smile all they want, but if the customer has been waiting for ten minutes, you can bet he or she won't be smiling back. An efficient check-in and check-out, coupled with that smile, will be the winning combination for pleasing your customers.

Key 4: Reliability. The obvious place to start with reliability is ensuring that the customer's reservation is there and correct when he or she arrives. However, this is certainly not where reliability should end. Some other key reliability factors include, but are not limited to:

- A television that works
- Adequate guestroom lighting (especially in work or reading areas)
- Towels and tissues
- An accurate and prompt message service system

Reliability means that when room service says, "It will be up in 15 minutes," the tray arrives in 10 to 12 minutes—not 30 or 45 minutes. Reliability means that when someone calls a guest, the message is taken and delivered. Reliability is a combination of all these factors that gives the guest a comfortable feeling that "this place works."

Key 5: Acceptability. People like to be accepted. Does your operation convey acceptance or do your guests feel as though they are processed? Are they viewed as outsiders instead of guests? Does the word "welcome" still exist in the vocabulary of all your guest-contact personnel? Are the employees also acceptable to your customers? Rude attitudes, shabby appearances, and so on can take a perfectly reliable operation and turn it into a very unacceptable environment for your customers. Make sure your customers feel accepted.

Key 6: Empathy. Not all of your customers will arrive at the front desk in a good mood. Be sure your personnel are trained to deal with difficult guest attitudes and are capable of recognizing those who might have just been through a trying experience. The importance of empathy and making sure your guests feel accepted can be related in the following true story.

I was invited to give a presentation at a distant resort area. Having had other commitments, it was necessary for me to take a very late flight, and there was no time to shave or clean up. Arriving at the resort after a six-hour flight, unshaven and having had the two drinks on board, I wanted to check in quickly and get some rest before the early morning presentation. Unfortunately, my suitcase had been lost by the airline. By the time the lost-bag forms were completed, it was after 1 A.M. when I entered the hotel. Trying to check in at the front desk proved to be an equally trying experience in this first-class resort.

A night auditor, sitting behind the front desk sorting through index cards, peered at me over his bifocals. The look was easily readable: "If I ignore him, maybe he'll leave." After all, I was unshaven and had no suitcase. Finally the auditor decided to take on his role as front desk agent and came to the desk, but he continued to sort his little cards and mumbled, "I'll be with you in a minute. I want to finish this batch." To say the least, I was not feeling particularly "accepted" at this point. After a brief exchange, in which I indicated that I would appreciate an efficient check-in, the night auditor asked, "Do you have a reservation?" My response was, "Yes, it was guaranteed by both my host (the resort's owner) and my American Express card." The auditor's response was, "I don't see it—are you sure you had a reservation for the 29th?" By now, a full ten minutes had passed and still no registration card, no key, no room—the night auditor had made things even worse by moving from no "acceptability" to no "reliability."

I won't go into the details of how Mr. Night Auditor learned empathy or how to hustle, but I will tell you he is no longer with that resort!

Key 7: Uniqueness. Because you so often hear the expression, "They are all about the same," wouldn't offering some uniqueness make sense? It does not have to be totally different (like a double-decker London bus for a limo), but you should have something that tells your market, "This is the place that has great food" or "hustling personnel" or "a good piano bar" or "the six-foot, four-inch doorman." Offering customers something that can be identified with you will give your product or service a recognizable edge.

Key 8: Class. Class has many definitions. One of the most applicable to the service industry is *the ability to function with grace under pressure.* The handling of an irritated executive by an experienced front desk agent can be a demonstration in class for all to observe. Class is also a feeling within the property that comes from the employees' overall esprit de corps. Class is *not* an arrogant general manager or director of food and beverage who is unable to extend a helping hand to a lower-level employee. Class is an attitude that you and your employees convey to customers when you offer your product or service. If you have class, your customers will know it and react positively.

Key 9: Beat-the-System Offer. Survey after survey indicates that most people do not like a regimented environment, or what "the system" offers. One technique in obtaining positive customer reactions is to make sure that your customers have at least one opportunity to "beat the system" (your system) during their visits with you. The opportunity may be nothing more than free after-dinner mints or the second drink on the house, or a discount.

Key 10: Value. Value is *quality at a fair price.* Just as most people want to believe they have "beat the system," no one wants to feel cheated. Over-pricing, poor-quality products, and inadequate service levels are "rip-off" signals that destroy the opportunity to offer consumers the strongest reason to be your customer—value. Today more than ever, the public is demanding quality at a fair price yet finding it increasingly difficult to obtain. Offer value and you will be successful. You will have given the customer the strongest possible reason to do business with you, and that signal will result in repeated purchases of your product or service.

Five Steps to More Competitive Marketing

The following five steps can help you market your property more successfully:

1. *Go out and look* at your strongest competitor's operation. That means looking at more than the rates and facility. Look at the competitor's staff—their level of desire, competency, enthusiasm, courteousness, and thoughtfulness. Set some stringent performance objectives.

2. *Make more sales calls—even if it's only one more.* Make going after revenue and customers the number one priority.

3. *Make deals.* Today, you need to make deals to maximize revenue. Unless every room is occupied, you are losing revenue.

4. *Change strategy.* There are a lot of ways to beat your competition, so don't hesitate to change strategy if it makes sense. If it doesn't cost you anything to offer it, do so. Even if it does cost you something, it might be less costly than losing the business. For example, shop your competition and find out the rates they are quoting in your valley periods, then adjust your rates accordingly. Go after and *steal* the business.

5. *Select and inspect.* Check a sales file *daily* and discuss it with the responsible employee. Every day, observe the front desk at check-in and the cashier at check-out. Be sure *your* guests are being taken care of properly. You work hard to sell them; make sure others are working hard to keep them coming back.

Key Terms

in-house profit center

REVIEW QUIZ

When you feel you have covered all of the material in this chapter, answer these questions. Choose the *best* answer. Check your answers with the correct ones found on the Review Quiz Answer Key at the end of this book.

1. Reducing consumer guilt is a way to:

    a. produce profit and revenue.
    b. distinguish your establishment.
    c. create positive consumer reaction.
    d. market an establishment more competitively.

2. Contracting a paperback rack is an example of earning money by:

    a. increasing productivity.
    b. investing $0.
    c. making a kid happy.
    d. redirecting your cash flow.

3. Which of the following is *not* a way to distinguish your establishment?

    a. making something perfect
    b. doing something unique
    c. applying a can of paint
    d. increasing productivity

4. Making sure the television works and that there is adequate lighting is an element of which key to positive consumer relations?

    a. efficiency
    b. neat and clean test
    c. reliability
    d. fresh and new signal

Chapter Outline

Research
Operations

Learning Objectives

1. Explain how research supports a property's overall marketing effort. (pp. 259–260)

2. Describe how operations can meet the expectations of guests, and summarize ways to handle guest complaints. (pp. 260–263)

Marketing, Operations, and Research

USING EVERY AVAILABLE MARKETING TOOL and sticking to an organized marketing plan are not enough to guarantee success in the hospitality industry. Marketing tools and plans cannot be fully effective unless they are: (1) based on sound research, and (2) supported by your operations team. This chapter focuses on the relationship between research, marketing, operations, and the guest.

Research

Research can, and should, play a major role in both operations and marketing. Research does not provide strategies, but it does identify issues that both marketing and operations need to address. Research supports the overall marketing effort by identifying:

- *What* is currently happening within the market (customer perceptions, needs, etc.)

- *Which* competitors are having an impact on the market (competitive strategy assessment)

- *What* is likely to happen to the market (environmental forecast)

- *How* the property or brand is performing within the market against the competition (see Exhibit 1)

In a very real sense, research provides balance and support to both marketing and operations.

Research results should be factual parameters within which marketing, operations, and development can function. These results identify key market and industry trends, competitive strategies, and implications upon which marketing strategies may be developed.

Research should also be used to objectively measure property performance, strategy execution, guest preferences, and guest responses to the property's marketing strategies. Once you've measured these variables, you can evaluate the effectiveness of the your property's overall marketing plan—how well marketing selected its strategies and how well operations fulfilled the expectations created by those strategies.

Research provides the basis upon which to rank, grade, and compare your property and your competition. Regardless of how the "scorecard" reads (share of

Exhibit 1   Focal Points of Research

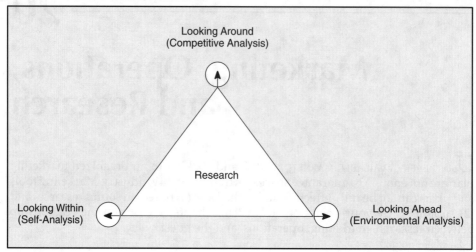

market, occupancy, average rate, covers, check averages, etc.), these results reflect guest reactions to the marketing message or promise, and to operations' fulfillment of that message. Analysis of guest needs and preferences must go beyond the research identification stage to convey an accurate assessment of guest expectations to both marketing and operations.

Operations

A marketing plan is developed based on the guest needs and expectations that were identified by research. A marketing plan cannot be executed successfully until operations delivers a product or service that meets guest needs and expectations as promised in the marketing. In order to ensure **customer satisfaction,** operations *must* meet guest needs by providing a level of service or product that matches the marketing message and related pricing.

Given the assumption that research, marketing, and operations act as a team, a number of practical steps can be taken to see that guest expectations are satisfactorily met. One useful tool that can be easily adapted to the hospitality industry lodging sector is an operations checklist. An operations checklist is based on the **guest's perspective,** not necessarily on the viewpoints of the property's marketing and operations staff members.

Operations Checklist (from the guest's perspective)

Preliminary Guest-Contact Points

_____   Advertising Display Boards—Are they clean and up-to-date? Do they show the correct telephone number and clear directions to the property?

_____ Limousine/shuttle/courtesy transportation—Are the vehicles clean and well-maintained? Is the service convenient for guests? Do the vehicles leave on schedule?

_____ Drivers/valets—Do drivers/valets have a clean, professional appearance? Do they have a sales-oriented, positive, friendly attitude?

_____ Facility Exterior—Are the buildings and outside areas clean and well-maintained? Are bushes and other landscaping well-maintained and free of debris? Are walkways well-lit, clean, and obstacle-free? Are parking and exterior areas secure and well-lit?

Major Guest-Contact Points (Front Desk/Lobby)

_____ Front Desk—Is the area clean and well-maintained? Does it project a feeling of activity? Are promotional materials visible and readily available without cluttering the counter?

_____ Front Desk Employees—Do front desk employees greet guests in a friendly, positive manner? Do employees efficiently help guests check in and check out? Do employees ask if departing guests would like to make future reservations?

_____ Telephone Operators—Are operators courteous and well-trained? Is there an adequate staff? Do operators consistently answer the phone within three rings?

_____ Bellstaff—Are bellpersons courteous and helpful? Do they look professional? Do they "hustle" to provide service to guests? Are they informative and sales-oriented without seeming too talkative?

_____ Restrooms—Do restrooms near the public areas have adequate supplies? Are the floors cleaned before and after meeting breaks? Are the counters wiped before and after breaks?

Food and Beverage Areas

_____ Breakfast Service—Is service fast? Do employees always offer coffee refills? Is a morning paper available? Do employees demonstrate friendly, courteous attitudes?

_____ Food and Beverage Employees—Do all food and beverage employees convey a friendly and helpful attitude toward guests? Does each employee have a clean, professional appearance? Are employees well-trained and efficient?

_____ Food Quality/Presentation—Does the food convey value, quality, and quantity? Is the presentation of the food attractive?

_____ Menus and Promotional Materials—Are menus and promotional materials on the tables or quickly presented to the guest? Are they up-to-date and accurate? Are they clean?

_____ Floors/Windows—Are floors clean and dry? Are they free of obstacles and safety hazards? Are windows and window treatments clean and well-maintained?

_____ Tabletops—Are all utensils, linens, and glassware clean and in their proper places? Is anything missing from the table set-up? Are tables and chairs clean and well-maintained?

_____ Check Presentation—Is the customer's check quickly presented when requested? Is the customer told how and whom to pay at that time?

Other Areas

_____ Gift Shop—Is the gift shop well-stocked with current issues of reading material? Do available items meet travelers' needs, such as toiletries or gifts for spouses and children? If credit cards are accepted, is this information adequately displayed?

_____ Recreational Amenities Areas—Are recreational facilities and amenities clearly promoted? Are directions to the facilities clearly visible? Are recreation areas clean and well-maintained? Are plenty of towels available in the pool area? Are supplies, such as rackets and balls, available for sports and game areas?

These checklist items are what the guest sees or experiences; the manner in which they are presented determines the guest's perception of your operation. Successfully addressing each of the checklist items should result in customer satisfaction with the marketing message and the property. *Always remember the customer's perspective!*

Recognizing that it is impossible to always meet every guest's needs, both marketing and operations personnel should be thoroughly trained to handle problems if they occur. Complaints and problems often indicate areas in which the operation is not fulfilling the marketing message. Some key questions to answer include the following:

- Does your property have clear refund procedures and guidelines for dealing with dissatisfied guests? Do employees understand these policies and procedures?

- Is there a guest comment card and/or a number or person a guest can call to have a complaint resolved?

- Are employees trained to respond to and take care of guest complaints immediately?

- Are employees trained to notify a manager or supervisor about all guest complaints?

Having a well-trained staff and procedures for handling guest complaints can help keep customers satisfied and result in repeat business. One way to ensure that procedures work is to develop a "listen and tell" system. Simply stated, each employee is trained to listen to guest comments and conversations for clues to guest dissatisfaction, such as, "The light bulb doesn't work," or "The faucet leaks." The employee then passes the information along to the appropriate person or department to promptly correct the problem—before the guest returns to his or her room, if possible. This approach reduces the need to placate the complainer and results in a satisfied guest.

Marketing does not drive operations nor does operations drive marketing—the guest drives both. Research is one way to determine guest needs and the best way to meet those needs. Marketing cannot work without researched information and operational fulfillment. Marketing, research, and operations form a dependent, mutually beneficial support system with research as a base, marketing as the means of communication, and operations as fulfillment; the result is customer satisfaction.

Key Terms

guest perspective
customer satisfaction

REVIEW QUIZ

When you feel you have covered all of the material in this chapter, answer these questions. Choose the *best* answer. Check your answers with the correct ones found on the Review Quiz Answer Key at the end of this book.

1. Research supports a property's overall marketing effort by identifying:

   a. what is currently happening within the market.
   b. which competitors are having an impact on the market.
   c. what is likely to happen to the market (environmental forecast).
   d. all of the above.

2. An operations checklist:

   a. may be hard to adapt to an individual property.
   b. evaluates the property from the guest's perspective.
   c. lists items or areas past guests have been dissatisfied with.
   d. all of the above.

3. Guest complaints:

   a. may indicate areas in which operations are not fulfilling the marketing message.
   b. can result in return customers if handled effectively.
   c. are impossible to eliminate entirely.
   d. all of the above.

Chapter Outline

Automation
    The Relationship to Marketers and
        Consumers
    Reservations Systems
    Property Management Systems
    Marketing Information Systems
    Travel Purchasing Systems and Beyond

Learning Objectives

1. Summarize the history of automation in the hospitality industry and describe automation applications and trends.

Note: This chapter presents speculation about the future. Although the speculation is based largely on current factual information, it is nonetheless speculation. For that reason, it is presented strictly for your information and enjoyment. The test materials for the course include no questions on this chapter.

Travel Purchasing Systems: Automation and Beyond

THE HOSPITALITY BUSINESS is not driven by operations or marketing, but rather by consumers. As a result of automation, consumers have come to expect ever more from marketing. The advances in computer applications in travel transactions, the purchase of travel, reservations services, front office systems, guest histories and relations, customer services, and research analysis are all changing the game called marketing in our industry. In fact, these computer applications will, in all likelihood, cause a marketing revolution in the hospitality industry. This chapter reviews these automation trends and predicts what the future will hold.

Automation

The hospitality industry is no exception to worldwide industrial trends when it comes to **automation:** the replacement of manual or personally performed functions by automated equipment such as computers. Granted, the hospitality industry is one of the last to be engulfed by automation, but, just as computer-driven assembly lines and robotics transformed the automobile and other heavy-manufacturing industries, automation is likely to have a dramatic impact on the hospitality industry. In fact, the impact will be in the very area that opponents of automation claimed to be sacred in the service industries: the people-contact areas. Automation will have some of its greatest impacts on the hospitality industry in the expediting of consumer purchasing decisions, changing consumer purchasing behavior, and providing new services to travelers.

Traditionally, automation was narrowly perceived as a tool for producing and analyzing budgets, reports, statistics, and accounts. Starting with these largely financial applications, computers began to creep into other areas of application such as sales reporting, rooms inventory control, and timekeeping. As telecommunications and computer technology grew, so did reservations systems and their ability to handle transactions. This, in turn, led to further inroads by computers, as computers were used to analyze the captured reservations data, thus providing marketing information. Further applications of automation and computer technology resulted in front-office systems that provided such marketing data as customer histories, patterns of use, and preferences. It became very clear that automation had entered the world of marketing in the hospitality industry.

The Relationship to Marketers and Consumers

These technological advances in computers, system development, and telecommunications continue to produce many different relationships between automated equipment (such as computers), marketers, and consumers. For marketers, automation has provided the valuable tools of **guest histories,** customer preferences, demographic and psychographic profiles, and the resulting improvement of services and delivery of such services to consumers. For consumers, their purchasing behavior has been affected by 800 numbers, central reservations offices, pricing based on statistical analyses of supply-and-demand periods/ratios, and a host of conveniences made possible by automation. These conveniences include the presentation of multiple choices instantly displayed on CRTs, express/automated ticket purchasing, express check-in and check-out, automatic traveler's check- and cash-dispensing machines linked nationwide, and one-stop trip purchasing, to name just a few. Today, consumers can simply dial an 800 number or even access their own CRTs and do all their travel/trip purchasing with one call—hotel room, car rental, airline ticket, events tickets, etc. How these conveniences are delivered to the marketplace and which industry players are alert enough to fully embrace and employ these automated conveniences are things to watch for as the hospitality industry makes exciting advances in the years ahead. Those businesses that recognize the automation trends and invest and adjust should be successful. Failure to recognize these trends will likely result in losing touch with consumers and losing sales. Think about it. Today, consumers opt for the convenience of an **automated teller or transaction machine (ATM)** to access their cash. Why shouldn't they expect the same convenience when checking in or out of a hotel, buying an airline ticket, or renting a car?

Reservations Systems

Airline, car rental, and hotel reservations systems all have evolved into performing much broader functions than their original function of enabling a consumer to make a purchase or a rental. Today, airline systems have become travel purchasing systems with immense capabilities. Car rental systems have evolved into highly sophisticated data banks that can generate everything from car-preference to purchase-preference histories. Hotel reservations systems have turned into marketing and information management systems that store guest history and preference records.

Before we look at specific reservations systems as they have evolved into travel purchasing systems, let's put reservations systems into perspective. Basically, reservations systems have become collectors or gathering points of vast amounts of consumer, product, and marketing data. Exhibit 1 depicts reservations systems in this collector or gathering role.

One of the first phases in the evolution of reservations systems was simply the *purchase facilitator* phase, which is often associated with an 800 number and central reservations facility. The second phase was an expansionary one that might be termed the *data collector* phase. The third evolutionary phase was the organized

Exhibit 1   Reservations Systems as Collectors

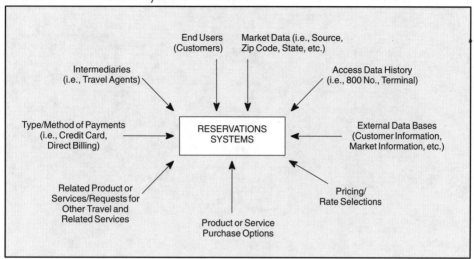

process of recasting this data into usable marketing and operations data—what is often referred to as the *management information* phase.

Many expansions of reservations-system capabilities paralleled the development of computer hardware and software. Today, one could argue that the ability to interface external data bases with reservations systems, thus providing data back to consumers, is the fourth phase of system development. The instantaneous or simultaneous relationship of data in all transaction outlets and locations may be thought of as another key phase or breakthrough—call it phase five. These five phases are shown in Exhibit 2. Regardless of terminology or the number of phases involved, these developments were, and are, major changes to what was originally simple purchase-facilitating systems.

There are many different reservations systems in the travel industry. One often hears about Westron in the hotel industry. This hotel-related system was one of the pioneers. Its capabilities were often used as a model for the development of many other hotel reservations systems. Today, Holiday Corp. has the Holidex system, Hilton the Hiltron system. The rental car industry has the "Wizard of Avis" and the "Hertz System." For years, airline reservations systems were dominated by American Airlines' SABRE system and United's APOLLO system. Later in the chapter we will discuss these systems and look at others that promise to have a major impact on how travel is marketed in the years to come.

Property Management Systems

Just as automation has influenced the purchasing process, so too is it influencing how the product or service is operated. **Property management systems, front office systems,** and back-of-the-house automation can be complex subjects in themselves. This section is intended to simply relate the relationship of property management

Exhibit 2   Major Phases of Development and Growth of Reservations Systems

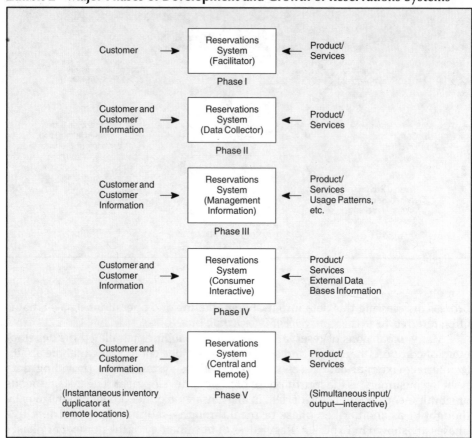

systems to marketing. There are dozens of property management systems and firms in the business, and dozens of hardware and software suppliers. Our concern is their significance to marketing and consumers.

Marketing directly benefits through applications of data that come from property management systems. Revenue maximization can be the big payoff from having a property management system with related software technology that can provide accurate forecasting. The ability to make rate adjustments daily, even hourly, based on historic profiles is one of the benefits of such systems. Knowing when to sell up or when to discount can be invaluable to maximizing revenue. Other benefits include better rooms inventory control, more accurate management of room blocks, and yield management capabilities.

The importance of automation to marketing and consumers also includes better service through guest histories and related recognition programs. Today, a consumer often can count on the same room, same seat, and same car preference as a result of guest or user history and preference systems. Property management systems have also enhanced the ability of hotels to offer express check-in, express check-out, and even automated check-in and check-out. This same technology has allowed for automated airline ticketing and car rentals.

To understand the significance of all this technology to hospitality marketing, marketers must closely monitor consumer acceptance and use of automation and understand how automation has changed consumer behavior. If consumers put a high value on any particular aspect of hospitality automation, marketing and operations must respond. Banks that didn't offer 24-hour access through automatic teller machines found that their customers deserted them, despite their fine "personal" service, for banks that offered this convenience. Hoteliers, especially those of the old school, will need to open their minds and be flexible in their attitudes about automation in order to keep up with and serve their customers. Customers and their desires are the true driving forces today in the hospitality industry.

Marketing Information Systems

Automation has also spurred numerous applications of data and information for marketing purposes. Today, the sales department in a hotel can act with some sophistication in profiling customer behavior, analyzing meetings patterns, prioritizing accounts, and generating leads. Marketing can assess promotions by tracking patterns of consumer response, identifying geographic and demographic segments, and pinpointing the types of consumers who responded and why, where, and how they actually responded.

Selection of media based on key feeder market data, and selection of a creative approach based on identifiable potential customer likes and dislikes, is now at our fingertips and demanding to be used and applied. Marketing partners such as travel agents and tour operators can be selected and evaluated based on automated records of performance, market preferences, and even demographic and psychographic clientele profiles. The influence of automation continues in virtually every aspect of marketing from research sampling to media selection.

The elements of a marketing information system include key group trends such as location preference and history, frequency of use, type and number of rooms, and spending patterns. For corporate accounts, these can be categorized by dollar volume, market, size, or other measurement. Promotional programs and travel agency productivity can also be included as part of the detailed data output. Again, the purpose of all these applications is simply to be better in marketing your product or service and, most important of all, to keep up with and understand how to reach consumers.

Travel Purchasing Systems and Beyond

All the pieces are identified and the major players are emerging for what many believe will be a revolution in the marketing of travel. The technological developments in hardware and software have evolved to a remarkable level of sophistication.

Let's take another look at the origin of today's travel purchasing systems. In the 1960s, airlines created reservation systems and in the 1970s began aggressively installing them in travel agencies. Rental car and hotel reservations capabilities were added to make the systems multi-product/service in nature. When the U.S.

government deregulated the air carriers in the 1980s, most airlines decided to treat their reservations systems as separate businesses and spun them off into new companies. This was followed by the merger or acquisition of systems as the airline industry sorted out and consolidated. In the 1990s, through interlinks and networking, the airline reservations systems became global in nature.

The Galileo reservations system had its origin in the United Airlines' APOLLO reservations system. Galileo and SABRE (a reservations system that originated with American Airlines) have more than half of the market share of CRTs today. There are a variety of ways hotel chains link and participate in these various global systems. The most common is in the form of an agreement directly with the system or through a "switching" service/company.

Today, system enhancements include everything from quicker/instant information access to video displays, to interlinks with on-line services to personal computers. On-going technical enhancements in inventory control and various marketing programs are constantly changing the delivery capabilities of these systems. Prodigy, CompuServe, and America On-line all include travel information services that allow subscribers to check airline schedules, view resort facilities, check visa requirements, and book their own travel arrangements. The amount and type of information available to today's traveler is virtually unlimited.

Naturally, marketing your product or service through these global distribution systems, networks, and services means access to the consumer and potential gains in market share. If you are not participating, you are simply not visible to the electronic consumer or travel intermediary.

Going beyond the traditional boundaries of airline-reservations-system automation has become a reality. The linking of consumer-related services, hospitality industry services, home banking systems, and even manufactured travel-related products is not only technologically feasible but in progress today. Because of the interest of hardware suppliers and software services, the world's technology experts are dreaming up ideas on how to enhance the purchase and marketing of the hospitality industry's products and services. Today you can sit in your home, office, or car and—via a PC and monitor—select everything from your airline seat to the view desired from your resort room. You can press a button and receive your tickets (if required) or access code, traveler's checks, etc.

Today's technology is revolutionizing travel marketing and purchasing. Advancements in technology and consumer demand all point to a TPS (total Travel Purchasing System). The total system will encompass more than imagined, as the technologies of reservations systems, automated banking, fiber-optics, and telecommunications are linked with new microprocessing technologies to form a super TPS capable of providing everything from your boarding passes to your travel advance, your room key code to your car access code. The future of travel automation is now.

Key Terms

ATM	guest history
automation	property management systems (PMS)
front office systems	

Chapter Outline

The Historic Foundations of Corporate
    Marketing Strategies
        Internally Driven Forces
        Externally Driven Forces
Corporate Strategies
Strategic Assessment
The New Paradigm

Learning Objectives

1. Explain the historic foundations of corporate marketing strategies.

2. Describe how internal and external forces helped shape corporate marketing strategies.

3. Describe the forces likely to have a significant impact on the hospitality industry and hospitality marketing in the twenty-first century.

Note: This chapter presents speculation about the future. Although the speculation is based largely on current factual information, it is nonetheless speculation. For that reason, it is presented strictly for your information and enjoyment. The test materials for the course include no questions on this chapter.

22

The New Paradigm

UNDERSTANDING CORPORATE MARKETING STRATEGIES in the hospitality industry requires an insight into both internal (within the industry itself) and external (sociodemographic and psychographic) factors affecting these strategies. During the twentieth century many external trends and internal industry occurrences helped shape corporate marketing strategies. As we move into the twenty-first century, new driving forces will influence hospitality corporations' overall marketing strategies. This chapter will discuss the historic twentieth-century forces that will continue to influence the future, and provide a strategic assessment of the trends shaping the twenty-first century and the implications of those trends for marketing in the hospitality industry.

The Historic Foundations of Corporate Marketing Strategies

A brief historical review is essential to understanding the evolution of most corporate marketing strategies in the hospitality industry. Historically, the hotel was a lodging property that served the person traveling to urban centers. In the 1950s one of the first alternative corporate strategies to hotels was the invention of the roadside lodging property—or "motel"—by Kemmons Wilson: Holiday Inn. Thus, two major product segments emerged in the hospitality industry: the hotel, a downtown product, and the motel, a highway or roadside product. One was geared for business travelers, the other was aimed at the family market. With this development came the beginning of large-scale market segmentation in the hospitality industry.

In the early decades of the twentieth century Marriott, Stouffer, and other companies grew from root beer stands, ice cream shops, and coffee shops into legitimate restaurant companies. The evolutionary strategy that took both Willard Marriott and Vernon Stouffer from one simple, small food establishment into the full gamut of food service facilities continued until it manifested itself in the next logical service to travelers—providing beds. This became the multiple-product strategy: providing multiple services with integrated, generally related, products to consumers.

As these early hospitality entrepreneurs began to succeed, demand for their concepts outstripped their resources for expansion. The answer for bringing more of their products and services to the market was quickly found in another pioneering corporate strategy called **franchising,** an expansionary strategy. The phenomenal growth of Holiday Inn best exemplifies franchising in its heyday. One need only look at other franchising companies within the hospitality industry such as

McDonald's, Burger King, and Wendy's to see how successful franchising is as a strategy for growth.

These basic market segmentation, multiple product, and expansionary strategies nurtured growth in the hospitality industry throughout the twentieth century. These three strategies are the foundation of today's corporate marketing strategies. Internally driven forces and externally driven forces made these strategies dynamic rather than static.

Internally Driven Forces

The early strategies of today's hospitality corporations were internally driven. Simply stated, it was the driving force of entrepreneurs, the desire to see their businesses grow, and new ideas that were the principle corporate strategies. This occurred during a time—the 1950s and 1960s—in which quantitative units and growth rates were the only buzz words known in hospitality companies. In fact, not until the early 1970s did "strategic planning" even become a part of the vocabulary of hospitality corporations. This internal strategic drive resulted in further market and product segmentation. It took on different meanings for different companies. For Holiday Inns it meant locations that were at logical stopping points along the highway. Later, for Hilton and others, it meant entering the marketplace with an "inn" product and expanding this product through franchising. For the hospitality industry as a whole it meant the birth and development of what would, one day, be known as the age of brand proliferation—the 1980s. Ramada Inns, Quality Inns, Sheraton Inns, and Hilton Inns emerged, along with larger companies such as Sheraton Hotels, Hilton Hotels, and Inter-Continental Hotels.

It is evident that a dual strategic thrust existed—internally driven product diversification and externally demanded market segmentation. However, in the 1950s and early 1960s the motivator or cause was internal, and growth in the number of units was the game.

Externally Driven Forces

Long before John Naisbitt wrote or even conceived of *Megatrends*, major external forces were in place that would have a lasting impact on the strategies of corporations in the hospitality industry. These external forces were large enough to influence and shape corporate strategy as it related to markets, products, quality, levels of services, pricing strategies, and so on. Those who stayed in step with these trends would become the industry leaders and growth companies of the 1980s. Key external forces can be succinctly listed:

- Population trends (growth, mix, and movement)

- Growth of affluence (wealth, discretionary income, etc.)

- Emergence of classes (low, middle, upper-middle, upper)

- Development of transportation systems (interstates, airports, "hub" airports, etc.)

- Tier qualitative segmentation of values, tastes, and psychographics

• Internationalism of commerce; global perspective versus national isolationism

What is significant is not the importance of each of these external forces, but the fact that components of each (a wealthier America, an older population, the emergence of "yuppies," etc.) were strong enough to cause everything from today's supply of luxury accommodations to a surge in the budget motel lodging segment. In the late 1980s and early 1990s the hospitality industry lived up to its label as a dynamic industry. The savings and loan crisis, real estate reevaluations, the falling away of weak companies, and constant changes of ownership (not just of properties, but of entire chains) were prevalent throughout the last decades of the twentieth century.

Corporate Strategies

As you have read, there is no single overriding factor that determines a hospitality corporation's marketing strategies. Rather, multiple internally driven and externally driven forces combine with a company's historic roots to determine its strategies today. There are as many ways to categorize strategies as there are corporate strategists in the industry. The perspective presented in this section is based on participation in planning processes within several of the companies used as examples, and from 25 years of study and observation of other corporations in the industry. The first strategy categorization might simply be termed *horizontal expansion.*

Corporate Strategy I: Horizontal Expansion. The hospitality industry encompasses food, beverage, lodging, and travel-related services. Therefore, horizontal expansion simply means expanding from one line of hospitality product or service—for example, food—to another—for example, lodging. For instance, Marriott now encompasses many hospitality services: food, lodging, retirement communities, etc. Holiday Inn now offers multiple lodging brands. Other hotel chains now include restaurants, resorts, and gaming and casino operations.

Corporate Strategy II: Geographic Expansion. At first, hospitality companies developed within a relatively small radius of their origin. For example, Marriott was known primarily as a Washington D.C.-area company until the late 1970s. But its rapid growth in lodging west of the Mississippi helped it develop into a national brand in the 1980s. Holiday Inn was a mid-south company, Ramada a southwestern company, La Quinta a Texas company. A combination of factors—market growth opportunities, sales of franchises, and the unit-growth mentality of the 1960s and 1970s—caused many local and regional hospitality firms to emerge with national—and ultimately international—status. The same is true of restaurant firms, such as Denny's, Wendy's, Burger King, and Arby's. For airlines, mergers and route system expansions created regional and then national carriers. Southern, Mohawk, Northeast, and Hughes AirWest all were absorbed into larger carriers, while Eastern, Pan Am, and others disappeared as brands.

Corporate Strategy III: Product Hybridization. Perhaps because of Holiday Inn's phenomenal growth and the entry of other motel developers into the marketplace, it wasn't long before traditional high-rise hotel companies began developing and franchising low-rise "inns." Hilton Inns and Sheraton Inns are two examples of **product hybrids** (variations on base products) that developed in the late 1960s and early 1970s. Product hybrids also were natural strategies for companies that began simply as motels; soon there were high-rise motels called Holiday Inns, Ramada Inns, and Marriott Inns. Motel product hybrids continued to appear as high-rise and mid-rise facilities offering more services than had the traditional motel.

Corporate Strategy IV: Specialization. Just as Holiday Inn began with the idea of offering families affordable accommodations, other entrants into the marketplace began as specialists categorized by price or service levels. For example, Motel 6, Days Inns, La Quinta, and Budget Inns began with a specialized product offering limited facilities—essentially guestrooms only. In the food segment of the industry came fast-food, salad bars, pizza parlors, specialty restaurants, steak houses, and seafood eateries. Specialization also went upscale in both pricing and services offered. Today there are all-suite companies such as Embassy Suites, and a plethora of luxury-only hotel chains. Interestingly enough, some of these specialized products and services were the result of what is perhaps one of the most commented-upon corporate strategies: product "tiering."

Corporate Strategy V: Product Tiering. **Product tiering** was an initial corporate response to growth limitations and the aging of corporations' prevalent products. The limitations of growth could have resulted from market saturation or could have occurred when the actual economics of the original concept no longer worked or were not as lucrative as an alternative approach. Ramada developed a three-tiered approach in the early 1980s: Ramada Inns, Ramada Hotels, and Ramada Renaissance Hotels. Each of these product tiers reflected different pricing, different levels of service, and operational variations. Holiday Inns, Holiday Inn Hotels, and Holiday Inn Crowne Plazas represented Holiday Inn's original product tiering. Other companies soon followed with various forms of product tiering, manifested in an upscale movement from inn to hotel to super hotel. Product tiering also influenced companies such as Marriott, which de-emphasized inns and franchising and opted to go in other directions with hotels and mega-hotels (1,000 rooms or more) called Marriott Marquis. Marriott Marquis was followed by a low-rise lodging product, Courtyards by Marriott, and extended-stay and all-suite products. Radisson, Choice Hotels International, Hyatt, and other lodging chains all developed types of facilities with varying levels of services, amenities, and pricing structures. This was simply the lodging industry's response to the mega-forces of population growth and demographic, economic, and psychographic segmentation. Product tiering was rampant in the industry by the early 1980s and continued to expand in the 1990s.

Corporate Strategy VI: Product Branding. **Product branding** is the most recent corporate strategy. This is a result in part of the proliferation of tiering and the subsequent consumer and franchise confusion it caused. The confusion was the result of a considerable amount of product relabeling mixed in with some genuine product tiering. An establishment looked like a motel and smelled like a motel, but often had another name. As a result of this confusion and of an even stronger force or marketplace dynamic known as consumer awareness, product branding emerged. Ironically, this occurred as the hospitality industry, one of the world's oldest industries, was just entering the era of brand identification. The focus of product branding is to clearly define what a product or service is, in terms of level and quality of service, location, price, and other key consumer-oriented factors such as the psychographic appeal of "prestige" or "thrift."

There are a number of clear examples of today's product branding. To understand these, one might think of a hospitality corporation as analogous to General Motors. For example, Holiday Inn has followed the General Motors product branding concept and now offers multiple brands, such as Crowne Plaza, Holiday Inn, and Holiday Inn Express—everything from a Chevrolet to a Cadillac. Marriott has adopted a similar strategy, with Marriott Hotels, Marriott Resorts, Marriott Marquis, Courtyards by Marriott, and Fairfield Inns. Other companies have elected to develop what might be analogous to the Porsche or Jaguar concept: one product of high quality—one brand, no variations. Examples of hospitality corporations with one-brand strategies include Four Seasons, Ritz-Carlton, and Westin, to name a few. These brands may change ownership, but their labels and names depict a very specific product positioning.

Corporate Strategy VII: Non-Franchising. Usually, firms do not franchise in order to keep greater control over the quality, ownership, and management of their properties. Often these firms are strong enough financially that franchising is unnecessary. Examples of lodging chains that do not franchise are few. Four Seasons, Westin Hotels, La Quinta, and Motel 6 are such examples.

Corporate Strategy VIII: Franchising. Franchising companies are more prevalent in the hospitality industry than non-franchising companies. Holiday Inn, Radisson, and Choice Hotels International are examples of lodging firms that are large franchisers. McDonald's, Burger King, Wendy's, Dunkin' Donuts, and Arby's are leading franchisors in the fast-food area. Today it is possible to purchase a franchise for virtually everything from a travel agency to a destination resort.

Corporate Strategy IX: Brand Collection. During the late 1980s and the 1990s "brand collectors" emerged. These were companies primarily driven by investors who took advantage of the relatively low prices needed to acquire chains or brands that had growth potential through global franchising. Companies such as Hospitality Franchise Systems (owner of the Howard Johnson, Ramada, and Days Inn brands) and Choice Hotels International (owner of Quality Inns, Comfort Inns, and Comfort Suites brands) are now among the largest in the industry.

Corporate Strategy X: Management Contract Companies. Another byproduct of the lodging industry sort-out of the late 1980s and early 1990s was the growth of large "**management contract**" companies. These are firms that specialize in managing hotels and motels for owners such as banks, insurance companies, trusts, pension funds, partnerships, or individuals. Examples include Richfield Hospitality Group, Interstate Hotels, American General Hospitality, and Carnival Hotels and Casinos.

Corporate Strategy XI: Vertical and Horizontal Integration. Vertical and horizontal integration are corporate strategies that involve a hospitality company in more than one component of the hospitality business. One example is the Carlson Company and its subsidiaries. Carlson is the parent of the Radisson hotel chain, and its line of hospitality products includes the world's second largest travel agency group, a cruise ship company, and a restaurant company, among others. Unlike the period before 1980, when integration in the hospitality industry meant a firm owned hotels and restaurants or an airline and a hotel chain, deregulation has provided hospitality companies the opportunity to gain competitive edges by owning or investing in multiple components of the industry.

Corporate Strategy XII: Singleness. Some hospitality firms have chosen to develop just one product or service, forgoing product segmentation, tiering, and vertical and horizontal integration strategies. Four Seasons, for example, has opted for a single product of all first-class hotels with ownership and management control. La Quinta is following this strategy at the value-priced segment.

Corporate Strategy XIII: Value-Related Products and Services. Residence Inns and Embassy Suites exemplify lodging concepts developed to respond to specific value and psychographic trends among consumers. As the sophistication of the consumer continues to develop and is expressed in new product and service demands and desires, corporations will identify and satisfy these demands and desires with appropriate and timely strategies. Other examples of value-related products and services include the variety of credit cards and credit services, such as gold cards and platinum cards; the variety of air travel options, such as all-first-class fares and budget fares; and new airline brands.

Corporate Strategy XIV: Global Positioning. The oceans, political ideologies, and other traditional trade barriers no longer seem insurmountable hurdles for the hospitality industry. Holiday Inn, Radisson, Marriott, Hospitality Franchise Systems, Accor, Choice Hotels International, and others have products throughout the world. The signs of fast-food chains can be seen in most international cities and airports. As the brands originating in the United States expanded globally, foreign brands also entered the market—Meridian, Trusthouse Forte, Sofitel, Nikko, and others. Investment reasons, risk levels, growth strategies, and reasons for expansion all vary by corporation and by market. These are influenced by many different social, economic, and political trends and events. These corporations' perspectives are as varied as the products, services, and markets they serve.

Corporate Strategy Implications. The once relatively simple family-driven businesses and single-branded lodging concepts that made up the hospitality industry in the first two-thirds of the twentieth century have given way to much more complex business concepts and multiple branding. Some businesses with family origins grew enormously, such as Marriott, while others were acquired or merged, such as Stouffer (whose hotels and resorts now bear the Renaissance brand). The global ownership of physical assets, brand switching, short-term management contracts, changes of ownership, brand collection, global brand expansion through franchising and joint ventures, and vertically integrated travel and hospitality companies are all changing the dynamics of the industry and accelerating its pace of change.

To the consumer, the hospitality industry gets more confusing, as his or her favorite hotel switches brands, changes management, or is replaced with a new concept or product. To the marketing professional, it's more challenging to bring in new customers and retain existing customers because of internally driven industry dynamics. But there is yet more challenge for today's hospitality marketers, in the form of new externally driven forces or trends to which marketers must respond. Let's briefly look at some of the key strategic trends that will impact the hospitality industry in the future, and the marketing implications of these trends.

Strategic Assessment

Earlier in the chapter a number of key internal and external forces were listed that shaped the hospitality industry and influenced marketing during the twentieth century. As we look to the future there are forces that are likely to have a significant impact on both the industry and the marketing of it in the twenty-first century. They are:

- Globalization

- Technology

- Behavioral pendulums

- Consolidation

- Vertical and horizontal integration

- Branding

There are many other important marketing forces to assess in the years ahead, such as global distribution systems, networks, communications media, and emerging market segments. However, the forces just listed appear to be the major trends, or **megatrends,** right now. But the hospitality industry currently is one of the most dynamic industries on earth and we're in a period of rapid change. In other words, a new megatrend could develop at any time.

Globalization. The marketplace is becoming increasingly more global. As business investment and business and related travel flow across every region of the globe, multinational and cultural positioning will be essential to attracting market share in the hospitality industry. Linkages and networks to major origin markets—the geographical areas where large numbers of travelers come from—will be necessary for a hospitality company to remain competitive in the world marketplace. As new businesses and business investment flow to new regions, leisure travel will also develop in these regions. Economic growth in Asia, the Pacific Basin, Latin America, and China will provide impetus to a more diverse travel market. Understanding these regions and knowing how to market on a multinational and culturally diverse basis will be essential for marketing success.

Technology. Integrating the latest technologies into a company's business practices is an all-encompassing survival strategy. Marketing as well as operations must keep pace with technological developments to not only remain competitive, but—more importantly—to meet the changing needs of consumers. New technologies that reduce costs and provide consumer conveniences should receive the highest priority. Implementing these technologies will allow marketing to attract consumers and gain market share. In addition, as globalization accelerates, being "plugged in" to the right global distribution systems will be a competitive advantage. Providing the technologically "latest" in guest conveniences, security, and safety will be key marketing advantages as well. The implications and stakes are immense in the technological area. Technology that facilitates the purchase process, and having the technology customers desire in guest amenities and services, are not just operational niceties but marketing necessities in the twenty-first century.

Behavioral Pendulums. The prolonged recession of the late 1980s, economic uncertainties of the early 1990s, forced career changes, and new ways of doing business, combined with the resultant human psychological consequence of stress, have caused deep behavioral changes in consumers that are likely to remain, not only in North America, but wherever in the world economic turmoil occurs. Unless we enter into a new age of global wealth, the overriding concept of "value" will remain with us throughout our marketing lives. Value in good economic times will weigh more heavily toward quality; in times of economic uncertainty, value will be price-oriented. For marketers, the key will be knowing when and where to change the marketing message to be in line with the direction of as many behavioral pendulums across the globe as possible.

Consolidation. Whether through mergers and acquisitions or through affiliations and agreements, consolidating with other companies may prove essential for a hospitality company's survival. Establishing a marketing relationship with the components of the industry that can help you either distribute your product/service or provide you with brand presence will be a necessity. The big are likely to get bigger and the specialized likely to get better. Whether a company is big or specialized, it will rely more on its booking sources (suppliers of customers—i.e., travel agents) and preferred consumers (key corporate accounts). The farther you reach the more likely you will be able to attract market share from the growing international feeder markets—those economically emerging areas that are now beginning to generate more travelers. The bottom line is that "critical mass" in both product and promotions will be advantageous—that is, the larger you are, the more marketing clout you will have in the marketplace.

Vertical and Horizontal Integration. Vertical and horizontal integration will take on a new meaning in the twenty-first century. Marketing survival will be more closely connected to agreements, coalitions, mergers, joint ventures, acquisitions, and expanded distribution channels. This all will be driven not just by economies of scale, but, more importantly, by the consumer's expectations of "single-source conveniences." Consumers will prefer one-stop shopping or one-call or one on-line service to handle all of their air, hotel, and car rental arrangements, rather than making three separate trips/calls. Survival will necessitate developing the right affiliations with other suppliers within the travel industry, stretching marketing expenditures through extensive co-ops (joint marketing or service offerings with travel partners—for example, an American Airlines/Renaissance Resorts package offer), and building other affiliations that extend your brand presence and build customer loyalty.

Branding. Branding will become increasingly important as consumers seek to sort through the plethora of new market entrants around the globe. Brands that are clearly identified, have a distinct positioning, and are consistent in multiple global markets will emerge as the winners. Developing a global brand image with universal appeal will be another key to successful marketing.

The New Paradigm

Under the new paradigm, marketing takes on new meaning. Under the new paradigm, "urgency" or "critical" are replaced with "immediacy" and "act now." Customers will expect immediate action. Loyalty is replaced with "you've got one chance to keep me as a customer." Brand loyalty will be won by performance—this time and every time. Competitiveness now means providing what is most convenient and best for the customer. Today and throughout the twenty-first century, marketers must be proactive and react immediately to survive. Fundamental change must occur on demand. Understanding multifunctional marketing tools and selecting the correct ones will be critical to winning. There will be little room for mistakes or defects, and few second chances. Individual marketing superstars will be replaced by all-star teams (and teamwork) whose focus will shift from being "just good enough to win" to "continually improving so as to never lose." Most important of all, the ability to change, to adapt to the new, and to understand the diverse will form the basis for success.

Key Terms

franchising

management contract

megatrend

product branding

product hybrid

product tiering

royalty income

vertical and horizontal integration

Bibliography

Abbey, James R., and Milton T. Astroff. *Convention Sales and Service.* Dubuque, Iowa: Wm. C. Brown Co., 1983.

American Hotel & Motel Association and School of Hotel, Restaurant, and Institutional Management. *Commercial Lodging Market, Phase Two.* East Lansing, Mich.: Michigan State University, 1968.

Arnold, David. *The Handbook of Brand Management.* Reading, Mass.: Addison-Wesley, 1992.

Aronin, Robert A. "U.S. Travel Industry." Unpublished Manuscript, 1976.

Berrigan, John, and Carl Finkbeiner. *Segmentation Marketing: New Methods for Capturing Business Markets.* New York: HarperBusiness, 1992.

Berry, Leonard L., and A. Parasuraman. *Marketing Services: Competing Through Quality.* New York: Free Press, 1991.

Bogart, Leo. *Strategy in Advertising.* New York: Harcourt, Brace and World, 1967.

Boyd, Harper, William and Massy. *Marketing Management.* New York: Harcourt Brace Jovanovich, 1972.

Chase, Cochrane, and Kenneth L. Barasch. *Marketing Problem Solver.* Radnor, Pa.: Chilton Book Company, 1977.

Clancy, Kevin J., and Robert S. Shulman. *The Marketing Revolution: A Radical Manifesto for Dominating the Marketplace.* New York: HarperBusiness, 1991.

Coffman, C. DeWitt. *Hospitality for Sale.* East Lansing, Mich.: Educational Institute of the American Hotel & Motel Association, 1980.

Drucker, Peter. *Management—Tasks, Responsibilities, Practices.* New York: Heineman, 1974.

Feig, Barry. *The New Products Workshop: Hands-On Tools for Developing Winners.* New York: McGraw-Hill, 1993.

Hayden, Catherine. *The Handbook of Strategic Expertise.* New York: Free Press, 1986.

Holloway, Robert, and Robert Hancock, eds. *The Environment of Marketing Behavior,* 2d ed. New York: John Wiley and Sons, 1969.

Kotler, Philip. *Marketing Management.* Englewood Cliffs, N.J.: Prentice Hall, 1972.

Lele, Miland M. *Creating Strategic Leverage.* New York: Wiley, 1992.

Levitt, Theodore. *The Marketing Imagination.* New York: Free Press, 1986.

Linneman, Robert E., and John L. Stanton, Jr. *Making Niche Marketing Work: How to Grow Bigger by Acting Smaller.* New York: McGraw-Hill, 1991.

Lodish, Leonard M. *The Advertising & Promotion Challenge: Vaguely Right or Precisely Wrong?* New York: Oxford, 1986.

Lundberg, Ronald E. *The Hotel and Restaurant Business,* 3d ed. Boston: CBI Publishing, 1979.

Magrath, Allan J. *The 6 Imperatives of Marketing: Lessons From the World's Best Companies.* New York: AMACOM, 1992.

McIntosh, Robert. *Tourism—Principles, Practices, Philosophies.* Columbus, Ohio: Grid, 1972.

McKay, Edward S. *The Marketing Mystique,* rev. ed. New York: AMACOM, 1993.

McNeill, Daniel, and Paul Freiberger. *Fuzzy Logic: The Discovery of a Revolutionary Computer Technology and How It Is Changing Our World.* New York: Simon & Schuster, 1993.

Michalko, Michael. *Thinkertoys: A Handbook of Business Creativity for the '90's.* Berkeley, Calif.: Ten Speed Press, 1991.

Myers, James H., and Edward Tauber. *Market Structure Analysis.* Chicago: American Marketing Association, 1977.

Nykiel, R. A. "Away from Home Eating Trends." Washington, D.C.: Marriott Corporation, 1973.

———. "Cruise Market Trends." Washington, D.C.: Marriott Corporation, 1974.

———. "Factors Influencing the Domestic and International Hotel Development Process." Paper and speech to the Business and Economics Graduate Program, Industrial College of Armed Forces, Washington, D.C., 1975.

———. "The Incentive Travel Market." Washington, D.C.: Marriott Corporation, 1972.

———. "The Japanese Travel Market—Outbound." Washington, D.C.: Marriott Corporation, 1973.

———. "Market Segmentation and its Applications to Sales and Advertising." Washington, D.C.: Marriott Corporation, 1973.

———. "Marketing Planning Process." Washington, D.C.: Marriott Corporation, 1973.

———. "The Next Thirty Years—A Study of Significant Quantitative and Qualitative Trends Affecting the Business Climate and Lifestyle in America." Washington, D.C.: Marriott Corporation, 1972, 1973.

———. "The Prospects for Future Growth in International Pleasure Travel." Washington, D.C.: Marriott Corporation, 1973.

———. "A Qualitative Study of the Domestic Lodging Market Needs by Segment." Washington, D.C.: Marriott Corporation, 1973.

———. "The Vacation Market's Preferences and Needs." Washington, D.C.: Marriott Corporation, 1973.

———. "Vertical and Horizontal Integration of the Travel Business." Washington, D.C.: Marriott Corporation, 1974.

Powers, Thomas F. "The Competitive Structure of the Hotel/Motel Market." A paper presented to the Council on Hotel, Restaurant and Institutional Education, 1969.

Rapp, Stan, and Tom Collins. *MaxiMarketing: The New Direction in Advertising, Promotion, and Marketing Strategy.* New York: New American Library, 1988.

Ray, Michael, and Rochelle Myers. *Creativity in Business.* Garden City, N.J.: Doubleday, 1986.

Reis, Al, and Jack Trout. *Marketing Warfare.* New York: McGraw Hill Book Co., 1986.

———. *Positioning: The Battle For Your Mind.* New York: McGraw Hill Book Co., 1981.

———. *The 22 Immutable Laws of Marketing: Violate Them at Your Own Risk!* New York: HarperBusiness, 1993.

Russell, Thomas, and Glenn Verrill. *Otto Kleppmer's Advertising Procedure.* Englewood Cliffs, N.J.: Prentice Hall.

Schwartz, Peter. *The Art of the Long View: Planning for the Future in an Uncertain World.* New York: Doubleday Currency, 1991.

Sherlock, Paul. *Rethinking Business-to-Business Marketing.* New York: Free Press, 1991.

Summer, J. R. *Improve Your Marketing Techniques: A Guide for Hotel Managers and Caterers.* London: Northwood Books, 1985.

U.S. Government Printing Office. *Directory of National Trade Associations of Businessmen.* Washington, D.C., 1980.

U.S. Travel Data Center. *The Importance of Tourism to the U.S. Economy.* Washington, D.C., 1975.

Vavra, Terry G. *Aftermarketing: How to Keep Customers for Life Through Relationship Marketing.* Homewood, Ill.: Business One Irwin, 1992.

Wahab, S., L. J. Crampon, and L. M. Rothfield. *Tourism Marketing.* London: Tourism International Press, 1976.

Willett, George. *A Whack on the Side of the Head: How You Can Be More Creative.* New York: Warner, 1990.

Wilson, Aubrey. *New Directions in Marketing: Business-to-Business Strategies for the 1990's.* Lincolnwood, Ill.: NTC Business Books, 1992.

Glossary

A

ACTION PROGRAM

A list of actions that must be taken to fulfill the marketing plan. It includes target dates, approved expenditures (as differentiated from unapproved estimated costs), and the person(s) responsible for implementing each action.

ATM

Automated teller, transaction, or ticketing machine.

AUTOMATION

The computerization of manual functions.

B

BENEFIT AND NEED SEGMENTATION

Divides a market into groups of consumers on the basis of the benefits they seek, the needs they expect to satisfy, and—in some instances—the factors they hope to avoid.

BOOKING PACE

The rate at which a group's room block is filling up.

BRAND

The name associated with products or services that conveys a specific perception related to the needs of consumers.

BUSINESS MIX

The major market segments from which your guests come; for instance, 30 percent group, 60 percent transient, and 10 percent leisure.

C

CARRIER

A public transportation company, such as an airline, steamship line, railroad, or bus line.

CHANNELS OF DISTRIBUTION

Vehicles through which travel-related products and services may be marketed by suppliers or purchased by consumers.

CHARTER

The bulk purchase of any carrier's equipment (or part thereof) for passengers.

CHRONOLOGICAL WORK PLAN

A listing of action steps to be taken in date order, with identification of responsibility.

CITY PAIRS

Cities (such as Boston and New York, or Washington, D.C. and New York) between which a heavy travel pattern exists; knowing major city pairs and understanding relationships between metropolitan statistical areas are essential for assessing the best use of marketing expenditures on a geographic basis.

CLOSE

To end the sale of a room category or rate.

CLUB FLOOR

Usually a separate floor of upgraded rooms and services in a major hotel.

CO-OP ADVERTISING

Joining with others to advertise products, services, and/or a region or market.

COLLATERAL MATERIALS

Print-based materials that assist in the marketing of products and services. Some examples include brochures, tent cards, posters, directories, maps, guides, menu inserts, flyers, and entertainment promotion pieces.

COMPETITION

Any business concern, product, or concept that competes for customers in your market.

COMPETITIVE RESEARCH

Marketing research that compares your product or service to the products or services of competitors and tries to discover how consumers perceive and experience your product/service offering in relation to the competitors' products/services.

CONSUMER'S PERSPECTIVE

The consumer's attitude toward a product or service that centers on the needs that it satisfies.

COOPERATIVE PROMOTION

A promotion involving two or more suppliers who join together in a common promotion for their mutual benefit.

CORPORATE RATE

A discounted rate given to a company because of its volume usage.

COST-PLUS THEORY

The recognition of the need to price or sell a product or service in periods of low demand by discounting the price beyond fixed and variable cost levels to stimulate sales.

CUSTOMER NEEDS

What a customer really looks for or wants in a product or service.

CUSTOMER PERCEPTIONS

The ways in which the customer, in his or her own mind, looks at a product. They include the customer's image of the product. Customer perceptions often differ from management's beliefs and perceptions.

CUSTOMER SATISFACTION

Meeting the identified needs of each guest with a level of service and product quality that matches or exceeds the expectations created by your property's marketing message and related pricing.

D

DATA BASE MARKETING

A sales and marketing methodology that sells and promotes by selective direct mail with the objective of increasing sales and profits.

DELIVERY PACKAGE

The essential tools, including required forms, copy, photos, fact sheets, and biographies, to ensure that you are ready to effectively execute public relations programs.

DEMOGRAPHIC PROFILE

Demographic data describing characteristics of consumers related to specific products or services.

DEMOGRAPHIC SEGMENTATION

The division of a market by like characteristics such as sex, age, income, home ownership, marital status, occupation, and education.

DIRECT MAIL

Promotional letters, advertising pieces, catalogs, or any other sales-oriented correspondence mailed to prospective customers.

DISCLAIMER

Usually a statement in fine print that defines the conditions of an offer.

E

END USER

The ultimate consumer of a travel product or service.

ENVIRONMENTAL RESEARCH

Marketing research that focuses on external forces (economic, social, political, technological, etc.) that are having or will have an impact on your product or service in some manner.

EXPOSURES

The number of consumers actually hearing or seeing your advertising.

F

FEEDER CITIES

Principal cities within a geographic region that tend to "feed" travel to each other. For example, in the western region of the United States, travel from Los Angeles feeds Palm Springs, Las Vegas, Phoenix, and San Francisco, and vice versa.

FLYER

A printed announcement of a special event or promotion, usually created for quick distribution by mailing it or leaving it at a location for passersby to pick up.

FOCUS GROUP

A marketing research technique that combines personal-opinion solicitation in the form of group discussion with a structured set of questions.

FRANCHISING

A method of growing a brand through selling the rights to use the brand name and related services.

FRONT OFFICE SYSTEMS

The computerization of front office functions, including items such as rooms management, housekeeping, rooms availability, rates, etc.

FUNCTION SPACE

The meeting room space in a hotel.

G

GEODEMOGRAPHIC SEGMENTATION

The division of a market along geographic and demographic dimensions; for example, linking the number of people with similar characteristics (age, income, etc.) with specific geographic locations.

GEOGRAPHIC SEGMENTATION

The division of a market generally by region, zone, state, district, metropolitan statistical area, or postal zip codes.

GLOBAL DISTRIBUTION NETWORK (GDN)

The entire electronic travel network; it includes travel agents, the global distribution system, switching companies, central reservations offices, and individual hotels.

GLOBAL DISTRIBUTION SYSTEM (GDS)

The computer systems that travel agents use to book airline seats, rental cars, hotel rooms, and other travel reservations and services.

GROUND SERVICES

All the services received at a destination (excluding method of travel to the destination), such as rooms, food, beverage, and local tours.

GUEST HISTORY

A record of a guest's purchase patterns and preferences.

GUEST PERSPECTIVE

How the guest views your products or services.

H–I

HEAVY USER

A recurrent consumer of a product or service who can be identified through demographics and other market segmentation techniques.

HOTEL REPRESENTATIVE COMPANY (HOTEL REP)

A firm that provides reservation and marketing services for independent hotels and hotel chains that do not operate their own central reservations offices.

IN-HOUSE PROFIT CENTER

Any area of an establishment that generates revenue.

INCENTIVE TRAVEL

A trip offered as a reward.

INFLATION RATE-PLUS FACTOR

A method for increasing rates or prices that is based on the premise that increases in rates should be at the inflation rate plus a percent target.

INTERMEDIARY

An individual or firm that facilitates transactions between travel consumers and travel suppliers. There are two types: commercial (those earning commissions) and captive—those who make travel plans for others as part of their regular jobs (for example, secretaries) and do not earn commissions.

INTRODUCTORY PROMOTION

A promotion designed to introduce a new product or service to the market.

L—M

LEVEL OF EXPECTATION
The quantity or quality of your product or service, as expected by your customers; a basic premise of advertising is that you never promise more than your product or service can actually fulfill.

MAILING LIST
A collection of names and addresses maintained on a computer to generate mailings.

MANAGEMENT CONTRACT
A contract to provide management for a hotel, motel, or other facility for which fees are paid to the management company.

MARKET RESEARCH
Marketing research that seeks to quantify and segment market demand.

MARKET SEGMENT
A portion of the total market wherein all of those particular customers have something in common. There are many ways of segmenting a market; the most widely used is by demographics—i.e., sex, age, income, education, etc.

MARKET SHARE
Your product's or service's piece of the total market for that product or service, usually expressed as a percentage or on a point scale.

MARKETING
Selling a service or product by focusing on the needs of the buyer.

MARKETING PLANNING
The organized process of studying the market, identifying and measuring its trends, developing objectives and supporting programs, and using the available facts in combination with the experienced judgments of the marketing team. The process includes the development of targets (timing, costs, results expected) and the monitoring of actual achievement against those targets. The purpose of marketing planning is the achievement of maximum desired results, through the efficient application of effort and resources.

MARKETING STRATEGY GRID
A presentation/analytical marketing tool designed to help you select strategies to improve your market share and gain on the competition.

MEDIA
The vehicles—newspapers, magazines, radio, television, and so on—by which you can advertise.

MEETING PLANNERS
Usually association, corporate, or training company executives whose major goal is to plan and execute successful conventions, conferences, or meetings.

MEGATREND

A massive qualitative or quantitative trend that has a substantial impact on an enterprise or society.

METROPOLITAN STATISTICAL AREAS

A geographic segmentation technique that divides a market into areas within a large county or within a number of small counties; the core of such an area is usually a major city.

O – P

OBJECTIVES

What you want to achieve with your marketing efforts. Example: By next year, increase our business in the pleasure travel market by 10%.

OPEN

To begin the sale of a room category or rate.

PACKAGE TOURS

Inclusive travel arrangements designed to fit the requirements of a particular group of travelers; package tours may be either escorted or unescorted.

PACKAGING

The combining of more than one hospitality product or service into a single purchase item for a single price.

PER DIEM

The amount of money that individuals can recover from their organizations for travel expenses.

PERSONAL SALES

Direct person-to-person selling.

PLACEMENT

Where your advertising actually appears, be it a time slot on radio or television, an outdoor billboard near an airport, or a spot on a page in a specific issue of a magazine or newspaper.

PLATFORM

The item-by-item list of things that directly support your ad proposition.

PREFERRED RATE

A specially discounted rate for a frequent customer—usually based on volume and set lower than the corporate rate(s).

PRESS KIT

A communications folder usually containing two pockets, the left used for background information, the right used for a press release.

PRESS RELEASE

A formatted document, usually one to two pages, presenting concise and pertinent information on a topic/event deemed newsworthy.

PRICE PROMOTION

A promotion in which the incentive to purchase is based on price.

PRICE SEGMENTATION

Identifies groups of consumers within a market whose purchase of products or services is within the limits of certain dollar amounts.

PRODUCT BRANDING

Labeling a product with a name by which it is marketed and identified, such as Embassy Suites or Residence Inns.

PRODUCT HYBRID

A variation on a base product, such as a high-rise inn or motel.

PRODUCT OR SERVICE RESEARCH

Marketing research that usually focuses on your product's/service's strengths and weaknesses in relation to the products/services of competitors.

PRODUCT TIERING

A variation in degree of a company's product quality or level of services, such as Ramada Inn, Ramada Hotel, and Ramada Renaissance Hotel.

PROMOTION

A creative marketing idea that is aimed at maintaining or increasing business and supporting the overall marketing effort.

PROPERTY MANAGEMENT SYSTEMS (PMS)

Computer systems that help managers with a variety of management tasks, including room inventory, control, guest histories, and rate management.

PROPOSITION

The strongest factual statement you can make on behalf of your product or service.

PROSPECT RESEARCH

Marketing research aimed at providing a profile of present and future guests.

PSYCHOGRAPHIC SEGMENTATION

A method of subdividing a market based on like needs and psychological motivations of consumer groups.

PUBLIC RELATIONS

A marketing tool that is the communications vehicle between your firm and current customers, potential customers, and the variety of other audiences in the marketplace.

PUBLICITY

One facet of public relations, it comprises the gratuitous mentions or exposures a company receives from announcements, events, and press releases.

Q–R

QUESTIONNAIRE

A data collection vehicle similar to a survey but usually briefer and less complex in content.

RATE PYRAMIDING

The concept of offering a variety of rates and/or ranges from which consumers may select; also includes the opportunity to sell up.

REGION

A geographic subdivision within a country, often defined by natural borders such as mountains, major rivers, etc.

RESPONSE RATE

The percentage of the total audience mailed to that replies.

RESTRICTIONS

Limitations and requirements that must be adhered to in order to qualify for an offer; for example, "Tickets must be purchased three days in advance."

RETAIL TRAVEL AGENCY

A company that sells carriers' tickets and wholesalers' or operators' tours to consumers.

RETAILING

With regard to hospitality packaging, the selling of a travel product, service, or package directly to the consumer.

REVENUE MAXIMIZATION

Achieving the highest potential revenue through management of market mix, pricing strategies, and yield management.

ROOM CATEGORY

A grouping of rooms that has been determined by type (standard, deluxe, etc.) or location (view, beach-front, and so on).

ROYALTY INCOME
The fee paid to a franchisor by a franchisee for use of the brand name.

S

SEGMENT PROFITABILITY
The profitability of a particular type of consumer or market segment, determined by analyzing the revenues generated through the sale of products and services to that type of consumer or segment.

SELLING UP
Seeking to obtain a higher price for a room, sell a higher profit margin item, or obtain a premium price when demand favors the seller.

STOCK
The type of paper or material used for printed materials; usually defined by weight, grain, or texture.

STRATEGY
How you plan to achieve the objectives you have set. For example: To increase our business in the pleasure travel market by 10% within the next 12 months, we will: (1) increase outdoor advertising, and (2) shift some of our advertising to family magazines.

SUPER SAVER
A popular term for a deeply discounted rate or fare.

SURVEY
A structured research document designed to elicit consumer opinion, uncover facts, and gain insights on potential trends.

SWOT
An acronym for strengths, weaknesses, opportunities, and threats.

T

TELEPHONE SALES
A sales contact by telephone, whose primary purpose is to obtain a reservation for a room, a group commitment, or some other sale.

TENT CARD
An internal-promotion tool that rests on top of a table, desk, bureau, or other flat surface.

TOUR OPERATOR-RETAILER
A company that specializes in the planning and operation of prepaid, preplanned vacations, and makes these available to the public through travel agents.

TOUR OPERATOR-WHOLESALER

A company that services retail travel agents in the preparation of tour packages, ordering, billing, and advertising.

TOUR ORGANIZER

An individual, usually not professionally connected with the travel industry, who organizes tours for groups of people such as teachers, lawyers, etc.

TRADE MEDIA

A group of publications and/or broadcast media that follows a specific industry.

TRADE-OUT/BARTER

An exchange of your product or service for advertising coverage.

TRAFFIC DEPARTMENT

An area within a company that manages and schedules business travel for company employees.

TRAVEL CLUB

An organization that targets frequent pleasure travelers and offers club members special travel packages to travel destinations.

TRAVEL INTERMEDIARY

An individual or firm that facilitates transactions between travel consumers and travel suppliers. There are two types: commercial (those earning commissions) and captive—those who make travel plans for others as part of their regular jobs (for example, secretaries) and do not earn commissions.

TRAVEL MANAGEMENT COMPANY

An organization that provides travel management services on a contractual or fee basis to corporations, government agencies, associations, and other organizations with business-related travel needs.

TREND RESEARCH

Identification of quantitative and qualitative preferences and attitudinal and behavioral directions in which the market or segments thereof are moving.

V–Z

VERTICAL AND HORIZONTAL INTEGRATION

The interrelationship between two or more hospitality industry products or services performed or offered by the same firm.

WHOLESALING

With regard to hospitality packaging, the selling of a travel package to travel agencies, airlines, and other travel companies who, in turn, sell it directly to consumers.

YIELD

The comparison of actual revenue achieved to the theoretical total potential revenue.

ZERO-BASE BUDGETING

A budgeting concept in which no expenditure is justified just because it was expended last year. Every expense is re-analyzed and justified each year on the basis that it will yield more favorable results than spending the same amount in another way.

ZONE

A geographic subdivision within a country useful for domestic marketing purposes; also, geographic subdivisions of the world useful for international marketing purposes.

Index

A

A. C. Nielsen Company, 15, 52
A Directory of Directories, 167
Abacus, 36
Activities and amenities
    guidebook or brochure,
    69–70
Advertising
    agencies, 91–93
    campaigns, 93–94
    checklist, 92
    clutter, 109, 136, 166
    cooperative, 95
    display boards, 260
    guidelines, 87–89
    process, 89–90
    types of, 96–101
Air carriers, 27, 36–37, 277
Air Transport Association of
    America, 37
Airfares, 187–188, 189
Airline reservations systems,
    35, 36, 269, 272
Airlines, 27, 36–37, 277
All-inclusive packages,
    155–156
Amadeus, 36
America On-Line, 35
American Airlines, 272
American Express, 134, 135
American Express Travel
    Services, 35
American Hotel Association,
    5
APOLLO, 35, 36, 269, 272
Arbitron, 15, 52
Areas of Dominant Influence,
    15, 52
Association & Society Manager,
    123
Association Management,
    123
Association Trends, 123
ASTA Travel News, 123
Auto Europe, 156
Automation, 267–272
Aviation Daily, 124
Avis, 99, 100, 103
AXESS, 36

B

Barter agreements, 94–96
Beat-the-system offer, 255
Benefit
    ads, 99
    and need segmentation,
    15–16
The "Best Surprise Is No
    Surprise" ad campaign,
    101–106
Billing procedures, 77
Booking pace, 209
Boston Consulting Group, 57,
    58
Boston Consulting Group
    Portfolio Box, 57, 58
Boxes/rectangles, 57–58
Brand
    awareness, 97
    identifier ads, 97, 99, 100
    identity, 97
brands, 3–6, 278–279, 283
The Breakers, Palm Beach,
    Florida, 98
Breakeven chart, 199
Brochures, 69–70, 166–167,
    172–173
Budgeting, 43–44, 220,
    229–230, 240
Build promotions, 98, 132,
    133
Business Travel News, 124
Business travelers, 23–25
"Business Travelers' Weather"
    page, 109

C

Camel Scoreboard, 109
"Can-of-Paint" technique,
    253
Canadian Hotel and Restaurant,
    124
Captive intermediary, 33
Carlson Company, 39, 280
Carlson, Curt, 5
Carrier strategies, 187–188

Cash cows, 57
Channels of distribution,
    33–38, 46
Charter travel company,
    35
Checklist
    advertising, 92
    operations, 260–263
    public relations, 118
    sales, 80–81
    sales-tool, 69–78
Chronological work plan,
    222
Chrysler, 106
Circles, 55
City pairs, 12–13
Civil Aeronautics Board,
    36
Club Management, 124
Club Med, 27, 34
Club Universe, 27
Club-level rates, 182
Clutter, 109, 136, 166
Co-oping, 94–96, 282–283
Collateral materials, 165–174
Commercial intermediary,
    33–35
Competitive/market analysis,
    217–219
Competitive/market
    positioning grid, 185,
    219, 222–223
Competitive research, 53
Consolidation, 282
Consumer research, 52–53
Contact
    person, 121
    report, 71, 74
Contracted rates, 183
Convention movers, 35
Cooperative
    advertising, 95
    promotion, 133, 135
*The Cornell Hotel and
    Restaurant
    Administration Quarterly*,
    124
Corporate marketing
    strategies, 277–281

Corporate Meetings &
Incentives, 124
Corporate rates, 181–182
Corporate Travel, 124
Cost-plus theory, 196–197
Couples, 102
COVIA, 35
Credit cards, 143
Credit card companies, 27
CREST studies, 17–18
Cruise ship rates, 190

D

Data base marketing, 144–147
Dateline, 121
Decision tree, 55–56, 57
Delivery package, 115–116
Demographics, 15, 143, 231
Department of Commerce, 38
Department of Justice, 36, 38
Department of State, 38
Department of the Treasury,
38
Department of
Transportation, 36, 38
Deregulation, 36
Designated Market Areas, 15,
52
Desk manual, 78
Destination cities, 14
Direct mail, 147–149
Direct-contact public relations
methods, 116–119
Directories, 167–168
Disclaimers, 174, 187
Disney, Walt, 5
Distribution channels, 33–38,
46
District, 11–12
Dogs, 58
Dollar Rent a Car, 131

E

Ego/recognition promotion,
132
Electronic/on-line travel
service providers, 35
Electronic travel distribution
systems, 35–36
Embassy Suites, 99, 108–109
Employee
community service
recognition, 175–176
motivation, 122, 123,
174–176

Employee-Interest
promotions, 175
Employee-of-the-Month
programs, 175
End user, 23–25
English Bloody Mary, 251
Entertainment collateral
pieces, 169–170
Environmental research, 53
Escape weekends, 16, 158
European Civil Aviation
Conference, 39
Events timetable/workplan
form, 75–76

F

Fact sheets, 168, 169
Fallback, 130
Family packages, 16, 158
Fantasia, 36
Federal Aviation
Administration, 36, 38
Federal Maritime
Commission, 38
Feeder
cities, 11, 235
markets, 94
FIU Hospitality Review, 124
Flexible breakeven analysis,
198–199
Fly-cruise packages, 157
Fly-drive packages, 156–157
Flyers, 170–171
Focus groups, 54–55, 231–232
Food & Service, 124
Food Executive, 124
Food Service Director, 124
Form instructions, 78
Franchising, 275–276, 279
Frequent traveler profile, 18
Fresh and new signal, 253

G

G. E. Portfolio, 58
Galileo, 36, 272
Garfield, 108–109
Gemini, 36
Geodemographic profile, 18
Geographic
expansion, 277
segmentation, 11–15,
143
Gift certificates, 168–169
Give-away/sweepstakes
promotion, 132, 134

Global positioning, 280
Globalization, 281
Government rates, 183
Ground operators, 36
Group
rates, 183
rooms market mix form,
218
Guest
complaints, 262–263
services/guestroom
collateral materials, 171

H

Headline, 121
Helmsley, Leona, 106
Hertz, 39, 105, 176, 269
Hilton, 3, 4, 193, 276, 278
Hilton, Conrad, 3
Holiday Inn, 4, 5, 101–106,
137, 194–195, 275, 276,
277, 278, 279
Holiday packages, 160–161
Holidex, 269
Horizontal expansion, 277
Hospitality Lodging, 124
Hospitality Restaurant, 124
Hot Shoppe Cafeteria, 4
Hotel & Travel Index, 207
Hotel and Motel Management,
124
Hotel rates, 181–183, 184
Hotels, 124
Human scenario ads, 98–99
Hyatt, 5, 88, 97, 107, 108, 134

I

Iacocca, Lee, 106
Incentive Marketing, 124
Incentive travel company, 35
Incentive Travel Manager, 124
Inflation rate-plus factor,
197–198
In-house profit centers,
247–248
Inside signals, 252–253
Insurance Conference Planner,
124
Inter-Continental Hotels, 5
Interdepartmental
communication, 83–84
Internal
promotions, 136
public relations, 122

International Air Transport
   Association, 37
International Civil Aviation
   Organization, 39
International Union of
   Official Travel
   Organizations, 39
Interstate Commerce
   Commission, 38
Introductory promotion, 132

J–L

Johnson, Howard, 5
Key-contact assignment, 74
La Quinta, 277
Le Parker Meridien New
   York, 104
Level of expectation, 88–89,
   104, 106–107, 130
Line art and silhouette ads,
   100, 104
Linear diagrams, 55–56, 57
Lodging, 124
Lodging and Food-Service News,
   124
Lounge collateral materials,
   171

M

Mailing lists, 15, 144, 146,
   147–148
Major market ad campaigns,
   93
Management contract
   companies, 279
Manhattan cocktail, 5
Maps, 171–172
Market
   mix, 205–207
   research, 52
   segment profitability, 45
   segmentation, 5, 11–19,
      200–201, 221, 230–233
   food service, 27–29
   geographic, 143
   price, 18–19, 28–29
   profitable consumer
      segments, 44–45
   share, 57
   share data, 233
Marketing
   advertising and, 87–109
   budgeting and, 43–44, 220,
      229–230, 240

collateral materials and,
   165–174
data base, 143–149
expenditures, 235
expense budget form, 220
guest complaints and,
   262–263
ideas, 251–256
information systems, 271
mix, 235–236
objectives and strategies,
   216–217
packaging and, 153–161
plans, 44, 215–222, 229–241
pricing strategies and,
   193–201
promotions and, 129–139
public relations and,
   113–123
purposes of, 6
rates and, 181–190
research, 51–64, 230–236,
   259–260
revenue maximization
   and, 205–212
sales and, 69–84, 240–241,
   247–250
strategies, 46, 61–64, 88,
   184–186, 233–234,
   275–281
strategy grid, 58–64
Marriott, 4, 39, 193, 201, 277,
   278, 279
Marriott, Alice, 4
Marriott, Bill, Jr., 4, 106
Marriott, Willard, 4, 275
Master notebook, 90
McDonald's, 107, 137–138,
   169
Meal-of-the-month clubs, 178
Media selection, 94
Meeting/convention definite
   booking form, 74, 75
Meeting facilities brochures,
   172–173
The Meeting Manager, 124
Meeting planner, 25–26
Meetings & Conventions, 124
*Meetings & Expositions
   Magazine,* 125
Meetings News, 124
Megatrends, 276
Megatrends, 281–283
Menu specials, 172
Metropolitan statistical areas,
   12–13, 52
Mission statement, 216
MONITOR, 16–17

Montgomery Ward, 143
Motel/Motor Inn Journal, 125

N

Naisbitt, John, 276
Nation's Restaurant News, 125
National Air Carrier
   Association, 37
Nationwide ad campaigns, 93
Neat and clean test, 253
Northwest Airlines, Inc., 133
NOW accounts, 249, 250

O–P

Offer ads, 97–98
Omni Hotels, 135
Operations checklist, 260–263
Origin markets, 52
Pacific Area Travel
   Association, 39
Package plans, 183
Packagers/retailers, 34
Packaging, 34, 153–161
Payoff promotion, 138–139
Per diem, 19, 25
Perceptual map, 55, 56
Personal sales, 79–83
Photographs, 121
Platform, 88
"Please-come-back" letter, 78
Pleasure travelers, 25
Population market ad
   campaigns, 94
Post-meeting/convention
   report, 77
Preferred rates, 182
Premier Cruise Lines, 138
Presentation tools, 55–64
Press
   kit, 119–121
   releases, 120–121
Price
   offer ad, 97–98
   offer plus ad, 97–98
   packages, 160, 161
   promotion, 130, 131
   segmentation, 18–19
Pricing techniques, 193–201,
   207–208
Primary research, 51
Product
   hybridization, 277–278
   research, 52
   segmentation, 5

tiering, 278
Product/service touter ads,
  96, 98
Professional trust ad, 96
Profitable consumer
  segments, 44–45
Promo, 125
Promotions, 129–139, 175–176
Property management
  systems, 269–271
Proposition, 88, 239
Prospect research, 52–53
Psychographics, 16–18, 143
Public relations
  application of, 114–121
  checklist, 118
  dealing with the press and,
    117–119
  definition of, 113–114
  examples of, 122–123
  internal, 122
  measurement of, 122
  opportunities, 115
  tools of, 119–121
Public speaking do's and
  don'ts, 115–116
Publicity, 113
Pyramids, 55, 56

Q–R

Qualitative research, 51
Quantitative research, 51
Question marks, 57–58
Questionnaires, 54
Quotes, 121
Rack rates, 182
Ramada, 108, 137, 170, 278
Rate
  cards, 173–174
  comparisons, 186–187
  pyramiding, 199–200
  ranges, 184
  strategies, 184–186
  survey, 217
Rates
  carrier, 187–188, 189
  club-level, 182
  contracted, 183
  corporate, 181–182
  cruise ship, 190
  government, 183
  group, 183
  hotel, 181–183, 184
  preferred, 182
  rack, 182
  rental car, 188–190
  seasonal, 183

standard, 181–183
suite, 183
summer, 182
super-saver, 182
weekend, 182
Recreational facilities guide,
  174
Regional market ad
  campaigns, 94
Regions, 11
Release date, 121
Reminder/final confirmation
  letter, 71
Rental car rates, 188–190
Repeat promotions, 98
Reputation builder ads, 96, 97
Reservations
  department, 84
  systems, 268–269
Resort Management, 125
Restaurant Business, 125
Restaurant Hospitality, 125
Restaurants & Institutions, 125
Restaurants, USA, 125

S

SABRE, 35, 36, 269, 272
Sales, 69–84
  brochures, 69
  checklist, 71, 73, 80–81
  department, 69–84
  goals, 240–241
  ideas, 247–250
  image, 81–82
  negotiation, 79, 81, 82–83
  organizing, 69–79
  personal, 79–83
  telephone, 73–74, 83
Sales-tool checklist, 69–78
*Sales and Marketing
  Management,* 125
Salesperson appreciation
  clubs, 177–178
Scheduled carriers, 36
Sears, 143
Seasonal rates, 183
Second-honeymoon escape
  weekend, 16, 158
Secondary research, 51
Secretaries, 26
Secretaries clubs, 177
Segment profitability, 45
Self-testimonial ads, 96
Sell up, 193–194, 195–196
Selling down, 196–197
Series ads, 99, 103
Service research, 52

Share promotion, 131
Sheraton, 95, 106–107, 278
Shopping guides, 174
Situation identification ads,
  98–99, 101
Southwest Airlines, 160
Special destination/attraction
  packages, 159
Special-event packages, 159
Special-interest packages,
  158–159
SRI International, 17
Standard
  metropolitan statistical
    areas, 12–13, 52
  rates, 181–183
Stars, 57
Stouffer, 109
Stouffer, Vernon, 275
Successful Meetings, 125
Suggestive identifier ads, 99,
  102
Suite rates, 183
Summer rates, 182
Super-saver rates, 182
Supplemental carriers, 37
Surveys, 54
SWOT, 53
System One, 35

T

*Tableservice Restaurant
  Operations Report,* 125
Telephone
  answering instructions, 78
  assurance procedures,
    73–74
  sales, 73–74, 83
Tent cards, 174
Tentative confirmation letter,
  70–71, 72
Testimonial ads, 96, 106
*Texas and Southwest Hotel
  Motel Review,* 125
Thank-you process, 78
Theme packages, 159–160
Thomas, Dave, 106
Tie-ins, 132
Tour
  operators-retailers, 34
  operators-wholesalers, 34
Trade
  ads, 100–101, 105
  media, 123–125
Trade-outs, 94–96
Traffic
  department, 26

flows, U.S., 13
flows, world, 14
Travel
    agents, 26–27, 34
    clubs, 27, 35
    distribution systems, 35–36
    intermediaries, 23, 25–27,
        33–35
    management companies,
        26, 34
    packages, 34
    purchasing systems,
        267–272
    purpose of, 34
    regulation of, 38–39
Travel Agent, 125
Travel Management Daily, 125
Travel Master, 125
Travel Trade, 125
Travel Weekly, 125
TravelAge East, 125
TravelAge Mid-America, 125
TravelAge Southeast, 125
TravelAge West, 125
Travelers
    business, 23–25
    frequent, 18
    pleasure, 25
Tremont House, 5
Trend research, 53

Trends in the Hotel Industry,
    125
Trial promotion, 130

U–V

U.S. Census Bureau, 15, 143
U.S. flagged carriers, 36, 38
United Airlines, 39
United States Travel Service,
    38
VALS, 17
Value concept, 19, 136, 255,
    280, 282
Vertical and horizontal
    integration, 39, 280,
    282–283
VIP
    club card, 176
    clubs, 176–177
    reservation request form,
        70
VIPs, 70, 176

W

Waiters and Bartenders
    National Union, 5
Walk-in customers, 78

Walt Disney World, 138
Weekend
    packages, 157–158
    rates, 182
Weekly intelligence sheet,
    186, 187, 188
The Westin Galleria & Westin
    Oaks, 101
Westron, 269
Wilson, Kemmons, 4, 275
"Wizard of Avis," 269
Work plan example, 223–225
World Convention Dates, 125
WORLDSPAN, 36
Worldwide Lodging Industry,
    125
Wyndham Hotels & Resorts,
    158

Y–Z

Yankelovich, Clancy, and
    Shulman, 16
Yesawich, Pepperdine, and
    Brown, 17
Yield management, 208–210
Zero-base budgeting, 43–44,
    229–230
Zip codes, 14, 15, 52, 143
Zone, 11

MARKETING IN THE HOSPITALITY INDUSTRY

REVIEW QUIZ ANSWER KEY

The numbers in parentheses refer to the learning objective addressed by the question and the page where the answer may be found.

Chapter 1	Chapter 2	Chapter 3	Chapter 4
1. d (LO1, 4)	1. c (LO1, 11)	1. b (LO1, 24)	1. d (LO1, 33)
2. a (LO2, 3–5)	2. c (LO1, 14)	2. b (LO2, 25)	2. c (LO1, 34–35)
3. a (LO2, 3–6)	3. b (LO3, 14)	3. c (LO4, 26)	3. b (LO1, 35)
4. a (LO3, 6)	4. c (LO7, 18)	4. a (LO4, 27)	4. a (LO2, 38)
	5. d (LO7, 19)	5. a (LO5, 27)	

Chapter 5	Chapter 6	Chapter 7	Chapter 8
1. c (LO2, 43)	1. a (LO1, 51)	1. d (LO1, 78)	1. a (LO1, 88)
2. a (LO2, 43)	2. c (LO1, 53)	2. a (LO2, 81)	2. b (LO2, 94–95)
3. a (LO3, 44)	3. b (LO2, 54)	3. d (LO3, 83)	3. c (LO3, 96)
4. c (LO5, 46)	4. b (LO3, 57)	4. c (LO4, 83–84)	4. a (LO3, 104)
	5. d (LO3, 60)		

Chapter 9	Chapter 10	Chapter 11	Chapter 12
1. c (LO1, 113)	1. a (LO1, 129–130)	1. b (LO1, 144)	1. b (LO1, 153)
2. c (LO2, 117)	2. d (LO2, 132)	2. a (LO1, 145)	2. c (LO3, 156)
3. a (LO2, 121)	3. c (LO2, 133)	3. d (LO1, 146)	3. d (LO3, 157–158)
4. d (LO3, 122)	4. a (LO4, 136)	4. c (LO2, 149)	4. b (LO3, 159–160)
			5. d (LO3, 161)

Chapter 13	Chapter 14	Chapter 15	Chapter 16
1. c (LO1, 165–166)	1. d (LO1, 182)	1. c (LO1, 193–194)	1. b (LO1, 205)
2. d (LO1, 165)	2. b (LO2, 184)	2. a (LO4, 197)	2. c (LO3, 209)
3. a (LO2, 171)	3. a (LO2, 184)	3. a (LO6, 199)	3. a (LO4, 210)
4. b (LO3, 175)			
5. a (LO4, 176–177)			

Chapter 17	Chapter 18	Chapter 19	Chapter 20
1. d (LO1, 215)	1. c (LO1, 230)	1. a (LO1, 248)	1. d (LO1, 259)
2. a (LO1, 216)	2. d (LO1, 230–232)	2. b (LO1, 249)	2. b (LO2, 260)
3. a (LO1, 217)	3. a (LO2, 236)	3. d (LO2, 251–253)	3. d (LO2, 262)
4. d (LO2, 223)		4. c (LO3, 254)